UNSETTLED FRONTIERS

UNSETTLED FRONTIERS

Market Formation in the
Cambodia-Vietnam Borderlands

Sango Mahanty

SOUTHEAST ASIA PROGRAM PUBLICATIONS

AN IMPRINT OF CORNELL UNIVERSITY PRESS   ITHACA AND LONDON

First published 2022 by Cornell University Press

Library of Congress Cataloging-in-Publication Data

Names: Mahanty, Sango, author.
Title: Unsettled frontiers : market formation in the Cambodia-Vietnam
    borderlands / Sango Mahanty.
Description: 1st. | Ithaca [New York] : Southeast Asia Program Publications,
    an imprint of Cornell University Press, 2022. | Includes bibliographical references
    and index.
Identifiers: LCCN 2021013254 (print) | LCCN 2021013255 (ebook) |
    ISBN 9781501761478 (hardcover) | ISBN 9781501761485 (paperback) |
    ISBN 9781501761492 (epub) | ISBN 9781501761508 (pdf)
Subjects: LCSH: Borderlands—Economic aspects—Cambodia. |
    Borderlands—Economic aspects—Vietnam. | Cambodia—Economic
    conditions. | Vietnam—Economic conditions. | Cambodia—Emigration
    and immigration—Economic aspects. | Vietnam—Emigration and
    immigration—Economic aspects.
Classification: LCC HC442 .M38 2022 (print) | LCC HC442 (ebook) |
    DDC 381/.4109596—dc23
LC record available at https://lccn.loc.gov/2021013254
LC ebook record available at https://lccn.loc.gov/2021013255

For Matthew, Nisha, Kiran, and Ashwin

Contents

Preface

My engagement with Cambodia and Vietnam has followed a winding path. I first worked in these two countries between 2005 and 2007. As an analyst with the Bangkok-based Centre for People and Forests, my role was to engage with my Cambodian and Vietnamese counterparts to document early lessons from the community forestry projects that had started to emerge there.

The experience sparked my deep interest in this region's history and challenges. After I joined the Australian National University in 2007, I found opportunities to continue my research there. During 2009–2012, I collaborated with the Vietnamese Institute of Policy and Research in Agriculture and Rural Development to study how craft villages in the Red River Delta were coping with toxic levels of pollution. In 2011 I studied the prospects for community-run timber extraction in Mondulkiri, Cambodia. Then, during 2012–2014, I led a collaboration that studied the social entanglements of forest carbon schemes in mainland Southeast Asia (ARC DP120100270), where my field efforts focused on a scheme in Mondulkiri. It was during this last project that I witnessed the dramatic changes sweeping this province, arising from its transborder trading networks and crop booms—especially for cassava. This inspired my more detailed research on cross-border commodity networks, with the support of an Australian Research Council Future Fellowship (2014–2018, FT130101495).

Although my analysis in this book is strongly informed by my Future Fellowship research, it was these earlier engagements that created the foundations. They grew my knowledge about the histories, landscapes, political economy, and state-society relations of these two countries. This earlier work also enabled me to study the relevant languages, which I commenced in 2009 for Vietnamese and in 2012 for Khmer. I reached a basic proficiency in these two languages but have always worked closely with research assistants and interpreters during fieldwork (see below). Upland communities are not always fluent in dominant national languages, especially the elderly, so I sometimes engaged a local Bunong interpreter.

My long-standing networks in the two countries enabled me to gain the "red stamps" (S. Turner 2013) that are so important in studying a sensitive border region. In both countries my host institutions facilitated the relevant national- and provincial-level permissions. Yet the additional requirements of a borderland study set me on a steep learning curve. During my first visit to a Vietnamese border crossing in Tây Ninh, it emerged that our portfolio of permission letters was short on one crucial letter—from the provincial military office. Military officials quickly surrounded our small research team and instructed us to leave the area. We returned to the provincial capital, taking another week to organize the missing documentation before we could return to our field site. A further complicating factor with Vietnamese approval processes was the need for documents to mention all the localities where the researcher would go—down to the commune level. Yet the networks that I was studying traversed localities in a very fluid way. I quickly learned to routinely include most border communes and districts in my targeted provinces in these approval applications so that I could flexibly follow traders and other network actors.

Aside from the complications of official approvals, scholars of this region acknowledge that foreigners often face additional constraints during field research (Sowerwine 2013). I was the subject of official surveillance, especially in Vietnam's border districts and during visits to factories. In contrast, discussions with traders sparked less interest from the authorities—even though traders were among the most open and informative sources on such issues as illicit trade and corruption. Official surveillance usually eased over time, but overall this did mean that my data collection opportunities in Vietnam were more structured and did not allow as much scope for participant observation as was possible in Cambodia. In Cambodia, surveillance was less direct but nonetheless present, especially at border crossings and in areas of high timber extraction. A key constraint in Cambodia was that I had less opportunity for informal discussions with border officials than I hoped for, as they approached me with a high degree of suspicion. I had to discern their roles and actions from the few interviews that I gained, as well as observations and accounts from other informants, such as cross-border traders and villagers. Overall, as the interview material presented in this book shows, I was able to broach quite sensitive matters during many of our interviews. I attribute this to the warmth and communication skills of my research assistants and the possibility that a middle-aged woman of South Asian heritage may have seemed quite innocuous to participants.

Although the acknowledgments cover my complete network of collaborators, it is important here to explain my research assistants' contributions to the research process. Vietnamese research visas require a host organization employee to accompany foreign researchers (see Sowerwine 2013 for the associated challenges and benefits). I additionally recruited trusted and independent research assistants to work closely with me over the course of my fellowship project. Thus, in Vietnam, I had both an official research assistant (Hoàng Hải Dương) and an independent assistant (Phạm Thị Bảo Chinh). In Cambodia, a host organization chaperone is not required, so I worked only with an independent research assistant (Chap Prem). I similarly gained some of the data from my earlier forest carbon research, which appears in this book, with the support of independent research assistants (Suong Soksophea, Em Kanha, and Keo Bora). While all of these research assistants held tertiary qualifications, it was their experience working in rural communities, willingness to learn, and curiosity that produced a fruitful collaboration. In addition, I knew all of these collaborators from prior interactions, or they came through recommendations from trusted in-country colleagues. This was essential given that the research touched on sensitive topics, such as illegality and corruption. Data collection could not have proceeded with a collaborator who was scared to discuss these issues or would censor such discussions. All of these research assistants had a strong command of English, which was our primary medium of communication with each other.

To strengthen the integrity and quality of the data we collected, I trained my research assistants in the details and nuances of my research, including my aims, relevant concepts, ethical considerations, and my interest in granular details of content and emotion. This up-front investment of time not only built our relationship and trust before going to the field but also made my research assistants knowledgeable and active participants in the research. I carried out interviews, group discussions, and field observations with rather than through these research assistants (see also S. Turner 2013, 222). We would often reflect critically on the potential meanings of key phrases, such as the term *còn cái xác* (corpse) that some traders used to refer to other traders who had gone out of business (see chap. 3). On two occasions my Vietnamese research assistants undertook field interviews without me present. We carefully planned these ventures together and debriefed after their fieldwork. One of these assistants, Chinh, also remained in regular contact with selected traders, and farmers who held cross-border land leases. In these cases, where I was not present during interviews, my research assistants recorded them where permitted so that they could be transcribed and translated in full. In Cambodia, Prem also undertook short solo trips, for instance, to accompany a trader on a cross-border delivery—something that I would simply not have been able to do as a foreigner. In effect, the research effort was as networked as the commodity networks that we were studying. Our collaboration spanned several years, and I am still in contact with many of these people—including to check specific points of detail or my interpretation of terms in an interview or field note. These colleagues have been core and trusted contributors to the work that this book presents.

I collected the data set that underpins this book between 2012 and 2018. In total, this added up to interviews (including repeat interviews) with some three hundred informants, as well as detailed field notes, photographs, and a large database of media articles. In Cambodia, these participants included villagers; new migrants; village, commune, and provincial officials; staff from national agencies; and donor and project personnel. In Vietnam, my field effort concentrated on traders; factory and warehouse owners and directors; commune, district, and provincial officials; professional bodies; personnel in research institutions; and some national-level officials. In 2016, I also conducted a survey of 220 households in the Cambodian provinces of Mondulkiri and Tbong Khmum to extend my understanding of household livelihood patterns, strategies, and risks and the variegated ways in which individual families engaged with markets. Prem's senior university students implemented the survey under our close supervision.

The other significant data set for this book is archival material from the Archive Nationale d'Outre Mer (ANOM) in Aix-en-Provence, France, and Vietnam's National Archives No. 2 in Ho Chi Minh City. Accessing these similarly involved support from skilled research assistants. At ANOM, my colleague Katie Dyt helped me to navigate the catalog and to translate materials. In Ho Chi Minh City, Chinh and I worked with Lương Thị Mai Trâm to translate key archival documents. I also made use of primary and secondary sources from the École Française d'Extrême-Orient (EFEO) and the Bibliothèque Universitaire des Langues et Civilisations. The historian Margaret Slocomb also generously shared her raw archival notes from the Phnom Penh archives. I sought archival materials on a range of topics, including rubber, land governance, border delineations, Indigenous peoples, and economic institutions to govern trade—all of which helped to contextualize the story of rubber presented in chapter 1. My interactions with several historians (see the acknowledgments) ensured that I made full use of secondary materials and taught me to approach my archival sources historiographically.

Through this deep immersion in the historical and contemporary commodity networks of the Cambodia-Vietnam borderlands, the focus of my work subtly evolved and transitioned to a larger story of frontier market formation. It reveals how dynamic commodity networks are continually forming and reworking frontier markets within shifting landscapes of settlement, displacement, and state intervention.

Acknowledgments

My partner, Matthew Phillipps, and our children, Nisha, Kiran, and Ashwin, have been an integral part of the research journey that produced this book. They supported me during our many trips to Cambodia and Vietnam and through the highs and lows of my five-year writing process.

My wonderful colleagues at the Australian National University have helped me in numerous ways over the years. My corridor neighbors—Tô Xuân Phúc, Sarah Milne, John McCarthy, Colin Filer and Keith Barney, along with other colleagues in the Resources, Environment and Development Program—have been collegial and encouraging; they asked insightful questions and provided welcome advice. Our political ecology writing group reviewed and commented on aspects of this work; this group additionally included Matthew Allen, Maylee Thavat, and Siobhan McDonnell. Jane Ferguson was an excellent writing buddy, providing insightful comments on some early chapters. Our university is very fortunate to have a dedicated group of cartographers; Kay Dancey and Jennifer Sheehan patiently and deftly prepared all of the maps in this manuscript, while Sandy Potter enlivened me to the possibilities of Story Mapping around some of the stories appearing in this book. Thái Bảo and Phạm Thủy changed my life by teaching me Vietnamese. Chị Thủy in particular spent many additional hours over coffee helping me with my conversation skills. Many others at ANU have encouraged me and shared ideas, especially Judith Pabian, Philip Taylor, Ben Kerkvliet, Peter Chaudhry, Grant Walton, Katrin Travouillon, and those who are too numerous to name here.

Although I am not new to archival research, my past work on forest management in colonial India did not fully equip me to navigate French Indochinese collections. Katie Dyt generously shared her archival experience, helping me to search the collection at ANOM and to translate some key works. Katie's meticulous documentation system also served me well at the National Archive No. 2 in Ho Chi Minh City, where I worked with Phạm Thị Bảo Chinh and Lương Thị Mai Trâm. Early discussions on historical sources with Andrew Hardy (École Française d'Extrême-Orient, EFEO), Mathieu Guerin (L'Institut National des Langues et Civilisations Orientales, INALCO), and Frederic Fortunel (Université du Maine) were very valuable in navigating these sources. I am especially grateful to Margaret Slocomb, who shared her notes on early Cambodian rubber plantations from the Phnom Penh archives. Thanks are also due to Harriet Kesby, who helped with French translations in Canberra, and to Ben Neimark, who provided archival advice.

In Vietnam, my host organization was the Central Institute for Natural Resources and Environmental Studies (CRES) in the Vietnam National University, Hanoi. At the time of my research, CRES was led by Hoàng Văn Thắng, who provided invaluable guidance, while my CRES-based research assistant Hoàng Hải Dương provided essential support with field research and permissions. I was privileged to work with an exceptionally collegial and dedicated research assistant, Phạm Thị Bảo Chinh. Chinh put in long hours looking after everything from field logistics to endless phone calls tracking down elusive traders. She also worked independently on some interviews and archival research, including one field trip with Dương, which I discuss in the preface. In Tây Ninh, I particularly acknowledge the support of Hồ Thị Thuý Ngân at the Department of Natural Resources and Environment, who assisted our team in navigating district and commune authorities and arranged my factory visits and interviews.

My host organization in Cambodia, the Centre for Khmer Studies, is an important and lively hub for many international scholars. I am profoundly grateful for their support between 2012 and 2018. My interactions with the following people have helped me to sharpen my analysis and deepen my understanding of Cambodia: Alice Beban, Robin Biddulph, Jeremy Ironside, Sarah Rose Jensen, Pak Kimchoeun, Nguon Kimly, John Marston, Colleen McGinn, Laura Schoenberger, Kem Sothorn, Michael Sullivan, Chan Sophal, and Courtney Work. In addition to sharing his deep expertise on agrarian Cambodia, Jean-Christophe Diepart has helped me in countless ways, from sharing obscure historical references to swapping statistics. Sarah Milne deserves special mention here for introducing me to many of these people and for her significant contributions to my Cambodian research over the years. I am also indebted to the two reviewers of this book who provided invaluable advice and subsequently identified themselves to me: Sarah Turner and Jonathan Padwe.

The Cambodian fieldwork for this book was undertaken with my research assistant Chap Prem during 2016–2018. Prem always added important insights to our field findings, based on his wide reading and deep knowledge of Cambodian culture and politics. Prem's students, who conducted our household survey, did so with dedication and care: Hang Lyna, Horn Kunthy, Roeurn Mao, and Yoeurn Mariya. Data entry from the survey was undertaken by Han Haknoukrith. In my previous work, some of which is used in this book, my field efforts were supported by Suong Soksophea, Em Kanha, and Keo Bora. Pak Kimchoen particularly helped me to navigate provincial government approvals for this research and to access official statistics. My interactions with Jonathan Newby (International Center for Tropical Agriculture, CIAT) helped me to understand a lot more about cassava than I could have learned from my field research alone, and I thank him for his willingness to share information and insights.

Aspects of this manuscript have been presented and published elsewhere, and my analysis has greatly benefited from feedback during these events and review processes. I thank participants in the workshop on "Cross-Border Exchanges and the Shadow Economy" held at the International Institute for Asian Studies (IIAS), Leiden on December 14–15, 2015, especially Tak-Wing Ngo and my discussant, Pal Nyri. The ANU-CRES Workshop titled "Ethnographic Approaches to Cross-Border Livelihoods" in Hanoi, December 2014, allowed me to interact with some amazing scholars, leading to a special issue in *Asia Pacific Viewpoint* that I coedited with Philip Taylor. The EuroSEAS 2017 panel Resituating Transnational Commodity Networks, convened by Sarah Turner, discussed and provided useful feedback on my early analysis of cassava networks. The EuroSEAS 2019 panel "Borderland Crop Booms" enabled rich discussion with other scholars working on this subject, including Juliet Lu, Cecilie Friis, Jean-Christophe Castella, Miles Kenney-Lazar, Isabelle Vagneron, and Pin Pravalprukskul. I also acknowledge the questions and comments of several anonymous reviewers for related articles that were published by the *Annals of the American Association of Geographers*, *Journal of Contemporary Asia*, and *Transactions of the Institute of British Geographers*.

Several people have helped me to strengthen this book's narrative. Sophie Dowling was a superb editor. Her detailed edits to the entire manuscript were made with exceptional skill, warmth, and intelligence. Anna Hutchens's masterful coaching helped me to plan this writing project and to stay on track. Nisha Phillipps's critical but friendly reading of my chapters pushed me to find my own voice in this work. I am also indebted to Colin Filer, Francesca Merlan, and Janet Sturgeon for their valuable comments on my book proposal at a formative stage. Sarah Grossman at Cornell University Press was all that a prospective contributor could hope for in an editor, with her valuable advice and responsiveness.

The Australian Research Council Future Fellowship (FT13010149) that financed much of this research gave me the space and freedom to fully immerse myself in this work in a way that would simply not have been possible otherwise. Collaborative research in a prior ARC Discovery Project (DP120100270, with Tô Xuân Phúc, Wolfram Dressler, Peter Kanowski, Sarah Milne, and Luca Tacconi) laid important groundwork for this study by alerting me to the dramatic changes underway in the Cambodia-Vietnam borderlands. My most recent ARC collaboration with Sarah Milne, Tô Xuân Phúc, Keith Barney, and Philip Hirsch (DP180101495) contributes to my discussion of rupture in chapter 4. Although ARC funds enabled this research, the views expressed here are of course my own and do not reflect the views of the Australian government or the ARC.

Finally, I am deeply grateful for the generosity and time of all the participants in this research. Although this work stands on the shoulders of many, I take full responsibility for any errors or omissions.

Abbreviations

ACIAR	Australian Centre for International Agricultural Research
ACLEDA	Association for Cambodian Local Economic Development Agencies
ADB	Asian Development Bank
ANOM	Archive Nationale d'outre Mer
ANU	Australian National University
APCC	Association des Planteurs de Caoutchouc en Cochinchine
APCI	Association des Planteurs de Caoutchouc de L'Indochine
CCHR	Cambodian Center for Human Rights
CEDEP	Cambodia Export Diversification and Expansion Program
CGIAR	Consortium of International Agricultural Research Centers
EIF	Enhanced Integration Framework
ELC	economic land concession
FAO	Food and Agriculture Organization
FIDH	International Federation for Human Rights
LICADHO	Cambodian League for the Promotion and Defense of Human Rights
MARD	Ministry for Agriculture and Rural Development (Vietnam)
REDD+	Reducing Emissions from Deforestation and Forest Degradation
SLC	social land concession
Socfin	Société Financière des Caoutchoucs
SWAP	sectorwide approach
UNDP	United Nations Development Programme
WTO	World Trade Organization

UNSETTLED FRONTIERS

INTRODUCTION

Frontiers in Flux

The market is not guided by an invisible hand. It stems from tangled networks that bind the past with the present, human with nonhuman actors, and local with global processes. Like a rhizomic plant whose underground shoots constantly seek new terrain, these exchange networks continually expand, take root, and rupture to rework frontier lives and landscapes. This book explores these historical, social, and material relationships along the Cambodia-Vietnam border. It reveals the workings of these commodity networks and how they merge to drive frontier transformation.

Since the mid-1800s, the upland regions of Cambodia and Vietnam have witnessed successive, intensifying waves of incorporation, migration, and rupture—from the vast rubber plantations of the French colonial period to the enforced collectivization of the Khmer Rouge era, which violently disrupted long-standing communities. In recent decades, global commodity booms have created an unrelenting drive to exploit the land and resources of these frontier regions, bringing lowland migrants with them. Along with the waves of migration and settlement brought by these market processes, the frontier remains an unsettled space where people seek secure lives as they grapple with dramatic environmental and social change and volatile engagements with diverse commodities.

Surya's migration story exemplifies these processes and introduces some important themes that I explore in the coming chapters. I met Surya in 2013 in the village of Phum Prambei in Cambodia's Mondulkiri Province, near the border with Vietnam. Aged fifty-five, Surya grew up in Vietnam's Mekong Delta and identified as part of the Khmer ethnic minority known as Khmer Krom.[1]

He moved to Cambodia as a young man in the postconflict period of the 1990s, where he first lived in the border province of Takau, south of the capital, Phnom Penh. In 1997, Surya migrated upland to Phum Prambei, which was then a small Indigenous Bunong village and Cambodian military outpost. He followed his cousin who had moved there earlier and was running a small coffee stall. For his first few years, Surya survived by fetching water for the military and by collecting and selling various forest products to Vietnamese buyers. In the year 2000, when the area was beset with rice shortages, a Bunong family accepted his offer to give them rice in exchange for enough land to build a house and establish a small farm. As more of his family members moved to Phum Prambei, Surya started to think of it as his *srok kamnert* (homeland). Migration surged in 2005, when well-connected provincial elites started to grab and clear land around the village that they would resell to new settlers for USD 300 to 400 per hectare. Surya revealed that the "powerful ones" would take as many as one hundred to five hundred hectares each. New roads rapidly dissected the land and destroyed the Bunong community's sacred burial forest. Even as a relatively new settler, Surya keenly felt this cosmological and material disturbance, recounting, "After the burial forest was burned and the stumps were dug out, I dreamed about ghosts from the forest with dark bodies who said they had nowhere to live."

Surya's account of migration and land commodification in a rapidly changing border landscape highlights the historically and socially layered transformations wrought by novel and intensifying market engagements. The ghosts in Surya's dreams speak to the displacement of Indigenous Bunong communities and signal the deep social and material disruptions that are characteristic of frontier markets. Such transformations are not only seen in the Cambodia-Vietnam borderlands but resonate throughout the world's frontiers (Hall 2011; Watts 2012). In these sites of resource extraction for global markets, specific social and environmental trajectories can be diverse and dynamic but are equally consequential (Larsen 2015). Frontier markets therefore require urgent attention at a time that some call an "impossible present—a time of rupture, a world haunted with the threat of extinction" (Swanson et al. 2017, M2).

Although the Cambodia-Vietnam borderlands have long been part of regional exchange networks, French colonization intensified commodity production and trade.[2] The French introduced new modes of agriculture for international markets and earmarked these areas for commodity crops, such as rubber and coffee. European colonization therefore initiated the region's incorporation into global capitalist markets (Wolf 1982), producing both national borders *and* a frontier market.

My starting point is that markets are more than a forum where goods and services are exchanged for money (Mayhew 2015). Although price, money, and bargaining are important hallmarks of market exchange (Polanyi 1957, 267), such exchanges cannot be considered separately from their social and political-economic contexts (Applbaum 2012, 264). It is this social embeddedness that ultimately enhances the transformative power of markets, as I later illustrate (Polanyi 1957). Furthermore, market exchange does not completely supplant existing modes of exchange but melds with these in diverse ways (Turner et al. 2015; Wolf 1982). Drawing on this socially embedded, or "substantivist," view of markets, I study the relationships, actions, and innovations that occur in market networks to gain a granular but contextualized view of their functioning (Gudeman 2001, 146).

To understand the fine-grained social and material entanglements of market networks, I draw on Deleuze and Guattari's analytic of the *rhizome*. This term literally refers to a class of plant that propagates itself through a sprawling underground stem and root system, but Deleuze and Guattari (1987, 23) use it as a heuristic device to explain the tangled and unbounded character of various social phenomena that lack clear organizational hierarchies and points of "culmination." Through this lens, market networks sprawl without a distinct node of control and without an end point or climax. This does not imply the absence of power but rather that power is exercised indirectly through knowledge systems as well as institutional and physical apparatuses (Bignall 2008). Although the rhizome analytic resonates with other useful network analytics, such as actor-network theory (Latour 1987) and commodity-chain analysis (Hopkins and Wallerstein 1986), it brings attention to two important market features. First, it shines a light on the interactions *between* disparate commodity networks. Second, a rhizomic lens reveals that markets are in a continual state of flux without a clear beginning or end. The rhizome analytic invites us to examine markets as constantly in formation, through everyday practices that bind social and material worlds.

To move between this granular level of analysis and broader market relationships, I incorporate historical and political-economic analysis. From this perspective, we can see how frontier markets are not just unstructured networks but are closely tied to processes of state formation. At the same time, states can ultimately struggle to control markets, as the early history of Indochinese rubber (chapter 1) and contemporary state interventions (chapter 5) reveal. The friction between market facilitation and the market's rhizomic form ultimately causes crucial challenges for market governance (chapter 5). The book thus explores how locally grounded and diverse market actors interact with political and economic institutions to produce dynamic—and ultimately ungovernable—frontier markets.

I examine these processes in the Cambodia-Vietnam borderlands, a diverse landscape that spans 1,137 kilometers (see fig. I.1; Blanchard 1999). The preface

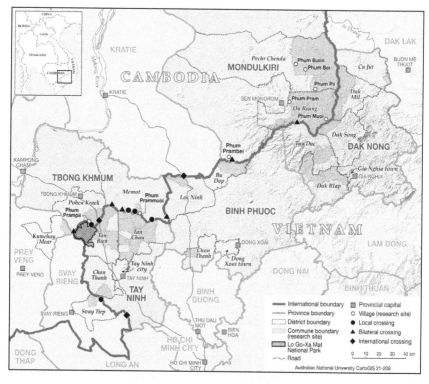

FIGURE I.1.   Study sites in Cambodia and Vietnam

outlines my research methods and fieldwork in detail, which centered on five adjacent upland border provinces: Mondulkiri (Cambodia), Đắk Nông and Bình Phước (Vietnam); and Tbong Khmum (Cambodia) and Tây Ninh (Vietnam). In Cambodia, I studied timber trade networks, as well as smallholder production and trading networks for cassava and rubber. I focused on smallholders to complement the substantial recent literature on estate agriculture (see Schoenberger et al. 2017 for a summary). In this book, the term smallholder refers to a farmer who operates on a limited land area that is typically family-owned and operated (Rigg, Salamanca, and Thompson 2016). Cambodia's national agricultural survey in 2014 found that the average size of such small family farms was 1.6 hectares (National Institute of Statistics 2015; Diepart 2015, 74). In Vietnam, I studied contemporary rubber and cassava processing industries in Tây Ninh, Bình Phước, and Đắk Nông Provinces. I selected these commodities both for their economic significance and their role in the spatial transformation of these upland provinces. My analysis of market engagements drew on French and Vietnamese historical records in the Archive National d'Outre Mer (ANOM) in Aix-en-Provence, France, and Vietnam's National Archive No. 2 in Ho Chi Minh

City. Collectively, these sources have enabled a rich exploration of past and contemporary market engagements, networks, and cross-commodity relationships.

The Cambodia-Vietnam Borderlands: A Historical Overview

Since the French commenced the delineation of territorial borders in the late 1800s, the international border between Cambodia and Vietnam has been in a state of flux. In 2019, a Vietnamese newspaper article reported on "new progress in [the] land border demarcation between Vietnam, Cambodia" in the form of a supplementary treaty to the 1985 and 2005 Treaties on the Delimitation of National Borders (Vietnam Pictorial 2019). The article expressed hope that the remaining 16 percent of this international border would be swiftly demarcated in the interests of regional security. In doing so, it inadvertently highlighted the border's unsettled character as a long-standing space of friction, complicated by state formation, markets, land dealings, and dynamic patterns of settlement and dispossession.

The Cambodia-Vietnam border extends from the "three borders" region in the north, where Laos, Cambodia, and Vietnam meet, to the Gulf of Thailand in the south (Blanchard 1999). The Vietnamese provinces along the border with Cambodia, from south to north, are An Giang, Đồng Tháp, Long An, Tây Ninh, Bình Phước, Đắk Nông, Đắk Lắk, Gia Lai, and Kon Tum. These sit opposite the Cambodian border provinces, from south to north, of Kampot, Takeo, Kandal, Prey Veng, Svay Rieng, Tbong Khum, Kratie, Mondulkiri, and Ratanakiri. My study sites in the Mondulkiri-Đắk Nông region were in the mountainous, or upland, border region. The landscape then undulated into lowland plains in my Tbong Khmum–Tây Ninh study sites (see Fig. I.1).

Under the French, these borderlands became a new frontier for commodity production and trade. For critical geographers, the term *frontiers* refers to resource-rich spaces that are being incorporated into global markets (Harvey 2003; Watts 2012; Cons and Eilenberg 2019). This departs from colonial notions of frontiers as borders or transition points between binary domains: order versus lawlessness (Curzon 1907), settler versus Indigenous populations, wilderness versus civilization (F. Turner 1920), and agricultural versus forested land. (The latter is still commonly used, e.g., in Chomitz 2007.) Yet these binary representations overlook the contested meanings, ongoing struggles, and transformations underway in frontiers (Lefebvre 1974). Examining the Cambodia-Vietnam borderlands as a space of frontier market incorporation foregrounds the continual reinvention of this space as new resources are discovered, introduced, and commoditized.

Novel territorial and labor configurations are crucial to these ongoing projects of market formation and state making (Larsen 2015, 2; Rasmussen and Lund 2018). In briefly explaining the complex history of this borderland frontier, I focus on some key themes: Indigenous history, how French colonization entrenched and expanded commodification and trade, and how land and labor interventions supported these processes.

The precolonial population of the Cambodia-Vietnam borderlands was predominantly Indigenous.[3] Bunong people lived in the mountainous Mondulkiri-Đắk Nông region (also pronounced Phnong in Khmer and Mnong in Vietnamese[4]), while Stieng people lived in the adjacent foothills (Xtieng in Vietnamese; Michaud, Barkataki-Ruscheweyh, and Swain 2016). Archeological and linguistic evidence shows that these two Mon-Khmer groups have long-standing relationships to this landscape that go back several thousand years (Keating 2016; White 2009).

Before French colonization, centuries-old trade and tributary networks—that also included Indigenous communities—traversed mainland Southeast Asia (Hickey 1982; Piper, Matsumura, and Bulbeck 2017). In addition to practicing shifting cultivation in small and scattered settlements, Indigenous peoples collected and traded such items as tree resin, honey, wild meat, antlers, elephant tusks, and animal skins.[5] As part of their tributary relations with lowland Vietnamese and Khmer kingdoms, these groups also conducted raids on neighboring villages to capture and exchange slaves (Hickey 1982, 34). These systems of tribute enabled Indigenous communities to gain a degree of political and social autonomy while exchange with lowland Khmer, Chinese, and Vietnamese peoples provided them access to valued material goods, such as salt, metal implements, and ceramic jars (Guérin 2003; Hickey 1982, 3).[6] Through such networks, Chinese and Vietnamese traders were extracting significant volumes of timber and other natural resources from Cambodia's border regions well before the French (Cooke 2004).

Territorial boundaries between Cambodian and Vietnamese kingdoms were fluid prior to colonization, as these involved tributary relationships around centers of power rather than firmly delineated borders (Stuart-Fox 1994). Indigenous populations resisted direct settlement and imperial control, in part by providing tributes to Cambodian and Vietnamese rulers (Blanchard 1999, 43; Hickey 1982). At the same time, territorial claims did figure in precolonial state making, such as the Vietnamese "advance southward" that annexed the Cham kingdoms of Central Vietnam by the 1600s and then wrested the Mekong Delta from Khmer control (Stuart-Fox 1994). Rather than a notion of sovereignty based on territorial borders, however, Blanchard (1999, 36) calls this a "border movement" to claim and incorporate new lands.

France defined and governed Indochina's territorial borders flexibly in order to progress its economic and strategic interests (Chhak 1966; Goscha 2012). Established through a series of treaties and complex negotiations, Indochina comprised the French colony of Cochinchina (established in 1862 with the Treaty of Saigon) and three protectorates: Tonkin (established 1883), Annam (established in 1884), and Cambodia (established in 1863) (Brocheux and Hémery 2009, 77; Thomson 1945). These territories all sat within France's broader territorial envelope of the 1887 Indochinese Union (see fig. I.2). A Hanoi-based governor-general held political, administrative, and budgetary powers over the entire Indochinese territory. Thus, although only the region of Cochinchina (which at the time encompassed my Vietnamese fieldwork sites) was under direct French control, Indochina as a whole came under new law-and-order institutions, territorial demarcations, regimes for property and labor, and the development of a monetary economy based on taxation and trade (Wells 2007).

France's trade interests and the development of French capitalism were central to the Indochinese colonization project (Brocheaux and Hémery 2009). French trade interventions first targeted existing modes of production and the region's abundant natural resources before moving to plantation agriculture. In Cambodia, they initially extracted revenues from rice production (Brocheux and Hémery 2009, 123), before turning to timber (Chandler 2008, 172). By the early twentieth century, the colonial state started to develop rubber as well as tea and coffee production (Brocheux and Hémery 2009). This pivot from initial modes of rent and resource extraction to agricultural commodity production came with new forms of land governance and infrastructure, such as irrigation, rail, roads, and ports (chap. 1; see also Aso 2018). In turn, the development of rubber and other plantation crops enabled the French administration to strengthen its territorial and political control in areas remote from Saigon. Meanwhile, French investment in border districts of Cambodia during the 1920s consolidated landholdings and commodity production by the same companies who were active in Cochinchina.

Indigenous-colonial relations need to be viewed with the caveat that they are gleaned from accounts by missionaries, explorers, military personnel, and administrators and therefore reflect these positionalities rather than those of Indigenous actors (Bourdier 2015, 49). These accounts suggest that land development for plantation crops started to bring Indigenous groups into friction with the French, with well-documented incidents of active resistance (chap. 1; see also Gunn 2014; Slocomb 2015). Under the guise of protecting Indigenous minorities and informed by Rousseauian notions of the noble savage, some in the French administration argued that Indigenous groups needed protection from the

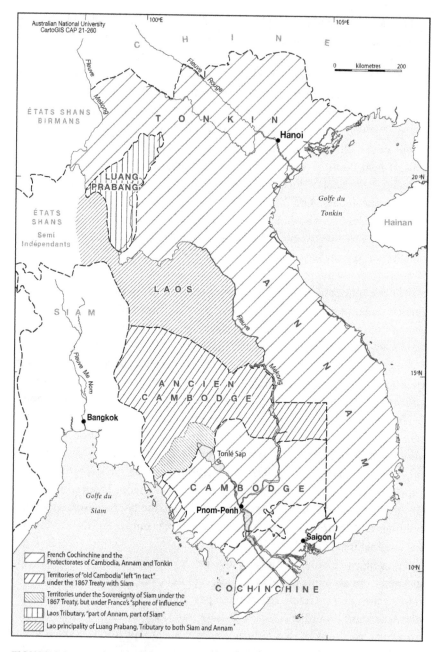

FIGURE I.2. The four territories of French Indochina, 1889.

Source: Based on ANOM, Aix-en-Provence, France (FRANOM_ 2PL_786)
Notes: Borders, territorial status, and names are as shown in the original 1889 map and reflect a historically situated, French colonial interpretation of territorial organization. The original map showed no borders between Annam and Tonkin. The map legend is an English translation of selected legend entries from the original French map.

exploitation and disruption wrought by modern market development.[7] The administration more broadly viewed the Bunong people as a security threat, citing their rebellions and attacks on Khmer and Stieng villages.[8] Administrators also claimed that Indigenous land use was destructive and inefficient, in order to progress territorial claims for colonial land-based projects, such as rubber (see also McElwee 2016; Salemink 2003).[9] These multifaceted and sometimes contradictory views nevertheless bolstered state efforts to control land and populations in these economically valuable spaces (Guérin 2003, 2009; Padwe 2009, 2020).

From the early 1920s until World War II, the French administration facilitated a major influx of Kinh (northern Vietnamese) laborers to rubber plantations on both sides of the Cambodia-Cochinchina border. Although the French viewed Indigenous labor as suited to the initial heavy work of land clearance, they preferred to deploy Vietnamese and some Khmer laborers for ongoing plantation work (Murray 1980). While I discuss the details of these labor arrangements in chapter 1, suffice to say that this process significantly shifted the demographic composition of the border region (see also Salemink 2003, 88–89). Rubber development moved hand in hand with new modes of state territorialization, enabling a greater state presence, active use of land, and the establishment of a governable population (Boucheret 2008). Yet a large population of increasingly disgruntled laborers on plantations also provided fertile recruitment ground for communist forces and others advocating for independence from the French.

It is not appropriate here to delve into the complex war history of this region, but some relevant points follow on how the conflict shaped the borderlands and market engagements. The armed independence struggle (also known as the First Indochina War [1946–1954]) that followed the end of World War II was a three-way contest between French, Khmer, and Vietnamese forces (McHale 2013, 368). Indigenous communities became involved because these parties aimed to mobilize them in different ways. For instance, the Vietnamese independence forces (Viet Minh) tried to enlist Indigenous communities in the independence struggle (Gunn 2013, 146; Jackson 1969). As French Indochina crumbled and the French resolved territorial control over Cochinchina in favor of the Vietnamese, Khmer-Vietnamese frictions over the Mekong Delta and lowland borders intensified (Blanchard 1999; McHale 2013). The ceasefire established in the 1954 Geneva Agreement also divided communist North Vietnam from the US-allied southern Republic of Vietnam along the seventeenth parallel line. The ceasefire was quickly overturned by armed conflict (Fall 1965). Blanchard (1999) documents a series of border incidents at this time. In 1956, Vietnamese troops chased members of Vietnamese politico-religious sects who were hostile to the Saigon regime into Cambodian territory. Vietnamese troops subsequently removed border posts on

May 2, 1957, and again in 1958, prompting a complaint by the Cambodian king, Norodom Sihanouk, to Vietnam's President Ngo Dinh. These examples show that during the 1950s and 1960s, the border region remained a space of friction between these newly independent states (Blanchard 1999; see also Owen and Kiernan 2006).

After independence, French investors did not immediately leave the region. Initially, they renegotiated their projects with the newly independent states of Cambodia and the southern Republic of Vietnam.[10] Many French companies had started to transfer their commercial interests from Vietnam in the 1940s and 1950s, but the Republic of Vietnam still permitted French owners to operate their plantations due to its budgetary reliance on rubber exports. By the 1960s, however, armed conflict forced many rubber plantations to close and French investors to withdraw (Pham 2019, 70). In Cambodia, French plantation owners similarly remained until conflict flared. As they withdrew, the sector started to diversify through land grants to Khmer businesses and smallholders (Fortunel and Gironde 2014; Slocomb 2010). By this time, smallholder rubber cultivation covered about ten thousand hectares in Cambodia (Delarue and Noël 2008, 1).

During the Second Indochina War (1954–1975), Indigenous groups were courted by competing interests. The Vietcong (communist Northern Vietnamese troops) engaged Indigenous groups to form a buffer against Cambodian incursions and to protect their supply lines along the Ho Chi Minh Trail (Gunn 2014, 147–8; McHale 2013; Salemink 2003).[11] Meanwhile the South Vietnamese Diệm regime pushed for Indigenous integration within a framework of modernization. US special forces also engaged central highlanders directly, attempting to mobilize these groups against the Vietcong (Salemink 2003, chap. 6). On the Cambodian side, Sihanouk launched a program of Khmerization—or integration—in the newly established provinces of Ratanakiri and Mondulkiri. He also deployed the Royal Khmer army to protect rubber estates and migrants—but these actions brought a backlash from Indigenous communities (Gunn 2014, 149; Padwe 2020, 91). This push to the northeast created space for the Kampuchean Communist Party (established in 1960, which became the Khmer Rouge) to recruit Indigenous groups to their revolutionary cause. They viewed the Khmer Leou, or upland peoples, as "original Khmer" who had survived "Indianization" (Coedès 1975; Gunn 2014, 150).[12] These groups therefore enjoyed a special place in Khmer Rouge rhetoric as natural revolutionary allies who were "nontraders" and held "class hatred." The Khmer Rouge simultaneously attempted to radicalize and peasantize these groups into settled agriculture, in order for them to more actively contribute to the revolution (Gunn 2014, 148; Kiernan 1996, 303).

Heavy bombing and defoliation during the Second Indochina War further shaped the borderlands studied in this book (Gunn 2014, 152). The United States sprayed around eighty million liters of herbicide from the air to remove canopy cover from suspected Vietcong bases and to destroy food crops (Robert 2016, 4; see also Nakamura 2007). The US campaign against the Vietcong also targeted the Ho Chi Minh Trail (see above) and border provinces of Cambodia. Defoliation and bombing affected an estimated 1.5 million hectares of forest (Robert 2016, 5). One estimate suggests that between 1943 and 1993, forest decline may have been as high as 43 percent, with a significant proportion of this forest loss occurring in the border region (De Koninck 1999).

In 1975, the same year that Saigon fell to North Vietnamese troops, the Khmer Rouge seized power in Cambodia and ruled until 1979. During this period of extreme violence, millions of Cambodians were internally displaced and killed, and private property was abolished. Populations in the southeast of the country were taken north (Greve 1993, 13), while Indigenous communities living near the border in Mondulkiri were moved to camps in a lowland district and forced to cultivate rice (Kiernan 1996). Cambodia's eastern border zone saw the expulsion and massacre of both Vietnamese and Khmer. In October 1977, there was a purge of suspected Khmer Rouge traitors with an armed incursion into Tây Ninh (Kiernan 1996) and massacres reported in the plantations of Kampong Cham (Fortunel 2013, 160). The east then gained significance as the base for Vietnam's defeat of the Khmer Rouge regime in 1979 (Jordens 1996; Kiernan 1996), after which Vietnam occupied Cambodia for a decade (1979–1989) (Chandler 2008).

After the Khmer Rouge was overthrown, many Cambodians returned to their previous homes, often searching for lost families (Greve 1993). A system of collectivized agriculture was then implemented in the lowlands, but this was abandoned by the end of the 1980s and reverted to individual household plots for cultivation (Diepart 2015, 12; Greve 1993; see table I.1). In Mondulkiri, Indigenous communities were permitted to return home when the Khmer Rouge was ousted, but many feared residual troops in the forests, stoked by warnings from government authorities (see chap. 3). During their extended absence from customary lands, the Cambodian military gained control over forests and land along the Vietnamese and Thai borders (Cock 2016; Le Billon 1999; Mahanty 2018).

The Khmer Rouge had shifted Cambodia's agricultural production toward cooperative rice farming and away from commodity crops (Slocomb 2010, 206). At the same time, natural resources, especially timber, were essential revenue sources for the Khmer Rouge in the 1970s. Vietnamese and Thai troops engaged in timber extraction during the Vietnamese occupation of the 1980s and, after Vietnamese withdrawal, the Khmer military and elite actors took over timber operations (Le Billon and Springer 2007). As Le Billon (2000, 792) describes it, an intricate interplay of factional interests meant timber exploitation became a key mechanism for capital accumulation by private as well as high-ranking government and military actors, who "were able to extract large benefits for turning a blind eye, protecting, or even organizing these activities." State officials and the military still have a tenacious hold over land and timber in contemporary markets (see chaps. 3 and 4).

Following this long period of conflict and upheaval, from the 1980s onward market formation in these borderlands has diversified with some echoes of colonial arrangements. For instance, the Cambodian government's 2001 amendment to the Land Law 1992 reflected the French preoccupation with plantation agriculture (see table I.1). The government has continued to support agricultural markets, emphasizing stable land tenure as an essential precondition for this (Royal Government of Cambodia 2004) as well as domestic value addition (Royal Government of Cambodia 2013, 8). A subdecree under the revised Land Law 2001 specifically opened new land concessions for plantation crops, such as rubber, bringing a new wave of rubber plantations but this time based on Vietnamese investment (see chap. 4). Other interventions have been more novel. The government's 2012 rapid land-titling initiative known as Order 01, which focused on small-scale farms, was an especially transformative intervention in frontier provinces. Across the country, teams composed of university students and state officials measured, mapped, and titled farms of up to five hectares. Many newly cleared agricultural lands were titled during this process in Mondulkiri (Mahanty and Milne 2016; see chap. 3). While French colonial state interventions served European capital, in contemporary Cambodia it is state and business elites, as well as large investors from Vietnam, China, and other parts of East Asia, that have benefited from more recent interventions.

A historical parallel is also visible in the direction of trade flows from Cambodia to Vietnam. While the French focused on natural resources and rubber, Cambodia's border provinces now export commodity crops, such as cassava, to Vietnamese processing industries in the east (Sopheap, Patanothai, and Aye 2012) and Thai factories in the west (CDRI 2009; Diepart and Dupuis 2014; Hought et al. 2012). These export opportunities have been integral to the country's tenfold increase in GDP between 1990 and 2016 (World Bank 2018). Even though manufacturing industries are a growing sector of the economy, agriculture remains a major contributor to Cambodia's GDP and rural livelihoods (Kem 2017; World Bank 2015).

By the time my research commenced in 2012, Vietnam's agricultural processing industries depended heavily on imports funneled through the Cambodia-Vietnam borderlands. From 2005, cassava and other crops flowed in growing volumes from Cambodian border provinces to the Vietnamese provinces of Bình Phước and Tây Ninh (FAOSTAT 2017), where processing factories and export

TABLE I.1 Key land governance instruments that have influenced postconflict market formation in Mondulkiri

REGULATIONS	PROPERTY RIGHTS AND ACCESS
1992 Land Law[†]	Allows registration and sales based on "possession"; enables "concessions" for land over 5 hectares
2001 Land Law[§]	Enables systematic land registration to promote tenure security, land markets, investment
2003 Sub-Decree No. 19 on Social Land Concessions[*]	Provides for the nontransferrable allocation of state lands to poor/displaced families for residential and/or farming use
2005 Sub-Decree No. 146 on Economic Land Concessions[††]	Major growth in agricultural concessions until moratorium in 2012
2009 Sub-Decree on the Procedures of Registration of Land of Indigenous Communities[§§]	Indigenous communal title for registered Indigenous bodies.
2012 Order 01BB on Measures for Strengthening and Increasing the Effectiveness of the Management of Economic Land Concessions[††]	Supported by a rapid land titling initiative (Order 01) that grants titles for many "possessed" lands (<5 ha)

Sources: Bidulph 2010 and 2014; Diepart 2015; Diepart and Schoenberger 2016; Desbarats 1995; Guillou 2006; Grimsditch and Schoenberger 2015; Milne 2013; So 2009; Un and So 2011; relevant legislation cited in footnotes.

Notes:

[†] Royal Government of Cambodia, Land Law (1992).

[§] Royal Government of Cambodia, Land Law (2001).

[*] Royal Government of Cambodia, Sub-Decree on Social Land Concessions No. 19, ANK/BK, March 19, 2003.

[††] Royal Government of Cambodia, Sub-Decree on Economic Land Concessions No. 146 ANK/BK, 2005.

[††] Royal Government of Cambodia, *Measures to Strengthen and Increase the Effectiveness of the Management of Economic Land Concessions,* May 7, 2012.

[§§] Royal Government of Cambodia, Sub-Decree on the Procedures of Registration of Land of Indigenous Communities, 2009.

warehouses mushroomed. Vietnamese processing industries initially targeted European markets but turned to China in the 2000s. The Vietnamese border was also an important conduit for timber destined for China, where demand for raw commodities has far outstripped any other market after the global financial crisis of 2007–2009 (Kaplinsky, Terheggen, and Tijaja 2011). The three focal commodities in this study—timber, cassava, and rubber—have been important in reinventing the postconflict frontier. Vietnamese and Chinese industries and traders have become key frontier protagonists and sources of demand for Cambodia's raw materials.

In this brief historical overview, four related themes tied historical markets to contemporary ones: Indigenous engagements, state formation, land governance, and labor mobility. Building on their prior exchange networks, Indigenous communities have engaged markets in diverse ways while enduring various forms of direct and indirect violence (Padwe 2020, 22). The contemporary frontier thus recreates aspects of the colonial "contact zone" (Pratt 1991). Migration and mobility have been central to this region's market formation story, initially facilitated by the French and now through organic migration to Cambodia's frontier provinces. Land interventions and commodification have reworked the borderlands, from colonial territorial interventions to post-independence land formalization projects. Colonial and contemporary states have played a crucial part in market formation. In the coming chapters, I explore these themes through the highly visible processes of market development of this borderland frontier.

Conceptualizing Market Formation

The preceding section outlined how processes of colonization, commodification and exchange have produced both a borderland and a market frontier. Central to my work is the idea that frontier markets are continually *in formation* as new resources are incorporated through everyday practices that bind social and material worlds. Although this view of markets is especially relevant in the Cambodia-Vietnam border region, I venture that it resonates in other postcolonial frontiers. As borderland scholars have long argued (Das and Poole 2004), the formative processes at the edges of markets also have the potential to expose their inner workings: the drivers, unruly characteristics, and fragilities that cause markets to change over time.

As noted in the historical overview above, European colonization drove market exchange for specific goods on the basis of price, money, and bargaining (Polanyi 1957, 267). Colonial administrations promoted markets by imposing new institutional structures to guide peoples' relationships with each other and with the natural environment (Wolf 1982, 19). Through these interventions, commodity markets overlaid existing ways of life with new mechanisms of resource access and trade that served to attract and benefit European capital and to create a waged and mobile labor force. In turn, markets served state formation by enabling colonial administrations to control territories and subjects; the two were mutually reinforcing (see chap. 1).

At the same time, colonial interventions interacted in complex ways with the cultures and trading networks that predated them, such as exchange relationships based on kin and tribute (Wolf 1982; see also Thavat 2010 on Cambodia; Turner, Bonnin, and Michaud 2015 on Vietnam). Scott (2009) suggests that colonial states had limited reach into upland minority cultures, but where they did, state interventions were not deterministic. Contemporary commodity markets continue to be embedded in community economies based on reciprocity, gift, and barter; these systems of exchange are conjoined because "no trade or market system exists without the support of communal agents such as shared languages, mutual ways of interacting and implicit understandings" (Gudeman 2001, 9; see also Polanyi [1944] 2001). Colonial land and labor institutions were therefore continually reinterpreted as local actors resisted, adapted, and even at times abandoned these impositions. Thus, across French Indochina, colonial land and market institutions were not rolled out seamlessly; they were reproduced and changed through everyday actions and interactions with diverse local populations (after Giddens 1984). Similarly, today, Hmong people in northern Vietnam combine subsistence activities with selective market engagements (Turner, Bonnin, and Michaud 2015); and Bunong communities maintain their connections to places that have been transformed by large-scale rubber concessions (see chap. 4).

Because of these contingent local engagements with institutions and markets, structural influences on the market are not deterministic but take hybrid forms as they meld with localized institutions and interests. The "actually existing" capitalism of this frontier (Brenner 1999) emerges from the interaction between capitalist political and economic institutions and the grounded social relations and practices that interpret and implement them (R. Foster 2002; Gibson-Graham 2006; Gregory 1982).

To better understand these dynamics, I compare frontier markets to the edgeless and proliferating network of Deleuze and Guattari's rhizome (1987). Deleuze and Guattari outline six core rhizomic characteristics that further help us to understand how frontier markets are constituted and reworked. These principles are *connectivity, heterogeneity, multiplicity, rupture, cartography,* and *decalcomania*.[13] Anyone who has pulled up a rhizomic weed has witnessed a rhizome's tangled and tenacious character. The interconnected nature of frontier commodity networks similarly seems to add to the market's expansiveness and endurance.

As discussed above, however, markets do not spread in a deterministic or completely unfettered way; they are shaped and recreated by enduring social institutions and historical legacies.

Although Deleuze and Guattari do not embrace these crucial structural legacies, their principles of cartography and decalcomania provide useful insights. In the principle of cartography, Deleuze and Guattari see rhizomic formations as a *map*—an interpretation—rather than a reproduction of an existing pattern or structure. This resonates with the institutional contingencies discussed above. The term *decalcomania* comes from an artistic technique where images are transferred from a specialized paper to other surfaces, such as glass and porcelain. By applying this concept to a rhizome, they suggest that a rhizomic form does not simply reproduce a pattern; instead—using the artistic metaphor—images are inevitably changed as they contact different surfaces that have specific qualities and resistances. This principle speaks to the landscapes and people that interact with and shape specific market networks. Finally, rhizomic structures are highly prone to instability and rupture—a crucial feature that has a generative role in market formation that I explore in later chapters. The rhizome therefore speaks to the interconnected, volatile, and locally molded commodity networks that constitute this frontier market.

The rhizome analogy resonates with existing approaches to understanding markets, such as commodity-chain analysis and actor-network theory, but adds the crucial dimension of cross-commodity linkages that is often overlooked in commodity studies. Commodity-chain analysis examines the "network[s] of labor and production processes whose end result is a finished commodity" (Hopkins and Wallerstein 1986, 159). This analytical method usefully exposes how capitalism is sustained by asymmetrical global structures of labor, production, and consumption (Bernstein and Campling, 2006; Gereffi, Korzeniewicz, and Korzeniewicz 1994). Later versions have considered how institutions that govern land and resource access contribute to unequal risks and benefits within commodity networks (Neimark 2010; Ribot 1998). By focusing on one commodity, however, this approach can miss broader connections, such as how market formation brings fundamental transitions to land and labor. A further limitation is the emphasis on direct actors in commodity-chain analysis, which masks the full complexity of commodity relations (Neimark, Mahanty, and Dressler 2016). For example, local officials may not appear as direct commodity-chain actors but can play a crucial role in mediating land access (see Mahanty 2019; chap. 3). My study incorporates these indirect players, who can play an integral role in market formation.

In addition to human actors, the characteristics of specific commodities and landscapes can actively shape market formation—as has been the case in the

Cambodia-Vietnam borderlands. For example, the key commodity crops of rubber and cassava require specific soils, climate, and cultivation requirements. Such biophysical features as elevation, rainfall, and proximity to infrastructure are also important. Actor-network theory helps us to look at such human and nonhuman actors by considering *actants*: any entity that "acts or to which activity is granted by others" (Latour 1996, 7). This concept takes us beyond the typical actors at the center of classical commodity-chain studies, such as producers, brokers, buyers, and consumers (e.g., Gereffi, Korzeniewicz, and Korzeniewicz 1994). Incorporating human, multispecies, and material actants helps to broaden this analysis to consider how cultivars, such as cassava, or material features, such as land, roads, national borders, or other pertinent agents, figure in market formation. The inclusion of nonhuman agents is controversial for some critical scholars, who worry that this will detract from their emphasis on exploitative social relations (Hornborg 2017; Lave 2015). Yet the two approaches can productively work together (see, e.g., Castree 2002; Rocheleau 2015; Tsing 2015; Vandergeest 2008). Attention to such material entities as cultivars, land, and infrastructure can provide a more holistic appreciation of commodity networks. This approach also gives agency to frontier landscapes rather than viewing them as passive settings in which commodity networks unfold.

The rhizome analytic is comparable to commodity-chain analysis and actor-network theory, but goes beyond their usual emphasis on individual commodities. A rhizomic lens adds attention to overall market formation processes where multiple commodity networks are involved. It also directs analysis to processes of market expansion and rupture and the contingencies that translate market institutions to local contexts. My analysis thus situates the analysis of specific commodity networks within a broader rhizomic view of markets.

Drawing on actor-network theory, the early stages of market formation involve disparate actants being enrolled into a supportive market network and then mobilized, to sustain production and reproduction over time (Callon 1986). Specific commodity networks may also rupture or fall apart due to dissonance (Callon 2010, 167). An example of this is discussed later, where fluctuations in the demand and price for certain commodities disrupt or "disarticulate" (Berndt and Boeckler 2009) cassava networks. In chapter 2, I show that instability also comes from new ideas and practices, such as recommendations from traders about new crops or cultivation techniques, or the emergence of disease. These frictions within different commodity networks are potentially influential in driving new modes of market engagement and the proliferation of new commodities. This is why it is useful to analyze both the trajectories of specific commodity networks, relationships between commodities, and structural factors that sustain market formation, such as land institutions.

In studying these dynamic qualities of the market, I explore whether there are limits to its continued reinvention and expansion in these borderlands. At a macro or systemic level, critical scholars have long recognized that unbridled market growth is ultimately untenable. This idea was integral to Marx's concept of the "metabolic rift," where capitalism would ultimately break down the socioecological metabolism that joins society to its natural and physical foundations (J. Foster 1999). Similarly, Polanyi ([1944] 2001) pointed out that the exploitative foundation of the market would ultimately pose social limits; people would resist and seek social protections from the market's unfettered growth. These cautionary observations about the limits to market growth call for empirical evidence of how these pressures are experienced locally and the different ways in which people respond. In chapter 4, I develop the idea that a key sign of market rupture is where disruption spills beyond a specific commodity network and accumulates through cross-network interactions in ways that irrevocably deplete resources and acutely threaten livelihoods in a broad section of the population.

Apart from these environmental and social stressors, individual decisions are also a potentially important source of disruption in specific commodity networks. This scope for agency is not well covered by either the structural approaches discussed earlier or networked analytics. Agency within the market can differ from traditional definitions that center on "the capacity of individual and corporate actors . . . to play an independent causal role in history" (McLaughlin and Dietz 2008, 105). In the frontier context, I find that personal actions by farmers, migrants, or traders that appear small and indeterminate can have broad and transformative effects when combined with and multiplied by the actions of others. This approach contrasts with neoclassical economics, where markets (and the economy) are studied as distinct domains of rational choice and decision making, divorced from social relations (Carrier 2018, 21).

Holly High (2014, 11) contributes to our understanding of these forms of agency through her discussion of desire, which she defines as a "force of actualization" that is both personal and social. From this perspective, agency within the market reflects the drive or capacity to take certain actions—actions that may be personally and even socially generative. This kind of framing is useful, for instance, in contextualizing how an individual migrant or a farmer adopting a new crop can influence frontier landscapes and markets. These personal actions are taken in the context of specific opportunities and constraints and have the potential to shift individual and collective lives in indeterminate ways. Agency may also be expressed through narratives and routine practices. For example, in Central Asian trading networks, Rippa (2019, 255) finds that traders actively construct and "perform" the market through their "regular contacts and virtual relations." As with other processes of knowledge production, such practices and beliefs reflect, entrench, and can even subtly alter lines of authority and power in market networks (after Jasanoff 2004, 4). These examples highlight the practical, discursive, contingent, and sometimes conflicted nature of agency—themes that I explore further in later chapters.

In summary, my rhizomic view of markets recognizes historical and structural influences as contingent rather than deterministic, and examines how specific commodity networks take form through granular, grounded social and material relationships. The rhizome lens reveals the complex connections between diverse commodity networks that compose this frontier market. It sheds light on the potential triggers for market rupture through cascading disruptions and entrenched inequities. Seen this way, markets are ultimately processual and contingent, with inherent qualities of complexity and change. This hybrid approach allows us to better understand "actually existing capitalism": the diverse ways in which markets take form in space and time through social structures, relationships, and agency (Hudson 2016).

Chapter Overviews

The chapters of this book explore historical and ongoing processes of market formation in the Cambodia-Vietnam borderlands, from French colonization to the period of my most recent fieldwork in 2018. They broadly follow a chronological approach, while pursuing the themes introduced in the preceding sections, of state formation, land governance, migration, and agency within frontier markets. My analysis shows how this rhizomic market is in a continual state of formation, or *becoming*, through proliferating and connected commodity networks. During the colonial period, these processes served European capital and now serve the interests of Cambodian elites and Vietnamese and Chinese capital. Evidence of social and environmental stress reveals potential limits to market formation, although this region has so far followed a tendency to "reinvent" the frontier by commodifying new resources (Rasmussen and Lund 2018). Frontier markets are shown as more than sites of incorporation into global capital; the frontier is a contact zone where hierarchically structured and complex historical, human, and material interactions are continually changing and reinventing markets.

After examining the historical development of large-scale colonial rubber plantations in the first chapter, I primarily focus on contemporary smallholder engagements with the market. As recent work on the global land grab focuses on large-scale agricultural production (see Schoenberger, Hall, and Vandergeest 2017 for a useful summary), the issues in this sector—such as ongoing land enclosures, primitive accumulation, and resistance—are well understood even if solutions are proving elusive. Although critical agrarian scholars have studied the effects of smallholder production on agricultural commodities, we are yet to understand how these engagements contribute to market formation more broadly. This book therefore supplements this literature by highlighting how smallholder market engagements intersect frontier migration and land use change—a set of relationships that warrants further and urgent study (Cohn et al. 2017, 351).

Chapter 1 examines the historical development of rubber production and trade, which was one of the first large-scale commodity crops to be cultivated on the Cambodia-Vietnam frontier during the period of French colonization. The chapter shows that this phase of market formation was facilitated by early processes of knowledge production, rubber's importance for state formation, and global political-economic transitions that sparked the 1920s Indochinese rubber boom. Because the French colonial state was a central player in the development of rubber, planters expected the administration to support them through innumerable crises, including land tensions, labor unrest, and price volatility. As rubber took hold, however, the market's rhizomic characteristics became evident: it was volatile, branched off into new arrangements and spaces, and became unruly and ungovernable. These developments catalyzed local resistance, which ultimately undermined the French administration.

In chapter 2, the Cambodian border province of Tbong Khmum provides examples of how the market's intersecting commodity networks mature over time. The French first targeted the area for rubber development, and in the 1960s smallholder settlement started to intensify, together with the production of agricultural commodities. At the time of research, Tbong Khmum had little to no forested land available for conversion. Consequently, the uptake of new crops—or commodity transitions—could not occur without smallholders purchasing new land, changing existing cultivation patterns, or migrating to upland areas. Commodity networks in Tbong Khmum evolved and intersected as farmers cultivated both old and new crops. These networks centered on rubber, cashew, and, later, cassava, pepper, and fruit trees. Vietnamese traders played an important part in developing these market networks. The chapter explores how the actions of farmers and these other actors have shaped specific commodity networks and, through these, contributed to the ongoing formation of the frontier market.

Chapter 3 studies the formation of contemporary cassava trading networks in the Cambodian border province of Mondulkiri, which neighbors Tbong

Khmum. In response to a boom in global demand for derivatives of industrial—or "bitter"—cassava over the last decade, large tracts of the Cambodia-Vietnam frontier have come under smallholder cassava cultivation to supply processing industries in Vietnamese border provinces. Subtle material and social variations in Mondulkiri have produced two distinct commodity networks that circulate dried cassava chips and fresh cassava tubers. Chapter 3 first distills the key actors and relationships in these networks and the negotiations and practices involved in mobilizing the cassava trade. It then turns to the specific role of migration in the development of new agricultural lands, where cassava has been a crucial pioneer crop. Once settled, migrants have employed a range of strategies to secure their landholdings, catalyzing land markets and new forms of credit. These commodification processes served to expand and deepen the frontier market, even as cassava networks became destabilized by disease and price volatility and farmers moved on to other crops. The chapter concludes that cassava networks have both adapted to and shaped diverse localities through related processes, such as migration and land claiming. The commodification processes that migration and cassava have set in train ensure that market formation continues even if cassava-specific networks are disrupted.

In light of the transformative processes associated with market formation in the preceding chapters, chapter 4 explores the theme of rupture. Focusing on two settlements in Mondulkiri, the chapter traces the emergence of a postboom rupture at the site of a large rubber concession, which interacts with accumulated environmental and social pressures, such as debt, soil, and resource exhaustion. Disparate social groups experience the effects of these transformations differently. While some farmers slip into precarity, lose their land, and migrate elsewhere in search of land or work, others seek new forms of value in the tired landscape by moving on to different crops and finding niches within illicit economies. There are synergies between the small-scale and gradual actions of smallholders and the large-scale developments that are more typical or visible sites of nature-society rupture. At the time of research, the breaking apart of market networks was catalyzing new market trajectories. As debt, land dispossession, and disease accumulated across different commodity networks, the prospects for "frontier reinvention" looked uncertain.

Chapter 5 examines how market governance is challenged by the market's rhizomic characteristics. This chapter returns to the crucial role of state actors and institutions in catalyzing new markets and in framing conditions such as land access. As markets evolve, however, state capacity to shape their direction and outcomes becomes highly contingent. This is first explored in the case of Cambodian value-chain interventions that attempt to enhance cassava production and processing opportunities and, through this, increase farmers' incomes and national revenues. These value-chain interventions have enrolled increasing numbers of farmers in cassava production, in particular through investment incentives that support contract farming. Yet they have been unable to address destabilizing influences, such as disease and price volatility. A similar pattern is observed in the second case study, a state-facilitated commodity network to produce petrol-ethanol fuel (called E5) for Vietnam's transport sector. In this second case, the state has engaged in market development to achieve environmental objectives but has been unable to grasp and manage this market's complexities, leaving the country with several defunct ethanol factories. The chapter concludes that the inherent complexities and instabilities of markets make them unruly and potentially ungovernable.

I show that over time globally connected trade has transformed this frontier, but local sociomaterial commodity networks continue to shape its specific form and effects. My hybrid approach contributes to ongoing methodological discussions on the intersection of structural patterns and local influences in market processes. It brings together the central role of historically and spatially situated actor-networks in market formation. Beyond this, my case studies illustrate the significance of agency in developing new commodity markets, particularly the actions of state actors, traders, and small-scale farmers. The networked character of market formation in frontiers means that even small-scale local actions, such as forest clearance by migrant settlers, can feed into regional and even global transitions, such as climate change. Capitalism's insatiable hunger for frontier resources produces enduring structures and institutions that shape the market's complex and granular networks, but stark social and environmental limits are now emerging.

RUBBER IN FRENCH INDOCHINA

From the late eighteenth century the French colonial administration sponsored extensive exploratory missions to assess and map Indochina's resources. These expeditions made the case that Indochina's frontier regions held great potential for agricultural development (Boucheret 2008, 45). Nonetheless it took more than favorable biophysical features to establish what would become a key plantation crop in the mountainous borderlands of Indochina: rubber, or *Hevea brasiliensis*.[1] Establishing rubber production required specialized knowledge about how to grow and harvest this new crop and the engagement of a diverse network of actors from administrators to scientists and private investors. Also essential were the political and economic institutions that the French administration created from the late 1800s onward. Colonial state making was in turn facilitated by *Hevea* cultivation, which opened and populated Indochinese frontiers. Although the French administration was central in establishing *Hevea*, it was French capitalists that propelled the crop's dramatic expansion during the 1920s. The interests of these two groups would ultimately diverge at pivotal intersections.

As established in the introduction, colonies such as French Indochina were crucial as a source of raw materials, labor, and wealth for European capitalism (see Wolf 1982). Building on my earlier historical overview, this chapter turns to the specific case of rubber; it examines the social, historical, economic, and political foundations that gave rise to large-scale rubber production in Indochina. French Indochina encompassed the northern and central regions of Tonkin and Annam, the colony of Cochinchina, and the Cambodian protectorate (see fig. I.2 in the introduction). In this chapter, I primarily focus on Cochinchina but also draw on examples from the Cambodian protectorate as large-scale rubber planta-tions were located along the borders of these territories. Although it is challeng-ing to uncover the precise configuration of actor-networks from historical data, we can discern who the significant actants were. One of these was the new cul-tivar of *Hevea brasiliensis*, whose large-scale cultivation in Indochina demanded new techniques and practices. Knowledge production by state and scientific ac-tors was therefore crucial in the early stages of rubber's development. Private plantation investors and financiers then expanded the sector with state support in the form of new land governance mechanisms and in terms of mobilizing capital and labor—interventions with lasting legacies that the following chap-ters elaborate on. These private actors in turn assisted the French administration to tighten their control of Indochinese territories and peoples, highlighting the close nexus between state and frontier market formation. Yet, even though the colonial state carefully nurtured rubber production, it was unable to govern the market as production and trade took hold.

The first phase in the development of the Indochinese rubber market involved the translation of the new cultivar, *Hevea brasiliensis*, to Indochinese conditions. This process took place before World War I, a period when the Indochinese econ-omy centered primarily on the extraction of surplus from the rice sector and natural resource exploitation—both of which needed little capital investment (Murray 1980). When the first *Hevea* seedlings reached Indochina from British Malaya in 1897 (Murray 1992), several actors helped to lay the sociotechnical groundwork for *Hevea*'s wider adoption. By 1907, larger commercial plantations started to develop in eastern Cochinchina's *terres rouges* (red soils), and by 1913 there were a total of fifty-one plantations, but most were not yet producing rub-ber (Brocheux and Hémery 2009, 127). These early endeavors established the nec-essary knowledge for *Hevea* to flourish in Indochina.

The basaltic red soil regions of Indochina's frontiers were viewed as ideal for *Hevea*, since these landscapes were densely forested and sparsely populated (Brenier 1914). These classic frontier conditions, however, also raised specific chal-lenges for the development of rubber that could only be addressed with state sup-port: the laying of infrastructure to areas remote from seats of commerce and government, the organization of land administration, and the mobilization of labor (Murray 1992; Thomas 2012). State policies in these areas helped to create favorable economic conditions for private investment and to reduce the financial risks that investors faced. In turn, as I elaborate below, rubber plantations helped to consolidate French territorial and political authority at the margins of Cochi-nchina (Aso 2018; Sowerwine 2011).

While state facilitation was important in these early stages, it was the dra-matic global increase in demand for rubber that fueled Indochina's rubber boom during the 1920s (Murray 1992, 47). Significant private investment in production, made possible by a rapidly expanding Indochinese financial sector, drove this post-World War I phase of the rubber market (1918–1929) (Murray 1980, 98). Large-scale, privately owned plantations of rubber, tea, and coffee increased in number during this period, but rubber dominated because of international growth in the motor vehicle industry, which boosted rubber demand (Brocheux and Hémery 2009, 126). At the peak of the rubber boom, there were 35,000 rubber plantation workers in Cochinchina (1928) and 10,200 in Cambodia (1930; Aso 2018, 112), and about 84,482 hectares were allocated for *Hevea* cultivation.

As the rubber sector became established, however, many challenges emerged. Issues such as price volatility, land conflicts, and labor unrest posed tangible threats to the Indochinese rubber market during the 1930s. For private plantation owners, the colonial administration was usually the first port of call for support, yet governing these changeable conditions demonstrably challenged state actors. The evidence I present in this chapter establishes that state facilitation of rubber production certainly did not amount to control or a capacity to govern the specific direction or outcomes of the rubber trade.

By introducing rubber, the French colonial state also introduced a global commodity market to Indochinese frontiers. Although this early history was more punctuated than today's rhizomic process of market sprawl, rubber production had three characteristics that are still found in contemporary frontier markets. Firstly, rubber production underwent temporal fluxes, in which the roles of different actors waxed and waned. Secondly, state formation and market formation were mutually supportive. Third, as the market took hold and spread to new terrains through an expanding array of actors, it took on a life of its own and became increasingly difficult for the French administration to govern. Indeed, the colonial administration's central role in introducing this commodity exposed it to existential risks when problems emerged. The chapter expands on these points in chronological sequence to examine the development of rubber production in Indochina, its mutually reinforcing role in state formation, and how international political-economic transitions and local land and labor challenges ultimately rendered this commodity network ungovernable.

Sociotechnical Foundations (Late 1800s to 1910s)

The research required for *Hevea* to spread as a major plantation crop in Indochina made it an important node for knowledge production (Aso 2018, 91). A diverse network of actants laid this groundwork to determine where to grow the new cultivar, how to establish and maintain it, and the most effective harvesting and processing techniques.

The French started surveying Indochina's social and ecological terrain well before rubber was introduced. The earliest written records on the Indochinese environment were in fact Chinese, but French Catholic missionaries who arrived in Indochina during the eighteenth century played an important role in documenting the region's geography prior to the establishment of French administration (Aso 2011, 52). To enlist local converts, missionaries who were posted to the northern and central highlands of Tonkin and Annam and to the outer reaches of the Cambodian kingdom gathered detailed information about local settings, languages, and customs (Daughton 2006; Michaud 2004). Starting in the 1870s, the colonial administration sponsored expeditions to document the geography of these Indochinese frontiers. The accounts and maps that these expeditions produced helped the French administration to plan its exploitation of Indochina (Boucheret 2008; Daughton 2006).

An example of such state-sponsored exploration is the work of Auguste Pavie (b. 1847), who led several exploratory missions between 1879 and 1895. In 1879, the new governor of Cochinchina, Charles Le Myre de Vilers, arrived with a stated desire to support reconnaissance missions to "unknown territories" on Cochinchina's borders (Pavie [1906] 1999, 81). De Vilers initiated a new periodical, *Excursions et Reconnaissances*, to share the knowledge gained from such expeditions—an indication of his enthusiasm to back such work. It was during de Vilers's governorship that Pavie, then serving in the Post and Telegraphs Office in the Cambodian town of Kampot, sought the administration's support for an exploratory mission to map and document little-visited areas of Cambodia (Pavie [1906] 1999, 82–83). De Vilers and subsequent governors supported several of Pavie's missions in Cambodia, Thailand, Laos, Tonkin, Annam, and Cochinchina. The many volumes that resulted from these missions recorded the culture, history, geography, zoology, and botany of these regions. While Pavie's missions are perhaps the best known and documented, numerous other explorers and scientists undertook similar work.

A second example is Henri Brenier's *D'Atlas Statistique de L'Indochine Française* (1914). This government-commissioned compilation presents maps and statistics on Indochina's biophysical, sociodemographic, and economic characteristics. Brenier (1914, 176) admitted that his scale of analysis, which was large for its time, made it impossible to achieve complete accuracy. Yet the atlas was influential in marking out the region's economic potential, including areas suited to rubber production. Specifically, Brenier's (1914) discussion of population relative to land and other geographical conditions proposed that areas of low population density overlaid soils that were highly suitable for rubber development: the *terres grises* (gray soils) and terres rouges (red soils), the latter usually lying under "lush jungle." Brenier's proposition about the compatibility of red soils and rubber was not new. In 1913, an entry in the annual report of the Association of Rubber Planters of Cochinchina and Indochina described "a vast vein" of red basaltic soils that traversed the Cochinchinese-Cambodian borderlands. This region was believed to be about one hundred kilometers in length and forty kilometers wide, spanning the (then) provinces of Baria, Bienhoa, and Thudaumot in Cochinchina and their bordering Cambodian provinces (*Les Annales des Planteurs de Caoutchouc de l'Indochine* 1913, 53). The administrative imprimatur on Brenier's account may have added weight to these existing views. A consensus thus emerged during the first two decades of the 1900s that red soils best suited *Hevea* because of their structure and fertility and because their elevation provided some protection from flood and disease. Although the clearance of such lands involved more labor, and some warned that these soils were easily depleted (Boucheret 2008, 54), the administration prioritized these border locations for the development of rubber.

Large-scale rubber production in Indochina called for new knowledge on how best to grow this novel cultivar. The challenges of propagating *Hevea* were already well known. Henry Alexander Wickham is often credited as the first to ship *Hevea brasiliensis* seeds to Britain's Kew Gardens for experimentation as a potential new crop for British colonies. Prior explorers, however, had already shipped seeds of different varieties back to Britain for propagation, albeit with mixed results (Dove 2011, 115). Scientific staff at the Kew Gardens finally achieved successful germination of wild Brazilian *Hevea* in 1876 after several failed attempts (Wolf and Wolf 1936, 161). The French drew on Britain's model for distributing *Hevea* seed throughout its colonies to test the crop in diverse growing conditions. British authorities had dispatched seed stock to their botanical gardens in Ceylon, Burma, and Singapore, followed by Malaya and British Borneo. These centers tested the optimal conditions for cultivation, the best methods and timing to "bleed" the *Hevea* trees, and coagulation techniques to make the latex easier to transport and trade (Wolf and Wolf 1936, 167–68).

Similarly, the Hanoi and Saigon Botanical Gardens and other state-supported research institutions were crucial to the successful propagation of *Hevea* in French Indochina. Propagation trials were carried out at three sites in 1897: in Ong-Yem, within the Saigon Botanical Gardens; at the Balland plantation near Giadinh; and in Annam by Alexander Yersin at the Institut Pasteur à Suoi-Giao (Chevalier and Le Bras 1955, 23). Aso (2011) carves out a particularly significant role for Yersin, an agricultural scientist who founded the Pasteur Institute at Nha Trang. Among the many crops that Yersin tested, *Hevea* arrived in 1897 in the form of saplings from the Saigon Botanical Gardens. He initially planted a

30-hectare trial crop in the institute's experimental plantation, before planting 307 hectares on his own land in 1914. This was both a commercial and scientific venture, which enabled him to experiment with different modes of soil preparation, seed propagation, plantation maintenance, and tapping techniques, as well as methods to process latex (Aso 2011, 13–14).

While these efforts in Indochina progressed, the French also maintained an empire-wide perspective on plantation crops. The scientist Auguste Chevalier was a key adviser on plantation agriculture across tropical regions of the French Empire, mapping out differentiated strategies according to environmental conditions and labor availability in various colonies (Chevalier 1949). In a late-career retrospective on the development of rubber, Chevalier proposed that Indochina compared favorably with production in British and Dutch colonies, as "the plantations [they] visited in Suzannah, Anloc, Lochninh etc. were splendid, filled with promise and could rival the most beautiful of English or Dutch possessions" (Chevalier and Le Bras 1955, 23). Chevalier attributed this to a conjuncture of "favorable circumstances," including "the presence of unoccupied lands which are sufficiently rich and not far from very dense populations of workers, likely to provide an abundant and skillful labor force; the arrival in these countries of considerable capital which was used to organize large plantations; and, from a technical point of view, the already old existence of scientific establishments in these regions" (Chevalier and Le Bras 1955, 124). Through these international scientific networks, *Hevea* was not just transferred but *translated*, in the sense described by actor-network theorists: new knowledge was produced on the cultivar and its cultivation from late 1890 into the 1910s, primarily driven by enabling networks of material actants, such as receptive soils, and human actants, such as scientists and government personnel (Aso 2011, 64).

Building on these efforts, private investors then tested *Hevea* under commercial conditions. Well ahead of the 1920s boom, small-scale investments in rubber plantations had already commenced. In 1904 the Société Agricole de Suzannah established Cochinchina's first commercial plantation, Suzannah. This was followed in 1907 by Xa Trach, which was established in Thudaumot Province by the Société des Plantations des Hévéas de Xa-Trach (SPHX; a Mr. Haffner, a former director of the Saigon Botanical Gardens, initially managed Xa Trach). Plantation numbers grew incrementally from 1910 up to the start of World War I in 1914. Chevalier observed that private plantations of this kind played a foundational role in extending knowledge about plantation management: "Two eminent farmers, E. Girard and A. Hallet played a prominent role in the period 1912–1920 as the first organizers of large plantations in Indochina and developers of the best farming techniques of *Hevea* in this colony" (Chevalier and Le Bras 1955, 24). These accounts reveal that scientists and plantation owners supported the knowledge production needed to expand *Hevea* cultivation in Indochina.

Early plantation owners further influenced the rubber sector by organizing rubber producers. In 1910, planters established the Association of Rubber Planters of Cochinchina, a body that served both knowledge production and market formation. This association was first called the Association des Planteurs de Caoutchouc en Cochinchine (APCC) but later broadened its remit to Indochina (Association des Planteurs de Caoutchouc de L'Indochine [APCI]). The association started as a loose collection of plantation owners who "met in Saigon in a room in the Continental Hotel with the aim of forming a group of Rubber Farmers in the Colony" (*Annuaire du Syndicat des Planteurs de Caoutchouc de l'Indochine* 1931, 9). A statute signed by the governor of Cochinchina in 1917 had syndicated the association to gain "more power and force" in light of the expanding plantation sector (11).

While syndication permitted a stronger advocacy role, the association's early emphasis was squarely on knowledge production. Before World War I, the association's annual reports are filled with debates on the most suitable cultivation techniques for *Hevea*, the best methods to "bleed" *Hevea* trees, processing innovations, and other aspects of rubber production. For example, in the 1914 annual report, a Mr. Magen, the director of the SPHX plantation asked, "Should we plough rubber plantations?" (*Les Annales des Planteurs de Caoutchouc de L'Indochine* 1914, 77). He extolled the benefits of first ploughing one side of the plantation and then a few months later ploughing the other side, specifying that these furrows should be one meter to the right and left of the trees. A later entry in the same annual report speaks to the optimal timing for bleeding *Hevea* trees: if undertaken when the trees are too young, the author states, the latex is of poorer quality and "barely pays the costs of cultivation and treatment" (89).

Another preoccupation of the association was the control of fire in plantations, as seen in this entry from the 1911 annual report: "In our issue from last March, we drew our farmers' attention to the necessity of periodically ploughing around trees, in order to hasten growth and we added *that it was the best insurance against fires* (emphasis in original). The frequency of fire incidents over the past months has made us insist on the importance of ploughing, from a point of view of protecting against fires that are so frequent for many reasons at the end of the dry season" (*Les Annales des Planteurs de Caoutchouc de L'Indochine* 1911, 198). In addition to fire mitigation regimes, these annual reports also discuss the causes of plantation fire, usually accusing "pirates" and "criminals" (1913) as well as "slash and burn" (or *ray*) cultivators (1912)—an early indication of the frictions between plantation owners, disgruntled workers, and Indigenous groups that were to escalate over time.

Finally, the association shared commercially significant information on rubber processing and quality. The 1913 annual report, for example, explains a new apparatus to measure the dosimetry of latex (the ratio of water present in a latex sample). The association also promoted technologies for coagulation, such as a technique where an alkali was added to collection cups to coagulate the latex. This edition went on to explicitly highlight the importance of technical information, stating: "It would be an error on the part of capitalists to not attentively follow this movement of inventions that either discover new functions of the product or ways to improve its quality" (*Les Annales des Planteurs de Caoutchouc de L'Indochine* 1913, 257). With this statement, the author frames rubber as a technical project as much as a commercial one, which was particularly important during these early stages of the establishment of rubber in Indochina.

As the production and trade of rubber progressed, the annual reports of the planters' association track a shift from the development of foundational knowledge on where and how to cultivate *Hevea* to knowledge regarding commercial *Hevea* cultivation and rubber processing. While state-sponsored exploration and science set the initial groundwork for rubber production, commercial plantation owners and such bodies as the Association des Planteurs de Caoutchouc de L'Indochine played a crucial role in the dissemination and commercialization of the crop. These groups were heterogeneous, and key individuals were at times influential, as the discussion has shown. Various state actors remained significant from the earliest stages of rubber development until the end of French rule—an outcome that the rubber market was intrinsically tied to.

Rubber in State Formation (1910s—1920s)

In addition to providing raw material for European industry, the French colonial administration supported rubber for its potential to generate state revenues and entrench French domination of the Indochinese peninsula (Boucheret 2014). The economic record is well documented, with rubber ultimately becoming the second-largest Indochinese export after rice, accounting for one-third of the total value of Indochina's exports during the colonial period (Boucheret 2014, 34). Rubber's role in assisting France to strengthen its administration of Indochinese territories and populations was realized well ahead of its economic potential, which only grew after World War I (see table 1.1). Through rubber, France signaled its ability to territorialize remote regions both to Indigenous subjects and to rival colonial powers such as Britain, who were competing to gain influ-

TABLE 1.1   Rubber output from Indochina 1900–1940 (in thousand metric tons)

YEAR	VOLUME	YEAR	VOLUME	YEAR	VOLUME
1900	0.3	1914	0.2	1928	9.8
1901	0.3	1915	0.4	1929	10
1902	0.1	1916	0.6	1930	11
1903	0.1	1917	0.9	1931	12
1904	0.2	1918	0.5	1932	15
1905	0.4	1919	3.0	1933	19
1906	0.5	1920	3.1	1934	20
1907	0.2	1921	3.7	1935	29
1908	—	1922	4.6	1936	41
1909	—	1923	5.7	1937	45
1910	0.2	1924	6.8	1938	58
1911	0.3	1925	8.0	1939	67
1912	0.3	1926	8.8	1940	72
1913	0.2	1927	9.6		

Source: B. Mitchell 2007

ence in Asia (Osborne 2016, 75; see below). In the process, colonization and its social and material networks produced a frontier market.

As noted earlier, the red soils that were targeted for rubber cultivation coincided with the outer reaches of Cochinchina and the border regions of the Cambodian protectorate. By facilitating large-scale rubber production, the French administration could simultaneously develop and territorialize these frontiers that were remote from the Cochinchinese capital, Saigon. Rubber cultivation additionally enabled the settlement of these areas by French farmers and plantation managers, as well as labor that was recruited in large numbers from the northern protectorates of Annam and Tonkin. In contrast, the ethnic minorities that lived in these areas, known by the pejorative term Moi (literally, "savages"), were deemed to be uncivilized and the "worst savages who have survived in Asia" (Forbin 1911, cited in Boucheret 2008, 55). Land and labor policies were therefore both essential to state formation. Yet ongoing frictions around land governance and labor conditions would prove the complexities of frontier incorporation and rule.

The colonial administration's taxation and trade regime created the conditions for Tonkinese and Annamese labor to be mobilized. These interventions preceded rubber's introduction by some decades but are briefly considered here. The administration's early emphasis on export-oriented agriculture, particularly rice, increased social differentiation and land shortages in Annam and the Red

River Delta (Murray 1980, 213). The local population was literally starved of live-lihood opportunities. Furthermore, the imposition of a personal tax on the na-tive Indochinese population in 1880, with successive increases to taxation rates, pushed small-scale cultivators to seek wage labor in plantations, mines, and in-dustry (Murray 1980, 228). Those unable to make tax payments became *corvee* labor for infrastructure projects, while the broader squeeze on rural livelihoods enabled the mass recruitment of indentured laborers, known as "coolies"[2] (Bro-cheux and Hémery 2009; Murray 1980; Slocomb 2007). The colonial adminis-tration thus actively created a mobile population that it could more readily control and mobilize for recruitment to rubber plantations in eastern Cochi-nchina and later Cambodia. The volume of workers recruited to plantations was large. In Cambodia, for instance, an average of 10,000 Tonkinese "coolies" ar-rived annually to work on plantations during the 1930s (Slocomb 2007, 58). In Cochinchina, Robequain (1944, 81) cites figures of 3,022 indentured workers in 1922, which increased to 22,352 in 1928, excluding women and children. He added that his figures were likely an underestimate. The proletarianization of the rural population and these modes of enforced and voluntary mobility served to consolidate the political and economic power of the French colonial adminis-tration (Murray 1980).

While the state created the preconditions for labor mobility, plantation owners undertook labor recruitment and transportation. Planters sought state support for these costs, arguing in an entry in the 1912 *Les Annales des Planteurs de Caou-tchouc de L'Indochine* for greater state support to defray the costs faced by plan-tations in hiring and maintaining laborers. The same article observed that although shipping companies had been granted tariff reductions for "coolie" "im-ports," the state had provided little help to planters. They made their case for state support on the basis that work on plantations would address the problems of poverty and hunger in the North (*Les Annales des Planteurs de Caoutchouc de L'Indochine* 1912, 15–19). Despite these appeals by private plantation owners, state support in the labor sphere remained mainly indirect. At the same time, the colonial state benefited from a growing frontier population of recruits from Tonkin and Annam that were seen as "submissive," "obedient," "respectful of authority," and "full of deference" (*Les Annales des Planteurs de Caoutchouc de L'Indochine 1913*, 8, cited in Boucheret 2008, 55).

In Cochinchina, the colonial administration provided support for French farmer settlers, even though large plantations dominated latex production. For its other colonies, the French metropolitan state recruited French workers and peas-ants to settle, acclimatize, and engage in manual labor. The metropole viewed Indochina as requiring more skilled French settlers who knew "agriculture or a trade, who [had] some resources, and who, instead of working with his hands, [would] supervise the work of the native . . . trained in his methods and disciplined to his needs" (Haussonville and Chailley-Bert 1897, cited in M.-P. Ha 2014, 23). In addition to making land available to French settlers (Murray 1980, 57), by the early 1900s the administration decided that young French women were also needed as wives. This was to give settlers a reason to stay and reduce the likelihood that they adopt Vietnamese concubines (M.-P. Ha 2014, 26–29). After World War I, veterans joined the ranks of these small settler farmers, with two thousand hectares of land reserved for their use in each province of eastern Cochinchina.[3]

Populating the Indochinese frontiers with Vietnamese and French settlers was integral to the fabric and formation of a French colonial society. Through this, the administration cultivated a nucleated and governable body of subjects as much as it did a space dedicated to rubber production. The case for frontier development was often justified as *mise en valeur*, a French term used to describe "development" in the sense of economic exploitation, which went hand in hand with the colonial administration's *mission civilisatrice* (civilizing mission) (Salemink 2003, 88). One important facet of this project was migration by ethnic Vietnamese, not just as a labor force for plantations but also for their capacity to teach Indigenous groups settled agriculture, commerce, and an industrial work ethic (Salemink 2003, 89). French settlers were a second important facet. Notions of model frontier subjects—also known as *bon colon* (literally, "good settlers")—reinforced these ideals of European colonial settlement. One such model farmer was Madame de la Souchere, also known as the "Princesse de l'Heveas" (Queen of Rubber), whose 1922 *Legion d'honneur* was awarded for her stalwart efforts to continue operating the family plantation alone after her husband's untimely death. Madame de la Souchere was cast as a moral and benevolent settler, the epitome of what the French bon colon brought to these remote regions (M.-P. Ha 2014, 214). French settler family farms thus show a political logic to the expansion of rubber into frontiers that went beyond economics alone. In contrast to Cochinchina, these family farms barely figured in Cambodia's colonial rubber sector (Slocomb 2007, 27), perhaps due to Cambodia's protectorate status and the delayed development of plantations there.

The French colonial administration began distributing land grants in 1874, thereby establishing the conditions for land territorialization. Such grants peaked under the Doumer administration (1896–1902) (Murray 1980, 62) and continued up to and beyond World War I (see table 1.2). About 94 percent of this land was held by companies, whose plantations became the mainstay of Indochina's latex production (Robequain 1944, 207); however, smaller farms of under forty hectares were important for the political reasons covered above.

The important place of frontier lands in state formation is evident from the high level of state oversight over land concession agreements in Cochinchina.

TABLE 1.2 Area of land (acres*) allocated to rubber cultivation in Cochinchina 1897–1920

DATE	1897–1900	1900–1910	1910–1915	1915–1920	TOTAL (1897–1920)
Acres	300	21,000	971,190	944,842	1,937,332

Source: Archival data cited in Boucheret 2008, 130.

* 1 acre = 100 square meters or 0.01 hectares

Concessionaires had three main pathways to gain land: (i) *grè à gré* (private agreements) signed between government and buyer, which were the main model for large Cochinchinese concessions; (ii) adjudication or public auctioning to the highest bidder, with the income going to the Cochinchinese budget (more common in urban and settled regions); and (iii) free land grants, which were especially used to encourage agricultural development in the terres rouges regions of the current Vietnamese border provinces of Tây Ninh and Bình Phước (see fig. I.2 in the introduction) (Aso 2018, 33). The state tightly controlled all of these land access systems. Both grè à gré and adjudication were governed by a complex set of regulations, while free land grants required sign-off at the highest level of the Cochinchinese administration. A concession granted by public auction to Adrien Hallet in 1918, for instance, specified that the lands must be developed in a timely manner: "The requested lands do not present any specific difficulties from a clearing or cultivation point of view. Therefore nothing opposes the speedy development of the future concession, the interested parties already possessing sufficient financial means. The quick development of these lands is essential in order to avoid claims of 'land grabbing' being made against the dealer/concessionary."[4] Another example from the 1920s is the allocation of 150 hectares to a Mr. Cremazy for the Phuoc Luc Concession.[5] This archival file was thick with several years of correspondence, including reams of letters between the provincial administrator and the governor of Cochinchina. Like the investors and administrators who wrote these documents, the documents themselves were material actants in the rubber network. They represented an agreement between the concessionaire and the land department based on maps, investigations, safety conditions, and other requirements. In both the Hallet and Cremazy cases, the documents contained several terms and conditions for the concession, with final approval granted by the governor, indicating oversight at the highest administrative levels.

A third important area where the rubber market intersected state formation was through Indochina's financial sector. Rubber was a capital-intensive sector, needing credit to cover the high up-front costs of plantations and to run operations until rubber could be tapped (Brocheux and Hémery 2009). An important—but indirect—state intervention in this sphere was the establishment of an Indochinese currency, the piastre. In his study of the Indochinese currency, Jean-Daniel Gardère (2010) documents the Bank of Indochina's minting of this new currency in 1878 and the events that followed. The piastre became legal tender across the Indochinese Union in 1885, helping to stamp French authority over trade in an environment where British and US currencies were also in use (Gardère 2010, 146). The establishment of a unique currency simultaneously served France's geopolitical and trade interests and took Indochina toward budgetary independence as a colony. The currency was closely intertwined with the inception of the Bank of Indochina in 1875 (153) and served to reinforce an administrative hierarchy within Indochina whereby the center controlled the currency (183). For example, when the French administration in the Cambodian protectorate experienced a shortage of money in 1890, it complained of Cochinchina's refusal to send sufficient coinage over the border. The option of minting a unique Cambodian currency was briefly floated, which, according to a colonial treasury official, "would have the advantage of staying mainly on Cambodia's territory" but was quickly ruled out as incompatible with Cochinchinese taxation requirements (*Letter from Indochina treasury pay officer to Resident Superieur, Cambodia*, August 12, 1890, cited in Gardère 2010, 158). The piastre also underpinned Doumer's taxation and financial reforms, which aimed to promote the colony's financial self-sufficiency through local budgets for each territory within the Indochinese Union (167). The piastre thus served both state-building and commercial interests.

While challenges to the colonial state-formation process were to come later, state support for rubber was intertwined with early efforts to control frontier territories. Central to this project was the population of Indochinese frontiers with governable French settlers as well as a mobile Tonkinese and Annamese population that appeared relatively amenable to control. The same actions that facilitated private investment in Indochina also enhanced trade and the colonial administration's budgetary autonomy from the metropole. Furthermore, the different modes of territorialization and subjectification in Cochinchina compared with Cambodia show that such state-formation processes, and rubber's place within it, were variegated between colony and protectorate. These processes continued to unfold during the rubber boom of the 1920s.

The Political Economy of the Rubber Boom (1920–1928)

The preceding discussion explains the introduction of rubber to Indochina and its significance for colonial state formation. I now turn to the Indochinese rubber boom in the 1920s, which emerged from a convergence of international economic conditions. Specifically, the mass production of automobiles and bicycles in the United States and some European countries created a global spike in demand for rubber. Efforts to stabilize the international rubber price were also significant, notably Britain's Stevenson Plan of 1922. These remote actants were thus influential in rubber's expansion in Indochina, as were French capitalists.

In the United States, the mass production of cars took off from 1913, enabled by the Ford Motor Company's new assembly line technology, which was initially used to produce its Model T vehicle (Hounshell 1984). After this key development, international demand for rubber grew very rapidly (see table 1.3). The US motor vehicle industry accounted for about half of global demand, with the rest going to the production of industrial parts, footwear, and medical and electrical instruments (Chevalier and Le Bras 1955). US and European tire companies also invested directly in rubber production by financing *Hevea* plantations in a range of countries (Wolf and Wolf 1936). The French tire company Michelin became a key player in Indochinese rubber, but other Indochinese producers also directly supplied US manufacturers (Chevalier and Le Bras 1955, 122). The promise of continued global demand for rubber provided by these technological and industrial developments helped to catalyze production in French Indochina.

Britain's Stevenson Plan of 1922 further boosted the growth of Indochinese plantations. After World War I, a global glut of rubber was created when a large number of colonial plantations started tapping latex, which depressed the international rubber price (Murray 1992). As Wolf and Wolf (1936) discuss in their historical study of rubber, postwar deflation simultaneously hit the US rubber industry with dramatic effects on demand for and the price of crude rubber. As Britain controlled about 75 percent of global production at the time, these price effects were most profoundly felt in British colonies. Winston Churchill, who was then the Secretary of State for the Colonies, explained the extent of this threat to British capital: "The whole industry in which . . . £100,000,000 of British capital had been sunk, was falling into ruin. . . . It was impossible for the Colonial

TABLE 1.3 World rubber consumption 1921–1929

YEAR	CONSUMPTION (TONS)
1921	320,000
1923	405,000
1925	512,000
1927	648,000
1928	729,000
1929	820,000

Source: Slocomb 2007, 110 and 113 (original source not shown).

office to witness the financial ruin of the rubber-producing colonies owing to the continual sale of their products below the cost of production" (quoted in Wolf and Wolf 1936, 220–21). Churchill appointed his personal financial advisor, Sir James Stevenson, to investigate the industry and recommend a course of action. Stevenson chaired a committee that proposed two related schemes: the first would restrict latex output at the plantation level, and the second would use duties to restrict exports (Wolf and Wolf 1936, 221).

When the Dutch and French—the other major colonial rubber producers— refused to participate in Stevenson's restrictions, the committee recommended that Britain proceed unilaterally with their output restriction and export duty scheme. The scheme, known as the Stevenson Plan, became law on November 1, 1922, and restricted British plantation owners to 60 percent of standard production or face higher export duties. While some illegal smuggling continued, the Stevenson Plan quickly buoyed the international rubber price, pushing it from USD 0.24 in 1922 to USD 0.36 in January 1923 (Wolf and Wolf 1936, 223). Without French and Dutch agreement to the plan, rubber's strong price together with growing industrial demand enticed Indochinese and Dutch colonial plantations to rapidly expand production and take up the slack left by British restrictions (Murray 1992, 47).

The Indochinese rubber boom of the 1920s thus emerged from the price effects of the Stevenson Plan, and from the rapid development of the automobile industry and mass production technology in the postwar United States. Indochinese production more than tripled in the decade between 1920 and 1930 (see table 1.1). Given the disadvantage that the Stevenson Plan inflicted on British planters, it was abandoned in October 1928 (Wolf and Wolf 1936). By this time, however, a significant volume of French capital had already reached Indochina. These companies aimed to grasp the lucrative opportunity that the Stevenson Plan provided to expand *Hevea*, while taking up incentives provided by the French administration which restricted non-French investment and provided favorable terms of trade to the metropole (Murray 1980, 199; see below). The strength of the Indochinese piastre, while the French franc was in crisis between 1920 and 1928, further drove speculative investment (Brocheux and Hémery 2009, 164).

The role of French capital in the rubber boom is illustrated by the case of Adrien Hallet. Hallet was a key player in a conglomerate of Franco-Belgian capital known as the Rivaud-Hallet Group. The group founded the Société Financière des Caoutchoucs in 1909 (Socfin, or, literally, the "financial rubber company") (Clarence-Smith 1997, 3). Initially a member of Socfin's board, Hallet rapidly expanded his influence and voting shares to become chairman of the company by 1923, a position he held until he died of sudden illness in 1925 at the age of fifty-seven. Socfin grew to be one of the most powerful holding companies in Indochinese rubber (Robequain 1944, 208), operating two major companies, the Société des Plantations des Terres Rouges (SPTR) and the Compagnie du Cambodge, as well as smaller holdings like the Compagnie des Caoutchoucs de Padang (Clarence-Smith 2010). Hallet was a prominent figure in Indochinese files on land acquisitions from 1910 until his death in 1925. For example, a cadastral entry from August 8, 1919, confirmed that Hallet was allocated 1,350 hectares in Thudaumot Province (near the villages of Luong-Ma, Lich-Loc, and Dong-Tuu, Thudaumot).[6] After Hallet's death, these lands were transferred to the Société des Plantations de Mopoli, which gave it to the Société d'Hévéas de Xatrach (which became the Société des Plantations des Terres Rouges in 1923).[7] This example highlights the intricate financial connections between Indochinese rubber companies, which served to complicate state regulation of company landholdings.

The French colonial state actively supported land access for companies like Socfin, as Hallet's case again illustrates. When Hallet arrived in Cochinchina in 1910, he already had plantation experience from British Malaya and Sumatra. He reportedly went prospecting in the basaltic hills near Loc Ninh, Thudaumot, where ten square kilometers of forest were marked off for his future development. The area was apparently so close to the Cambodian protectorate that "the border was pushed back a little on this occasion" (Robequain 1944, 205). Hallet's ease of land access and the readiness of state authorities to realign an inconvenient border illustrates their responsiveness to the needs of these large investors. Bolstered by state support, the Rivaud-Hallet Group acquired 32,000 hectares by 1930; employing some twenty thousand workers and producing an estimated 35–40 percent of the total latex flowing from Indochina (see also Bui 2012).[8] By 1939, the group's international landholdings had expanded to 141,500 hectares (primarily for rubber, oil palm, and coffee cultivation), accounting for about 3.5 percent of world rubber exports (Clarence-Smith 1997).

During the rubber boom, the French administration helped to establish the commercial and physical infrastructure needed to attract private capital to Indochina, including road, rail, and communications, as well as tax incentives and policies to regulate non-French investments in Indochina (Murray 1980, 167). Such infrastructure was built with a mix of corvee labor, provided by villagers in lieu of taxes, and direct state funding. The latter was key to road construction in the remote Cochinchinese terres rouges regions (Murray 1980, 260). Private capital then expanded and developed Indochina's rubber sector. Socfin was one of many companies that grasped these opportunities. During the boom period of the 1920s, other key companies included the Société Agricole de Suzannah, Société Agricole de Thanh Thuy Ha, Caoutchoucs de l'Indochine, and the Plantations d'An Loc (Murray 1980, 153). It is instructive that, by the 1940s, just three companies dominated the Indochinese rubber sector: the Rivaud-Hallet Group, the Michelin Group, and the Banque de l'Indochine (Brocheux and Hémery 2009, 127)—reflecting the dominant role of big French capital in Indochinese rubber.

The rubber boom of the 1920s thus arose from the political economy of global rubber markets as well as French Indochinese-metropolitan dynamics. The first provided the impetus for Indochinese *Hevea* plantations to expand, while the second delivered the means for this expansion. It was in the late 1920s that rifts became visible between large-scale investors and the French colonial administration.

The Ungovernable Market (after the 1920s Rubber Boom)

Although the administration was influential in the establishment of rubber production, it was unable to control the course of this sector. Once in train, rubber's production and trade had unruly and even ungovernable dimensions. Land allocations were at times conflicted, and speculation was difficult to control. When prices fluctuated, planters expected the French administration to provide support. Large plantations created aggregations of exploited and discontented workers, who appealed for labor reforms and ultimately posed an existential threat to French colonial rule. These ungovernable dimensions of rubber, a key commodity for Indochina, became increasingly evident during the late 1920s and 1930s when the interests of capital and state diverged.

In the early days of Indochinese rubber, land was easy and cheap to access—or even free—but unless the land was developed and cultivated within ten years, the authorities applied taxes (Murray 1980, 57). By 1914, with the beginning of World War I, only one-third of allocated lands had been "improved" or planted with rubber; the rest were unused, rented, or held speculatively (Murray 1980, 190–91). This pattern persisted after the war ended in 1918. The rubber boom between 1922 and 1928 fueled a "veritable land rush" (Boucheret 2008, 178) by metropolitan sources of capital, which invested an estimated seven hundred million francs between 1925 and 1929 to obtain plantations (Robequain 1944, 162). Yet the actual development of these lands lagged far behind, as the gap between allocated and cultivated land in table 1.4 reveals.

The administration perceived this sluggish development of concessions as speculative and a loss in taxation revenues (Murray 1980, 191). In the interests of gaining better state returns from the rubber boom, a 1926 review by the

TABLE 1.4   The gap between allocated and cultivated land for *Hevea* in Indochina 1927–1929 (in hectares)

YEAR	1927	1928	1929
Total allocated land area	66,984	78,773	84,482
Areas under rubber cultivation	26,122	28,237	29,920

Source: Boucheret 2008, 179.

inspector general of agriculture, Yves Henri, produced a bill that recommended various measures to more tightly regulate the size, timing, and development of concessions (Boucheret 2008, 183). While Henri's bill met resistance from large plantation companies, small farmers with holdings of less than 40 hectares (as defined by Robequain 1944, 207) supported his moves to prevent large investors from monopolizing land. Under Henri's bill, new concessions would be restricted to 300 hectares, concessionaires had to demonstrate their financial capacity to develop and cultivate the land, and strict time limits would apply for land to come under cultivation, imposed through a mix of taxes and fines (Murray 1980, 191). Between the release of Henri's bill and its passing into law by Governor Varenne in September 1926, some powerful companies had rushed to file anticipatory requests for new land. For example, on April 26, 1926, the Rivaud-Hallet Group's Société des Plantations des Terres Rouges applied for two areas of land in Thudaumot, of 600 and 995 hectares. Similar claims were lodged by Michelin and the Société Indochinoise de Commerce d'Agriculture et de Finance (SICAF), a plantation holding company created by the Bank of Indochina (Aso 2009, 246; Boucheret 2008, 189).

The Varenne regulations were short-lived due to resistance from rubber planters, particularly these large-scale investors, who used their connections to influence state actions. After enactment in September 1926, the Council of Ministers suspended the regulations only months later in March 1927. Crucial to this outcome was pressure from the newly syndicated Association des Planteurs de Caoutchouc de L'Indochine, who reframed the debate by positioning both settlers and large companies as victims of the political authorities, without any distinction. Plantation owners, notably Michelin, finally saw to the removal of Varenne in January 1928, because he posed a threat to their "dominion over their estates and labor" (Thomas 2012, 162). The manager of Michelin's Indochinese rubber operations explained Varenne's removal as a natural outcome, given the influence of a company of Michelin's stature: "The Governor is boss of the local officials and labor inspectors. The Governor has the Governor-General above him; and above the General there stands Michelin and Co. of

Paris. . . . As is well known, Michelin can ruin a bureaucrat's career . . . much as it can advance those of the officials with whom it is satisfied" (cited in Thomas 2012, 169). Thus, by the late 1920s, the same companies that had been enticed to invest in Indochina by the French colonial administration turned their power against a governor that sought to control them. This occurred both in the arenas of land and labor, as I detail next.

Local resistance to concession development further complicated the French administration's land governance. This resistance grew following the allocation of large land concessions in the Cambodian protectorate during the late 1920s. Slocomb (2007, 35), for instance, documents a petition from villagers in Kratie's Stung Trang District in 1927 that complained of the loss of rice fields and croplands as well as access to forest resources, such as timber. Similarly, the numerous concessions within the Mimot-Kantroy complex in Kampong Cham Province (now the Cambodian border province of Tbong Khmum) involved tense negotiations between companies and French authorities over the timing of development and the size of lands assigned to companies. Authorities there also received many local complaints about forced resettlement, loss of access to farming lands, and the tendency for companies to receive land allocations before disputes were settled and concessions formalized. A letter from the Resident of Kampong Cham, Desenlis, to colleagues in Phnom Penh outlined these tensions: "I still do not know d'Ursel's [the concession holder's] intentions, but the *chef du poste* at Mimot wrote to me that in the course of a private conversation with d'Ursel, he learned that he intends to clear as much as 5000 hectares in this dry season. . . . His coolies will find themselves in contact with the Stieng population . . . and conflict is inevitable" (quoted in Slocomb 2007, 41). Desenlis went on to say that he planned to write in stern terms to d'Ursel to "respect absolutely all the natives' *chamcar* [cultivation areas] and not to touch them under any pretext" (41). This was one of several land cases in the Cambodian protectorate, which typically involved direct appeals to French administrators by disenfranchised Khmer and Stieng populations and posed new challenges for state administrators.

Price volatility brought additional pressures for the French colonial administration. Although the Stevenson Plan had initially boosted global rubber prices, these remained volatile, particularly after Britain abandoned the plan in 1928. Although the French administration was ill equipped to address price stability, planters nevertheless pressed for and gained state support. During the price slumps of the late 1920s and the early 1930s, the Union des Planteurs de Caoutchouc, a new lobby group set up in 1931, "pushed hard for government handouts" (Thomas 2012, 165). Loans were issued from budgetary reserves to newly established plantations. For established plantations that had to sell their latex below production costs, an act passed on March 31, 1931, created an indemnification fund. A tax on French imports of raw and manufactured rubber backstopped these funds. The windfall in reduced input prices for European manufacturers was thus used to subsidize Indochinese producers (Robequain 1944, 206; see also Thomas 2012, 165). In 1936, the French administration provided further financial aid to Indochinese rubber planters, as well as tax concessions on rubber production, including the removal of a domestic 2 percent tax (Boucheret 2008, 362). Although Robequain (1944, 206) credits government support with saving Indochina's rubber industry, the relationship between business interests and the French administration was acrimonious at times, and the latter ultimately supported planters to cope with price collapses rather than being able to address the causes of price volatility.

International efforts to stabilize rubber prices were no less challenging. In 1934, the French metropolitan government joined a meeting of major rubber-producing countries in London that sought to stabilize global rubber prices by controlling global production levels. France signed the resulting agreement, which placed restrictions on rubber production as well as on the release of new land for plantations (Aso 2009, 248). Production quotas were to be adjusted from time to time by an International Rubber Regulation Committee, which included representatives from France, Britain, and the Netherlands (Wolf and Wolf 1936, 234). The inclusion of France and the Netherlands in this agreement was an advance on the Stevenson Plan, but colonial governments struggled to roll out quotas between their various colonies and among producers within each colony. Tensions also prevailed within the committee, where the British and Dutch wielded greater influence due to their longer history of rubber production and the large rubber volumes that their respective colonies still produced (Wolf and Wolf 1936, 235–237).

Meanwhile, in Indochina, plantation labor conditions became another major challenge, producing frictions between the French administration and company actors. Indentured laborers faced exploitative and violent conditions on both Cambodian (Aso 2018; Slocomb 2007) and Cochinchinese plantations (Murray 1980; Robequain 1945). These laborers commenced work in debt to their employers, because their contracts usually involved an advance payment to cover their initial travel to the work site and to support their families at home until wages started to flow. While recruiting agents trapped some into bondage, most were "free" in as much as they voluntarily entered contracts. Yet this apparent agency was constrained by the lack of employment options in their home villages, the livelihood pressures imposed by new colonial market and taxation regimes, and their initial debt on arrival (Slocomb 2018, 360–61). Plantation owners argued that these labor opportunities provided a solution to rural poverty, but sanitation and living conditions on plantations were very poor. Workers suffered from constant ill health, notably from malaria (Aso 2018; Murray 1980; Robequain 1944, 216), and plantation supervisors subjected them to arbitrary abuse and violence (see Thomas 2012).

Over time, these different forms of workplace exploitation and abuse loomed large in the plans and fortunes of the colonial state (Thomas 2012, 175). During the 1920s rubber boom, when labor recruitment was at a peak, the French administration enacted laws to regulate plantation working conditions, which covered all of Indochina but was particularly geared toward rubber workers in Cochinchina and Cambodia. Governor Varenne's 1927 edict set out standards for plantation worker salaries, contract durations, and daily rations (seven hundred grams of dry rice per man, woman, or child), and required plantation owners to provide "sound, convenient and hygienic" housing for all staff. The edict also mandated that a savings fund was to hold a 5 percent salary deduction for workers, "in order to protect the native against his own improvidence, gambling and tendency to acquire debts" (Robequain 1944, 78). Employers were also able to pursue cases of desertion by laborers (Slocomb 2007, 65). The French administration created the Inspection Générale du Travail to enforce these laws, but its legion of labor inspectors struggled against plantation owners who continually overstepped these regulations, because they perceived trade-offs between improving pay and working conditions and their own profit margins (Thomas 2012, 173). Although plantation owners expected the state to protect them from disgruntled workers as well as Vietnamese nationalists and communists, they were quick to resist the policing of labor conditions (Thomas 2012, 163).

It was in this complicated space of perceived responsibility with limited authority that the French administration became increasingly entangled in labor disputes to stabilize unrest (Murray 1980). On some occasions, state authorities had small and temporary impacts on plantation labor practices. For example, on the night of February 18, 1927, 280 Tonkinese "coolies" fled from the Mimot plantation and went to the Kratie residency to submit complaints of contract breaches and employer brutality (Slocomb 2018, 363). The resident superior referred the matter for investigation, and the manager, Verhelst, was found guilty of beating the workers, received a sentence of three months' imprisonment, and was then deported, while the plantation director was also fined. Regulation had a temporary impact, yet real change in working conditions failed to materialize. Six months later, demonstrations continued about working conditions and around 100 workers deserted the Mimot plantation (Slocomb 2018, 367). This particular incident was instrumental in the French administration's efforts to regulate plantation labor conditions. In general, however, exploitation and violence continued unabated in Indochina's largest plantations, where managers became adept at circumventing the "embarrassment and inconvenience associated with unwanted plantation visitations" by labor inspectors (Murray 1980, 280). Most large plantations maintained private prisons to hold "coolies" that had attempted to escape or failed to comply with their overseer's instructions regarding work, thus regulating their own lands and labor (Murray 1980, 280).

The French administration's weak regulation of plantation labor conditions contributed to large aggregations of disgruntled workers who became fertile ground for the anti-French resistance. Supported by communist organizations, workers staged at least eight major strikes between 1930 and 1937 (Murray 1980, 299). In Cochinchina, one of the best-known strikes occurred on Michelin's Phu Rieng plantation during the Tết (Lunar New Year) festival of February 1930. Prior to this event, the Revolutionary Youth League had dispatched one of their group members, Nguyen Xuan Cu, to Phu Rieng with the aim of recruiting plantation workers to the revolutionary cause. Nguyen established a key clandestine cell of the Revolutionary Youth League and also formed a worker's union that published the broadsheet L'Emancipation to publicize workers' struggles and coordinate a self-defense group. In the lead-up to the Phu Rieng strike, frictions intensified regarding labor conditions, including an attack by "coolies" on the brutal overseer M. Monteil on September 26, 1927. Other attacks ensued against supervisors that had a history of violence against plantation laborers, which attracted concern from other plantation owners as well as the French administration. The administration reluctantly acknowledged that these attacks were a "direct response to the abuse committed within the plantation" (Murray 1980, 300). According to Murray (1980, 306), events like the uprising at Phu Rieng produced "a significant shift in the terrain of the class struggle in Indochina" and bolstered the independence movement (see also Thomas 2012 on Michelin's plantation in Dau Tieng and Slocomb 2018 on Cambodia). These accounts reveal a nexus between labor exploitation, the administration's weak regulatory capacity, and the growth of anti-French resistance in Indochina. To diffuse this burgeoning unrest, the administration publicly downplayed these connections, representing them as isolated incidents on specific plantations or events that arose from the cruelty of particular plantation managers rather than a systemic problem (Thomas 2012, 167).

These pressures and controversies in the spheres of concession lands, rubber prices, and plantation labor conditions demonstrate that, having actively supported the formation of frontier rubber production, the French colonial administration struggled to effectively govern the rapidly evolving rubber market.

Rubber as Part of an Ungovernable Market Rhizome

The development of rubber production and trade in Indochinese frontiers rested on knowledge production through actor-networks and political-economic developments. Although the state was crucial in facilitating this process, market formation required a host of additional actants, such as scientists, explorers, and venture capitalists, as well as an imported cultivar, and the artifacts and technologies that mobilized land, labor, and international demand for rubber. The establishment of frontier rubber plantations served the French administration's need to gain territorial control and to settle Indochinese frontiers with compliant subjects. Yet, as production took hold, the rubber trade took on an ungovernable and volatile character that ultimately challenged state control and legitimacy.

The rubber case shows that the roles and significance of different actants in this market changed over time. Explorers mapped the terrain and conditions suited to rubber from the late 1800s. Scientists adapted *Hevea* cultivars and harvesting practices to Indochinese conditions in the early 1900s, while private finance was instrumental during the 1920s rubber boom. These transitions reveal the rubber market's elastic and dynamic character in its early stages and the how the roles of key actants changed as the market took hold and intensified.

While various actants rose and fell in prominence and specific state officials came and went, the French colonial administration was closely and continually involved. It supported expeditions that charted the localities to be targeted for rubber cultivation. Land administration and taxation regimes set the conditions to mobilize land and labor. State policies later attempted to regulate market conditions, such as time frames for land development, labor standards, and commodity prices. In short, it is questionable whether the industry could have grown without active state facilitation, given the level of financial risk involved for investors and the lengthy wait for profits. In return, rubber helped the French administration to control and populate frontier territories and thus served colonial state formation.[9]

For French Indochina, a coproductive relationship can be traced between market and state formation, although this relationship wavered over time. The red soils of the remote Cambodia-Cochinchina borderlands were integral to large-scale *Hevea* cultivation. Not only did rubber production increase investment and revenues (advancing the interests of both Indochinese and European capital); it provided a basis for the French administration to control and civilize these sparsely populated regions and Indigenous peoples, a project that the Cambodian royalty would continue in eastern Cambodia after independence (Padwe 2020, 92). Yet physical and sociopolitical disparities also created frictions (Scott 2008) in the growth of this market rhizome. The French first targeted western Cochinchina for rubber production—a region that fell under their direct administration and was therefore more conducive to establishing rubber, which needed state control of land, labor, and infrastructure. They later expanded rubber to the Cambodian protectorate. While the colonial administration observed the Cambodia-Cochinchina border at times, they could readily override it when necessary (Goscha 2012). In time, however, the ability of the administration to incorporate these borderlands within a governable colonial state would prove as elusive as governing the trajectory of the rubber market.

The rubber case illustrates some important and rhizomic aspects of markets. Despite the instrumental role played by the French colonial administration in the early stages of market development, after initial land enclosures were made and the rubber frontier established, the interests of private plantation owners and investors took precedence in ways that challenged the project of state formation. Rubber production and trade then followed twists and turns that proved to be well outside state control. Having promoted market formation, the French administration was expected to navigate intransigent land conflicts, price volatility, and labor unrest. Yet these developments emerged from the cyclical fluxes of global capitalism (in the case of price) or the actions of companies and local actors that the state seemed unable or unwilling to regulate. These risks and market instabilities proved highly problematic for the colonial state. The state's failure to regulate plantation labor conditions was perhaps the most striking example, which ultimately fueled resistance against French colonial rule.

In summary, this chapter puts forward a hybrid understanding of frontier market formation, where historical, political, and economic developments framed conditions but the market took hold through the influence and actions of critical actors and their networks. As it developed, the rubber industry evolved in directions that were influenced by many but ungovernable by one specific actor. Furthermore, the rubber case shows the mercurial character of frontiers, a theme that is explored further in chapter 2. The French considered Indochina a resource-rich periphery that was ripe for exploitation and development. Yet within Indochina, the low population and forests of western Cochinchina and eastern Cambodia were specific frontiers available to be populated and developed.

Several of these patterns persist in contemporary frontier markets. The next two chapters, which focus on the adjacent border provinces of Tbong Khmum–Tây Ninh and Mondulkiri–Đắk Nông (see fig. I.1 in the introduction), similarly find a continued connection between market formation and state formation. While this first chapter has concentrated on the dominant role of large plantations in French Indochina, however, chapters 2 and 3 turn our focus to small-holder market networks, which are also significant in contemporary agricultural commodity markets. Smallholder networks also provide novel insights into how and why this frontier market has incorporated different commodities over time.

MARKET FORMATION
IN TBONG KHMUM PROVINCE

Memot rubber plantation in Tbong Khmum Province is a former French colonial plantation (originally Mimot plantation), whose land and labor conflicts were examined in chapter 1. The road to the village of Phum Prammoui, one of my two study sites in this lowland province of Cambodia, winds through this plantation. An elderly Phum Prammoui resident that I interviewed shared that the first *Hevea* seeds grown in his village came from Memot plantation in 1982. Through this transfer, colonial rubber literally "reseeded" market formation in the postconflict period here. Yet, as Margaret Slocomb suggests in her history of Cambodian rubber, colonial legacies go beyond the physical presence of rubber in the landscape. French land governance institutions were the first to introduce notions of private ownership, land speculation, and a belief that land should be developed to extract profit and rents (Slocomb 2007, 154). Furthermore, this colonial plantation history shaped Tbong Khmum's settlement and demographic history, through waves of labor migration and, later, violent expulsions during the Khmer Rouge period. The contemporary frontier market is inhabited by these institutional and social ghosts, while continuing to evolve in distinctive ways.

Building on the preceding analysis of rubber production in French Indochina, I turn from large-scale plantations to smallholders, a category of farmer that is often defined by their relatively small landholdings, ownership and operation at the household level, and varying degrees of market integration (Rigg et al. 2016; see also Dove 2011). In upland Cambodia, smallholders can be Indigenous or Khmer, and their modes of market engagement are often differentiated along these lines in Mondulkiri (see chap. 3). In the areas of Tbong Khmum where I worked, however, there were no Indigenous groups present.

By tracing market transitions from the colonial era to the time of my field research in this province during 2016, I argue that Tbong Khmum is a continually "reinvented" frontier in the sense described by Rasmussen and Lund (2018): a space where new agricultural commodities are continually emerging and taking hold. A granular examination of market diversification reveals how this process of reinvention works, especially the influence of actor-networks and their differentiated roles, risks, and opportunities. As global commodity booms have driven market intensification in this province over the last decade, the search for new agricultural land and outmigration has taken these commodity markets to new frontier spaces in upland Mondulkiri. The Tbong Khmum case thus illustrates how diversification deepens the hold and complexity of the market—from single commodity networks to a market rhizome—while migration expands commodity markets into new locations.

Colonial and Postcolonial Market Formation

Former colonial rubber plantations dominated the landscape at both of my Tbong Khmum study sites. While the Memot plantation remained prominent near Phum Prammoui, the Krek plantation was located near the border village of Phum Prampii, my second study site in this province. One of the largest colonial plantations, Chup, was some distance from both of these sites and so did not feature in my research. As the following discussion and case studies show, despite the upheaval of the intervening periods of independence and conflict, continuity with the colonial past lingers in contemporary Tbong Khmum's market-formation processes. Building on the historical overview in chapter 1, I elaborate localized transitions here.

The plantations of Memot and Krek were established during the rubber boom of the 1920s but faced variable prices during the Great Depression in the 1930s and up to World War II. During the turmoil between World War II and Cambodian independence in 1953, the Cambodian rubber sector underwent several important transitions (Boucheret 2008, 631). As in Vietnam, communist agitation among workers in such plantations as Chup and Mimot figured in the country's political transitions to come (Fortunel 2013, 128; see chap. 1). Although the plantations remained in French hands after independence, the sector started to diversify. Under Sihanouk's regime, Cambodian citizens were granted their first concessions in the 1960s because rubber and rice were regarded as the "twin pillars of national development and economic independence" (Slocomb 2012, 101). These Khmer plantations were far smaller than their colonial precursors but targeted the same red soil regions in the border districts of Tbong Khmum. State-run rubber plantations were also trialed in the 1960s, but even at their peak in 1968 these covered a much smaller area of 4,540 hectares, about one-tenth of the land under French-owned plantations. During this decade, two thousand "family-scale" rubber plantations also emerged, each covering about five hectares (Slocomb 2012, 102) and marking the emergence of a new class of agricultural peasant in Cambodia (Fortunel 2013, 131). All major rubber plantations were nationalized in 1975 by the Khmer Rouge, but after the Vietnamese withdrew from Cambodia in 1989, the new government gradually divested former French plantations into the hands of state elites or private investors with senior state connections. More recently, the Krek plantation was acquired by the Cambodian-owned company Krek (Cambodia) Co. Ltd., and the Memot plantation by a Cambodian investor, Lim Sunleang, in 2008.

The labor migrations that were integral to the rubber sector and plantation development also shaped Tbong Khmum's social landscape. As detailed in chapter 1, under the French, the plantation labor force primarily consisted of "coolies" from Annam (central Vietnam), who were seen as more hardworking than Khmer, Stieng, or Bunong workers. This created a sizeable Vietnamese diaspora in the province, which was then known as Kampong Cham. When the outbreak of the First Indochina War in 1945 restricted the recruitment of Annamese coolies, plantations recruited Southern Vietnamese and Chinese workers instead and later turned to the more readily available Khmer and Cham workers (Slocomb 2007, 154). These transitions shaped the ethnic composition not only of the plantation workforce but also of the region—with associated frictions. When the Khmer Rouge seized power in 1975, they violently expelled the families of former Vietnamese coolies, although many had already left for Vietnam in the preceding years because of growing anti-Vietnamese sentiment and violence. An elderly informant, Tuan, who lived in the Vietnamese province of Tây Ninh, explained that families like his had previously worked on plantations, but they crossed to the Vietnamese border district of Tân Biên in 1973. "Before that," he recalled, "no one lived here—except communist guerrillas, South Vietnamese and American forces, and Pol Pot's people." In 1978, a Khmer Rouge incursion into Tân Biên killed six hundred local residents (interview with male Tân Biên resident, May 21, 2015). After Vietnam's reunification in 1975, the government encouraged migration to this region to bolster its border with Cambodia. As the population grew and cross-border trade recommenced during the 1980s, former Cambodian residents like Tuan became important brokers and traders, since they were fluent in Khmer and had useful knowledge about Cambodian patronage networks.

After colonial migration for plantation labor, the next major wave of migration to this eastern border was during the 1960s. During this time, Phum Prammoui was settled by migrants from the lowland province of Svay Rieng, which is located about one hundred kilometers southeast of Tbong Khmum (see fig. I.1 in the introduction). The land surrounding Phum Prammoui was initially covered in dense forests, which new migrants would clear to build housing and commence farming (group discussion with Phum Prammoui residents, March 24, 2016). In 1976, Khmer Rouge troops forced all the villagers to move to the neighboring province of Kratie to work on collective rice farms. When the Khmer Rouge fell in 1979, eight surviving families returned to Phum Prammoui to find that all the houses had been destroyed, and only scrubby forest and disused agricultural fields remained. They recleared the land to plant upland (dry) rice; those families with more working-age people at home could clear and gain more land. Farmers also started to plant cashew trees between their rice rows to sell to Vietnamese buyers. An elderly man, Arun, recalled that these trees were seeded from trees on his father's farm, planted before the Khmer Rouge period. It was Arun who gathered and propagated seeds from a few mature cashew trees that survived the fighting, which had otherwise razed the village. When his neighbors saw him successfully growing cashew, they asked him for seedlings, and gradually, through village and kin networks, cashew production became reestablished in Phum Prammoui (group discussion with Phum Prammoui residents, March 24, 2016). The *Hevea* seeds mentioned at the opening of the chapter were grown in parallel. As with cashew, family and village networks spread *Hevea* seedlings. Unlike cashew, however, which could be grown near houses and around fields, rubber required dedicated areas of land. Initially, villagers targeted any available and unclaimed land, but as this disappeared they had to reallocate land from other crops if they wanted to grow rubber. In Phum Prammoui, more and more villagers adopted rubber until, by 2003, there was a rubber boom. Only families with enough land and finances could grow rubber, however, because they had to wait five to seven years until the trees started to produce latex.

Contemporary Market Intensification

Vietnamese traders directly introduced cassava to farmers in Phum Prammoui during the 1990s. In 1996, the first Phum Prammoui family experimented with cassava cultivation after buying stems from traders and found that it grew well on their land. As cassava is propagated by planting short sections of stem from the mature plant, farmers could easily share their stems with neighbors and kin. Phum Prammoui farmers rapidly took up this crop, which also started to boom in the early 2000s. The overlapping rubber and cassava boom coincided with an end to available land for villagers looking to expand their cultivation area. By 2005, families had started to divide their land into smaller and smaller plots among their children. This was when villagers started leaving to search for new agricultural land in upland and less densely settled parts of the borderlands, such as Mondulkiri.

When I commenced my fieldwork a decade later in 2016, pepper had become another major crop in Phum Prammoui, requiring less land than other earlier crops. The first three or four families to cultivate pepper in Phum Prammoui bought vines from a neighboring commune in 2012–2013. After observing their experiments for a year or two, other farmers within and beyond this village started to adopt this new crop. The up-front capital costs of planting pepper were far higher than rubber, however, which limited the potential for the crop to boom to the same extent as cassava and rubber. Pepper required irrigation, and the vines had to be staked on timber poles and protected under shade cloth for the first few years (see fig. 2.1). Nevertheless, many middle-income and wealthy farmers took significant loans of up to USD 10,000 to plant pepper.

Unlike Phum Prammoui, Phum Prampii was mainly settled during the post-conflict migratory surge. Maly, an elderly Khmer woman who was in her seventies when we met, had moved from Svay Rieng Province to the border village of Phum Prampii in 1993 because she and her husband had very little land in Svay Rieng. In Phum Prampii, Maly could immediately buy 1.5 hectares of land, which she gradually expanded to 2.5 hectares. Even in 1993, Phum Prampii was covered in dense forests of old trees, where pigs, deer, and tigers roamed wild. There were already ten to twenty families in the area that had started arriving from Svay Reing in the mid-1980s. By the time Maly came to Phum Prampii, the villagers were mainly growing rice for their own use and made some charcoal to sell locally, but in the years that followed they tried out various cash crops, such as cashew, rubber, cassava, and sugarcane. Maly had tried to grow some of these before settling on cassava and rubber at the time of my research (interview with Khmer woman, Phum Prampii, March 12, 2016).

The market trajectory was also somewhat different in Phum Prampii, where cassava was the first major cash crop. An elderly Khmer man, Chakra, explained that he was the first to bring cassava stems to the village in 1992. He exchanged fifty kilograms of rice for some cassava stems from Vietnamese traders, who instructed him in cultivation techniques. After growing his first cassava crop, Chakra sold the fresh tubers for about 50 riel/kg (USD 0.01). He shared the stems

FIGURE 2.1.   New pepper poles in Phum Prammoui

Source: Photograph by author.

freely with other villagers and a neighboring village. By 1995–1996 many people had started to grow cassava (group discussion with Phum Prampii residents, March 22, 2016).

Like Phum Prammoui, what followed in Phum Prampii was a mélange of crop experimentation and uptake. These experiments were often instigated by Vietnamese traders, who promised to buy the new products that they recommended. Alongside cassava, villagers had also grown cashew but were advised by traders in 2004–2005 to cut their cashew trees and plant rubber. Some seedlings were sourced from Vietnamese traders, and villagers also accessed seed stock from the nearby Kraik plantation. When the price of rubber subsequently fell, these traders again suggested a change of crop—this time recommending farmers cut their rubber trees to grow sugarcane. Many followed this advice, but by 2014 those who had adopted sugarcane abandoned that crop to grow pepper. Cassava remained a constant through these crop shifts; farmers grew it on any available land—and between rubber seedlings—because it was easy to grow and provided an annual income while waiting for longer-term crops to yield.

Rather than follow the advice of Vietnamese traders to make wholesale crop transitions, Khmer farmers more commonly reallocated available land and cultivated multiple crops in parallel. For example, my 2016 household survey showed that in both villages, most farmers had introduced new crops in the past five years, but only 8 percent had abandoned an existing crop. As with Phum Prammoui, commodity networks in Phum Prampii intersected each other and grew into a deepening and increasingly complex market rhizome, driven by such actors as traders and early-adopting farmers.

Contemporary Market Proliferation through Socially Differentiated Networks

The granular case studies from Phum Prammoui and Phum Prampii that follow explore how Khmer farmers engage with market intensification and proliferation in differentiated ways, according to their assets and capacities. In each village I examine the diverse situation of landless villagers and farmers with small, medium, and large areas of land to understand their differentiated engagements with commodity crops and contributions to market formation. While Tbong Khmum was settled long before I conducted research there, these stories illustrate how the frontier is continually reproduced by the introduction of new commodity crops and novel modes of market engagement, and the different positioning of farmers in relation to market formation. Table 2.1 shows diverse cropping patterns in the two villages.

Phum Prammoui Case Studies

By 2016, smallholder cultivation in Phum Prammoui was characterized by a mixture of commodity crops, including cassava, rice, rubber, pepper, and cashew. Table 2.1 shows that among these, the most prevalent crops were cassava, rubber, and pepper. Most farming families grew more than one crop and thus participated in multiple commodity networks, with the majority growing two to three different crops. Importantly, adopting new crops such as pepper rarely involved wholesale substitution of existing crops; less than half of Phum Prammoui's farmers (about 44 percent) had abandoned a crop in the previous five years, choosing instead to retain a variety of two or more crops. Those with small landholdings, however, could grow a far smaller variety of crops.

Kin and social networks as well as transborder actors, such as Vietnamese traders, gradually introduced new commodity crops in Phum Prammoui and significantly shifted the overall market trajectory. Crops were often adopted by one or two farmers, and depending on their success, others would follow. This

TABLE 2.1 Cropping patterns in Phum Prammoui and Pham Prampii

	CROPS[#]	CASSAVA		RICE		RUBBER		PEPPER		CASHEW		OTHER[@]	
		%	HA	%	HA	%	HA	%	HA	%	HA	%	HA
Pham Prammoui	2.7	72	1.8	44	0.6	66	1.5	46	0.7	4	0.6	10	1
Pham Prampii	2.2	86	2	64	1.1	40	1.5	4	0.4	2	0.5	0	0

Source: 2016 household survey (Pham Prammoui: n=50/279 households, or 18 percent; Pham Prampii: n=50/297 households, or 17 percent).

Notes:

[#] Average number of crops grown per farmer.

"%" refers to the percentage of households growing a specific crop while "ha" shows the average area dedicated to the crop by those households.

[@] Typically fruit trees, such as rambutan and durian.

enrollment process reflects Diederen and his colleagues' (2003) proposition that agricultural innovation is led by early adopters and consolidated by subsequent adopters (unflatteringly referred to as "laggards"). Their study observed that such structural characteristics as land size, access to capital, and age were less influential in early adoption than behavioral differences, such as farmers' capacity to innovate and to make use of new external knowledge sources. In Phum Prammoui, however, both dimensions were significant, as the following case studies show: a landless family (Sita) and families with small (Nakry), medium (Montha), and large (Samnang) landholdings (see table 2.2).

SITA

Sita's story illuminates the precarious but central role of landless laborers in market intensification and proliferation. Sita was a fifty-five-year-old Khmer woman and sole parent to two adult daughters with no land. Her daughters had been the first to leave the village to work overseas—moving to Malaysia as nannies a few years before we met. They returned within a year because they found their host family cruel and the working conditions very harsh. One daughter then moved to Thailand for construction work, and another found employment in Phnom Penh as a garment worker. Sita continued to care for her grandchildren, who lived with her after her daughters left the village for work. The villagers did not look favorably on these choices—branding her daughters as prostitutes for living away in unknown circumstances. Sita found this distressing but knew that her daughters were saving to help her buy the timber she needed to upgrade her house. Sita tried renting land to grow cassava in 2014–2015, but the cassava earnings barely covered her input and labor costs, so instead she lived by selling her labor to other farmers. She also relied heavily on her daughters' remittances to get by. One of Sita's biggest worries was her health, particularly as she grew older. Over the previous two decades, medical emergencies had required her to sell land and take on loans. She constantly worried that illness would prevent her from earning daily wages to pay for necessities (interview with Khmer woman, Phum Prammoui, March 26, 2016).

Better-resourced farmers depended on Sita and other landless laborers to expand their cash crop production. Unlike the frontier migrants discussed later in this chapter, Sita's daughters had moved to off-farm work—echoing broader patterns in Southeast Asia (Kelly, Olds, and Yeung 2001; Rigg 2007). Their remittances enabled Sita to cover her own living costs and those of her grandchildren. Households such as Sita's contributed essential labor to new commodity networks, but she had limited influence and gained a very meager and insecure income from this work.

TABLE 2.2 Case studies of market engagement in Phum Prammoui

NAME	LAND OWNED (HA)	NUMBER OF CROPS	CROPS GROWN	HOUSEHOLD DEBT (USD)	NONFARMING ACTIVITIES
Sita (landless)	0	0	0	$550	Labor for other farmers
Nakry (small landholding)	1.2	2	Rubber, pepper	$5,000 (ACLEDA; repaid with loan from kin)	None
Montha (medium landholding)	2	2	Rubber, cassava	0	Rubber tapping for other farmers
Samnang (large landholding)	5.2	4	Rubber, rice, rambutan, cassava	$1,000 (ACLEDA; taken annually)	Lump-sum cashew harvesting in Ratanakiri

Source: Author's data.

Notes: Based on average landholdings in this village, the cases reflect four categories of landholding: (i) landless, (ii) less than two hectares, (iii) two to five hectares, and (iv) over five hectares.

NAKRY

Nakry's case reflects the trajectory of a small landowner with access to intergenerational wealth. A divorced Khmer woman in her fifties, Nakry had about 1.2 hectares of land, on which she had grown several crops in the preceding years. Nakry was born in a neighboring village and moved to Phum Prammoui through marriage in 1999 but later divorced her husband. Her only child, a son, was born in 2000 and was living with her ex-husband. Although her landholdings were small, Nakry was able to establish one hectare of rubber, which she planted in 2005 on land that was given to her by her father. She also had 119 pepper poles that she had planted near her house in 2015. Although the slump in rubber prices and the costs associated with establishing pepper gave her a net zero income in 2015, in previous years she had cleared around 2 million riel (USD 500). Her biggest liability was labor costs: "If I was able tap rubber myself, I could get more" (interview with Khmer woman, Phum Prammoui, March 25, 2016). Due to low returns in 2015, Nakry had turned to working for other farmers in 2016, clearing weeds in their cassava fields. She could earn about 15,000 riel/day (USD 3.75) from this work but still needed to periodically borrow money from her parents. Her daily wages were necessary to service the USD 5,000 loan that she had taken to plant pepper. She thought pepper would be a good investment because others were growing it, but the debt was a major burden in these first three years as she waited for the first pepper crop. In summary, although Nakry was growing multiple crops, she found it difficult to break even, and she was only able to move to new market crops, such as rubber and pepper, by taking on debt. She also relied on others' expertise and labor to tap latex from her rubber trees, which she paid for by doing work for other farmers.

Nakry's situation, like other small landowners, involved a fragile balance of activities. As Nakry lived alone, she had to hire workers to help with farmwork. Although Nakry had more land and financial resources at her disposal than Sita, she could easily tip toward an unviable situation where she was forced to sell her land—for instance, if she was unable to afford her loan repayments. Farmers in Nakry's circumstances contributed to the process of embedding new commodities, such as pepper, in Phum Prammoui but did so at considerable risk. Pepper and other capital-intensive crops cost at least USD 7,000 per hectare to plant and therefore required substantial loans (interview with male pepper farmer, Phum Buon hinterland, January 16, 2016). It was also difficult for Nakry to access the skills and knowledge needed to grow and market new crops, leaving her dependent on the labor and skills of others. These circumstances left farmers like Nakry particularly vulnerable to price shifts, such as the fall in pepper price in 2018.

MONTHA

With a slightly larger area of land and specialized knowledge about rubber tapping, Montha was a young, male Khmer farmer with a more secure outlook than Nakry. Born in a nearby village, Montha came to Phum Prammoui after marrying a local woman. Montha and his wife inherited two hectares of land from her parents and had no children. They grew a mix of crops and worked for daily wages around the village (see fig. 2.2). Montha and his wife had 160 rubber trees and also cultivated cassava on their two hectares. Aside from farming, Montha would work for his relatives, tapping rubber trees. His rubber-tapping skills, which he learned from his mother and father, who previously worked at the Memot plantation, were in high demand among farmers in Phum Prammoui. For a day of tapping (starting at 6:00 A.M. and finishing at midday) he would receive 12,000 riel (USD 3). He would then work on his own rubber trees in the afternoons. Montha and his wife could manage their own cassava planting and harvest and also did reciprocal (unpaid) labor swaps with relatives. In 2015 they produced 10 tons of cassava tubers, earning 6–7 million riel (USD 1,500–1,750), but in 2016, lack of rain, disease, and declining soil quality took their toll on Montha's yield and reduced his profit to 2 million riel (USD 500). The rubber price also fell from 2,000–2,500 riel/kg (USD 4–5) in 2015 to 1,800 riel/kg (USD 3.50) in 2016, but Montha remained optimistic

FIGURE 2.2. Montha in his small rubber plantation in Phum Prammoui

Source: Photograph by author.

about the prospects of profiting from his rubber crop. In general, this mix of activities usually left Montha and his wife with sufficient income to buy rice and other necessities and even save on occasion.

Although I classified Montha as a medium-sized landowner, his land area was only slightly larger than Nakry's. Yet his capacity to save money indicated far more secure circumstances. Key factors here were his specialized knowledge and skills in rubber tapping—gained from his parents—and his access to reciprocal labor networks during peak farming seasons, which reduced his costs. These factors had enabled him to withstand the price volatility of rubber and cassava in recent years, while still growing his wealth. Like Nakry, however, Montha was growing crops that were already established in the area rather than experimenting with new cash crops (interview with Khmer man, Phum Prammoui, March 25, 2016).

SAMNANG

For families with more than five hectares, farming was often mixed with other business activities. Samnang, a divorced Khmer woman aged forty-two, was born in Phum Prammoui and was only an infant when her family was taken to Kratie by the Khmer Rouge in 1976. On returning to the village in 1979, her family first claimed a small area of land where they grew rice (about 1.3 hectares) and were later able to buy a further 0.5 hectares. Over time, this small amount of land was distributed between Samnang and her two siblings. Samnang's family also held additional land that they had cleared on the border, but in 1985 Vietnamese soldiers "came with guns" and prevented Khmer farmers from cultivating that land. After receiving her share of family land and additional land purchases, Samnang eventually held about two hectares of land, where she grew rice, rambutan, and cashew. In 2014 she decided to cut her cashew trees and grow rubber instead as she thought it would provide a better return. By 2016, Samnang had bought more land—enough to grow 2.5 hectares of rubber, 1.6 hectares of rice, and about one hectare each of rambutan and cassava. She and her two siblings could collectively grow enough rice to feed the extended family for the entire year, but as the family grew, the rice sometimes fell short. Although her rubber crop was only four years old, she had already started to produce cuplump from her trees, a coagulated rubber product that smallholders produce in preference to liquid latex if they do not have local latex buyers, as it can be stored for longer periods.[1] Samnang's cuplump production earned about 120,000 riel (USD 30) every four days. Her younger brother transported their cuplump, rambutan, and cassava directly to a buyer across the border in Vietnam. They tried to manage their rubber production within the family rather than hire workers but did need additional labor for the other crops.

In 2016, Samnang and her siblings had started traveling farther afield to work on cashew plantations in the northeastern province of Ratanakiri during the harvesting season. This arrangement involved a lump sum payment, negotiated with the cashew plantation owner. They paid USD 1,000 to harvest a two-hectare crop, covered by a loan from the Association for Cambodian Local Economic Development Agencies (ACLEDA) Bank. After harvesting the cashew, they would sell it in the provincial capital, Banlong, clearing around USD 1,850 after costs. For this contract, she and her brother recruited workers from Phum Prammoui. Now that she had experienced success with this venture and was familiar with the requirements, Samnang discussed her plans to take on a larger harvesting contract for ten to twelve hectares. This would need a larger loan of USD 5,000–10,000 to cover the larger lump sum contract and to pay laborers, whom she would recruit in her village and transport up to Ratanakiri in a minivan. These arrangements also required moving to Ratanakiri for up to a month and a half. Samnang and her family were thus able to build on and deploy their capital to expand landholdings, plant high-value crops, explore lucrative labor contracting arrangements, and participate in an expanding range of commodity networks (interview with Khmer woman, Phum Prammoui, March 25, 2016).

These case studies and other data from Phum Prammoui reveal a dynamic commodity landscape that remained a frontier for new modes of market engagement. Regardless of the size of their landholdings, farmers typically grew multiple crops and were actively engaged across several commodities, as also observed in Vietnam's upland markets (Sikor and Pham 2005; Turner, Bonnin, and Michaud 2015). Those with small landholdings had a smaller range of crops and were more vulnerable to the price shifts that commodity markets experienced during my research. Most precarious were those with no land. Each case also illustrates the importance of knowledge, such as rubber-tapping skills, and kin and social networks, for instance, to reduce labor costs during harvests.

Phum Prampii Case Studies

Like Phum Prammoui, the history of market formation in Phum Prampii shows that this frontier was also continually reinvented by cross-border commodity networks that mobilized new crops. Both villages had similar crop innovation and dissemination patterns, and in each village, farmers participated in multiple commodity networks (see table 2.1).

I now trace how Phum Prampii villagers from different wealth strata have engaged with this evolving frontier market (see table 2.3). As with Phum Prammoui,

TABLE 2.3 Case studies of market engagement in Phum Prampii

NAME	LAND OWNED (HA)	NUMBER OF CROPS	CROPS GROWN	HOUSEHOLD DEBT (USD)	NONFARMING ACTIVITIES
Chann (landless)	0	0	0	0	Daily labor; seasonal labor in Kratie; raising chickens for sale
Chaya (small landholding)	1	2	Rice, rubber	200 (microcredit)	Seasonal labor in Kratie; hand tractor rental
Kiri (medium landholding)	4	1	Cassava, rubber	1,000 (ACLEDA)	Land rental; grocery business
Rachany (large landholding)	30+ ha	2	Cassava, rubber	0	Farming, land rental; tractor/truck rental

Source: Author's data.

Notes: Based on average landholdings in this village, the cases reflect four categories: (i) landless, (ii) less than two hectares, (iii) two to five hectares; and (iv) over five hectares.

these case studies reveal the circumstances of a landless laborer (Chann) and farmers with small, medium, and large landholdings (Chaya, Kiri, and Rachany, respectively).

CHANN

Born in Svay Rieng Province, Chann was a Khmer laborer in his forties who moved to Phum Prampii in 1993 because he had no land in Svay Rieng. Unlike Sita in Phum Prammoui, who lost her land through a distress sale, Chann's situation of landlessness was intergenerational. The violence inflicted by the Khmer Rouge left Chann and his wife orphaned, and neither could gain land in the post-conflict scramble when they returned to Svay Rieng. This meant that they lacked the resources of many other migrants to Phum Prampii who could buy land from villagers and officials that had already seized land. Instead, Chan and his wife started to work as laborers in exchange for rice—at that time receiving twenty-four kilograms of rice for six days of work rather than cash. Eventually, the *me phum* (village head) gave them a three-hundred-square-meter plot of land, which was enough to build a house (see fig. 2.3). They also started to clear a forest plot for cultivation, but another villager quickly seized that land from them.

After these setbacks, Chann and his wife resigned themselves to working as laborers. While landlessness had trapped his family into laboring, which gave them only about 100,000 riel (USD 25) per month, Chann observed wistfully that those who were wealthy could grow rubber and cassava. The work was precarious; Chann shared, "If they are not happy, they will dismiss us." His children had no opportunities to gain land either so had also started to work as laborers, at times moving farther afield to other provinces, such as Kratie, for seasonal work. Chann also raised chickens for sale. The family's combined income was used to buy sacks of rice that were stored and shared at the house, while other food was scrounged from their surrounding areas, such as wild leaves and frogs and crabs from the rice fields. Chann's disadvantage was multiplied by his family's lack of ID cards and birth certificates, which prevented them from accessing government services and voting. To Chann, it seemed that his family had been forgotten and abandoned by the village head (interview with Khmer man, Phum Prampii, March 22, 2016).

Like Sita in Pham Prammoui, Chann's case underscores the important but precarious role of landless laborers in market formation. Intergenerational landlessness represented a particularly entrenched form of poverty, which left families like Chann's unable to benefit from land allocations in the postconflict period as they lacked connections with government elites (see also Diepart 2015). His disadvantage was also multiplied by lack of access to state welfare. Yet the development of new commodity networks could not have occurred without the

FIGURE 2.3. Intergenerational landlessness in Phum Prampii: Chann

Source: Photograph by author.

labor of landless workers like Chann and Sita. His case highlights the inherent injustices and social frictions within market formation, which I touched on in chapter 1 and will return to in chapter 4.

CHAYA

The situation of small landholders in Phum Prampii and Phum Prammoui was broadly similar. Chaya, a twenty-eight-year-old Khmer woman, and her husband owned one hectare of land, which her husband had inherited from his mother. Chaya moved permanently to Phum Prampii in 2009 after marriage. She had met her husband the year before their marriage, when she visited the village as a seasonal laborer. They grew rice on one half of their land and had just planted rubber interspersed with cassava on the other half. Chaya had inherited a small amount of land in her home village in Svay Rieng, which she sold when she moved to Phum Prampii, allowing them to purchase a hand tractor with trailer, which they rented out to other farmers. Chaya and her husband also provided daily labor for other farmers, although she was at home with a young baby when we met. That year, her husband was planning to work as a seasonal laborer in Kratie, to clear land for a new rubber plantation. This would help them to manage their farming commitments and to save for Khmer New Year. Overall, Chaya and her husband's mixed farming and labor activities provided enough money to manage day to day, but she did not anticipate being able to expand their land-holdings or to add improvements, such as irrigation.

In comparison with Nakry in Phum Prammoui, Chaya's household had two working-age people at home, who were able to manage their farming activities. Like Nakry, however, their work for other farmers was an important supplement to their household budget. They also migrated seasonally to save for special occasions. Chaya and her husband engaged with multiple commodities across the market rhizome, but at some risk. For example, rubber would become a more uncertain venture after it grew too tall to intercrop with cassava, particularly given that its price was so volatile. In general, small landowners were a diverse category of farmers, with intricate differences in their circumstances and capacities. My 2016 household survey confirmed that most engaged in more than one commodity, highlighting that this group also played a part in embedding new market crops (interview with Khmer woman, Phum Prampii, March 23, 2016).

KIRI

Kiri, who owned four hectares of land, had a more diverse set of market engagements, which included off-farm activities. A Khmer man in his forties, Kiri grew cassava and rubber and hoped to grow pepper in the future. He and his wife also operated a small grocery business, which provided the largest share of his family's income. In the past, he cultivated a mix of rice and cassava but transitioned to rubber about five years before we met, because of its high price. When we spoke in 2016, pepper was selling well, so he planned to turn some of his land to pepper crops. Aside from the initial loan that he needed to establish rubber, he also needed annual loans for his cassava crop to cover labor costs and other inputs. Kiri also had sufficient land to rent out a small area to Vietnamese watermelon farmers between his cassava crops (see below; interview with Khmer man, Phum Prampii, March 21, 2016).

Kiri and other medium-size farmers operated across several commodity networks and had the land and capital to experiment with new crops. Kiri was not an early adopter of rubber and pepper but had sufficient financial access to act relatively early and decisively when prices looked favorable. He depended on hired labor, particularly since he had additional nonfarming activities to attend to, confirming my observation about the role of landless laborers and small farmers with insecure incomes in market formation. Kiri's case also illustrates the importance of price in farmers' decisions to adopt and abandon specific crops and their need for loans to cover the costs of establishing capital-intensive crops. These patterns were similar to those of large landholders, such as Rachany.

RACHANY

With over thirty hectares of land, Rachany's family was one of the wealthiest in Phum Prampii. Rachany was a Khmer woman in her forties and oversaw the family's farming and business activities, which included a truck rental business that she established in 2014. Rachany and her husband had both been born in Phum Prampii and started out as farmers. Over the years, however, they were able to accumulate about thirty hectares of land through inheritance, judicious land claims, and purchases. During 2016, she started distributing this land to her children. A few years ago, when she struggled to find transport to take her cassava crop to Vietnam, she decided to buy a tractor and trailer with a microcredit loan. People then started to ask if they could rent it. Seeing a business opportunity, she began to provide transport services on a regular basis, carrying cassava and other goods for villagers to Vietnam through the nearest major border crossing. She knew of two other small tractor rental businesses in the village, but hers had the advantage of larger trailers, enabling them to carry more cassava per load. These businesses competed with each other, but only tractors with trailers could traverse the more difficult "forest" roads (forest being a term loosely applied here to less developed agricultural areas). For Rachany's family, business was good; they were clearing about 2–3 million riel/month (USD 500–750) from the tractor rental, but if a tractor broke down, they could face sudden and large expenses. She reinvested some of her profits into rubber cultivation and in 2016 began renting out areas of land to Vietnamese farmers for USD 300–350 per hectare. Others followed this rental arrangement, leasing their land to Vietnamese farmers who grew short-term crops such as watermelon. Border police at a small crossing point near their village facilitated these leases, connecting prospective Vietnamese tenants with Khmer farmers for a commission (interview with Khmer woman, Phum Prampii, March 21, 2016).

Rachany's role in the market went beyond crop production to connecting local producers with Vietnamese buyers. As such, she was also well informed about opportunities for new commodities in Vietnam and price trends. For instance, she was among the first to start renting out land to Vietnamese farmers—a different kind of commodity network based on land commodification—because she had the land and networks to do this. Thus, farmers in Rachany's situation had the resources, knowledge, connections, and land to engage early in new commodity networks.

Phum Prampii and Phum Prammoui both followed a similar pattern of early market formation and continual elaboration. The predominance of multicropping showed that new crops and commodities did not replace earlier ones but built on and interacted with earlier commodities in complex ways. Within this evolving market, villagers' opportunities and risks differed markedly according to their circumstances. Small farmers could easily slip into precarity and landlessness if prices dropped or in the face of other emergency expenses, while medium and large farmers had the greatest capacity to experiment with and adopt capital-intensive crops. For those with little land and financial access, such crops as cassava were relatively easy to adopt. Cashew was also amenable to planting in small isolated plots. Rubber could be grown by relatively small farmers, but the most capital-intensive crop of pepper remained the preserve of those who could gain—and service—large secured loans. Thus, the cultivation requirements of specific crops made them important actants in these market networks, shaping their accessibility to farmers in terms of land, labor, and capital requirements.

The most recent market elaborations of cross-border land rentals and seasonal harvesting contracts were similarly initiated by the wealthiest farmers, who had the land and networks to act on price signals and new market opportunities. At the other end of this spectrum were people like Chann, who, unable to gain land, were consigned to laboring their whole lives—a pattern that was passed on intergenerationally. Yet market elaboration depended strongly on these precarious workers. Knowledge networks and credit were also important in these market proliferation processes.

Traders and Credit Providers

By providing new knowledge and cultivars, cross-border actors such as Vietnamese traders enabled the proliferation of new commodity networks. As with rubber in the French colonial era, the groundwork for crop adoption was also laid by a range of other actors, notably state-sponsored scientists and extension workers. Taking the example of cassava, Vietnamese cassava research centers developed and disseminated the industrial cassava cultivars now grown in Cambodia and Vietnam. Crop scientists had actively promoted cassava as a crop that was well suited to poor farmers due to its ease of cultivation and low investment needs (interview with Vietnamese cassava scientist, Đồng Nai, April 12, 2015). The new varieties and cultivation techniques they developed were rolled out through Vietnam's extension system, but cassava's dissemination to Cambodia was primarily facilitated by Vietnamese traders.

Cross-border traders from Vietnam ranged from very small to large-scale in terms of their volume of trade, usually indicated by the size of their available transport. However, the smallest Vietnamese traders—often with family histories of relocation from Cambodia—were highly influential in crop transitions because of their close relationships with Khmer farmers. To encourage cultivation of new crops like cassava, traders promised to return and purchase the crop on a lump sum basis. They would visit partway through the growing season and calculate an overall payment figure for the crop based on visual estimates of the likely crop yield before it matured. The purchase price at the end of the season would factor in the costs to the trader of providing Vietnamese labor for cassava harvesting, as well as transport. It was these small-scale operators, harvesting anywhere from five to thirty hectares of cassava in a season, that historically provided planting materials to Khmer farmers (interview with Vietnamese trader, Tây Ninh, April 19, 2015). Many cited them as instrumental to their initial uptake of cassava production (group discussion in Phum Prambei, December 11, 2013; interview with Khmer man, Phum Prampii, April 15, 2016).

The importance of small Vietnamese traders as knowledge translators was evidenced by their detailed understanding of Khmer farming operations. A small trader called Duc, for instance, shared that he frequently gave advice to Khmer farmers about which cassava variety to grow and what techniques to use if he found their cassava field lacked productivity (interview with Vietnamese trader, Tây Ninh, April 15, 2015). Duc spoke fluent Khmer and was well attuned to local conditions, including the seasonality of production as well as cultivation conditions. In another example, a trader named Truong explained that the seasonality of production in Cambodia made it more difficult for Khmer farmers to keep their own seed stock: "In Vietnam, farmers can keep their cassava stems, but in Cambodia the crop is harvested just before the rains, so their stems are not suitable yet for planting—they would need to grow bigger in order to use it for reproduction, say one month longer. But they have to harvest cassava before rain sets in, so the farmers must buy stems for planting from Vietnam" (interview with Vietnamese trader, Tây Ninh, April 15, 2015). For Vietnamese traders to give advice on cropping, they needed a relationship of trust with Khmer farmers, which was cultivated through their knowledge of Khmer and their family migration histories (interview with Vietnamese trader, Tây Ninh, April 19, 2015). Thus, small-scale traders were able to establish direct relationships that facilitated crop and market diversification in Tbong Khmum.

While cross-border networks introduced knowledge about new crops, farmers often required loans to engage in new commodity networks. This made credit providers important players in market intensification and proliferation. According to my 2016 household survey, about 70 percent of households held debts in both Phum Prammoui and Phum Prampii. Larger loans of over USD 2,000 were typically drawn from the ACLEDA Bank or other large institutions, while the growing number of small microfinance institutions in rural Cambodia provided smaller loans. Average loan sizes were smaller in Phum Prampii (USD 1,445) than Phum Prammoui (USD 3,016), due to Phum Prammoui having larger areas of capital-intensive crops, such as rubber and pepper.

The emergence of debt introduced disruptions in market formation that affected small and medium farmers in particular. Dramatic price falls for rubber and later pepper left these categories of farmers struggling to maintain repayments (see also chap. 4). Some took loans from family or smaller microfinance institutions to service debts with other larger institutions, such as ACLEDA. By late 2017, stories emerged of farmers who had lost their land due to loan defaults. Others looked for new ways to maintain their payments, such as seasonal labor in neighboring provinces. These trends highlight that agricultural innovation is not simply about early and late adoption of ideas but occurs within a broader context of market formation. New knowledge, such as that provided by traders, could in one sense be viewed as an engine for market enrolment and mobilization, along with price signals. The Phum Prammoui and Phum Prampii case studies add, however, that innovation can also rest on the exploitation of landless laborers and escalating debt. Building on these insights about how the market was embedded and elaborated, I next consider the mechanisms that spread Tbong Khmum's market rhizome to new agricultural frontiers.

Expanding the Market: Outmigration and the Desire for Land

As market formation intensified and available land diminished in Tbong Khmum, people started to leave for less densely populated areas, such as the upland border districts of Mondulkiri. Migration to less settled frontiers and market expansion moved like two partners in a dance. I was able to explore this dynamic because the new migrant settlement of Phum Buon in Mondulkiri was largely populated by people from my study districts in Tbong Khmum. The migratory connection between my two study sites allowed me to explore why people migrated, the conditions in their source regions, and migrants' role in transplanting and extending commodity networks from established agricultural landscapes into new spaces.

More broadly, lowland provinces such as Tbong Khmum have been a key source of migration to Cambodia's upland frontiers (Diepart and Ngin 2020). Although Cambodia has a falling rate of rural-rural migration (CRUMP 2012, 53), migration continues at high levels to frontier provinces such as Mondulkiri (Diepart 2015; Hecht et al. 2015). This is typically driven by migrants from land-poor provinces moving in search of land (Diepart 2015, 21; see fig. 2.4) and is

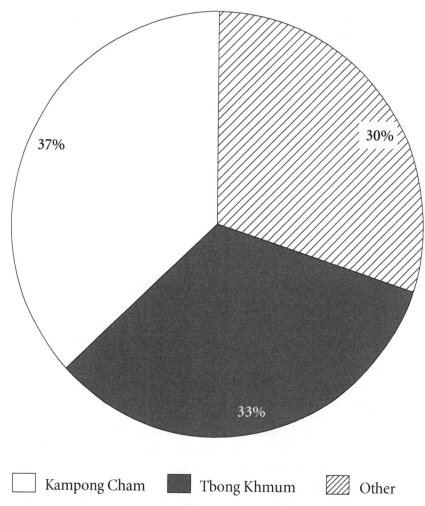

FIGURE 2.4. Source of migrants to Phum Buon, Mondulkiri Province

Source: 2016 household survey.
Note: Figures refer to the origin of household head.

largely unregulated apart from a registration system with local authorities that new migrants typically address with an informal payment (interview with male village official, Phum Prambei, December 13, 2013).

Migration in this contemporary context is organic and self-driven, unlike the mass recruitment for colonial rubber plantations (see chap. 1) or Vietnam's post-war migration schemes that aimed to populate upland and border regions (see De Koninck 2000; Hardy 2003). Although lowland-to-upland migration experiences have been well studied in Vietnam, less is known about the motivations and experiences of Cambodia's frontier migrants and their engagements with existing Indigenous communities. Their stories provide insights on the migration process, while the resulting disruption to Indigenous lives and relationships to land in Mondulkiri is discussed in chapter 4.

Migrants to Phum Buon most commonly cited land shortages and soaring land prices in their home villages as their reason for moving. The land squeeze in source districts often arose from the intergenerational fragmentation of land-holdings, while rising land values in these established locations made it unaffordable to purchase new land. This was reflected in the account of a Phum Buon settler who had migrated from the district of Ponhea Kraik: "I moved because I needed land for my new family—there was a shortage in my commune. And also the quality of soil was decreasing there. By selling one hectare there, I could buy three to four hectares up here. Here it costs four to five thousand US dollars per hectare now, but in [Ponhea] Kraik it costs ten to twenty thousand US dollars" (interview with Khmer woman, Phum Buon, March 14, 2016).

According to Diepart (2015), such shortages initially arose from inequities in the immediate post–Khmer Rouge period—as seen in Chann's case—where land was allocated through political connections and on the basis of available household labor. These holdings were then "fixed" at this level by the 2001 Land Law, which prohibited the clearance of peripheral and forested lands. Subsequent land markets were only accessible to better off farmers (Diepart 2015, 17). By 2016, farmers in Phum Prammoui had an average landholding of 2.7 hectares, while 12 percent of villagers were landless. In Phum Prampii, land holdings were 2.3 hectares on average, but the rate of landlessness was higher at 18 percent. Landlessness and land fragmentation among small landholders were two key reasons cited by Tbong Khmum migrants who left for such frontier settlements as Phum Buon (see fig. 2.5). Two case studies of migrants to Phum Buon illustrate these dynamics.

Kunthea

The quest for land and land security were a major motivation for upland migration, as Kunthea's story illustrates. In 2016, Kunthea and her family were relatively recent arrivals in Phum Buon. After a day in their cassava field, Kunthea, her husband, and son returned in the late evening to their shack at the edge of Phum Buon, where the road became a twisted and rutted track. Kunthea, a Khmer woman aged thirty-eight, was born in Ponhea Kraik District, Tbong Khmum. The family moved to Phum Buon in 2013. Before that they lived at the Thai border for about six years, where their second child was born and where they rented land to cultivate peanuts and soybeans. They first left Ponhea Kraik because they lacked farming and residential land. Kunthea shared, "We were so

FIGURE 2.5. New settlers in Phum Buon came from Tbong Khmum and other land-poor provinces

Source: Photograph by author.

poor and saw others from the village going there [to the Thai border]. We hoped our life would be better." Although Kunthea's neighbors from her home village had the money to establish themselves in their new location at the Thai border, she recalled, "For me, there was only enough for food and daily living costs." When her youngest child became sick with a chest infection, the family went back to Ponhea Kraik to get help. While there, she was able to sell her parents' half-hectare of land, which gave her enough money to buy five hectares of land in Phum Buon from some former Ponhea Kraik neighbors. This cost 2.5 million riel (about USD 625). She added, "We took a risk because the land was not titled yet." When the teams of students working on the land titling initiative known as Order 01 arrived later that year (see introduction), only part of Kunthea's land was titled, because some of it was still uncleared.[2] Life in Phum Buon had been hard for Kunthea's family. They started cassava farming by borrowing stems from other villagers. Their first harvest yielded about 70 sacks of dried cassava, and they could save their own seed stock. In the second year they harvested 120 sacks, but that was also the year that Kunthea's youngest child passed away. Most of their income went to health care and funeral costs for their son. In their third year, their land was flooded, so the farm only yielded 90 sacks of cassava. She concluded, "Life has been tough, but here it is better because we have our own land and do our best to work on it" (interview with Khmer woman, Phum Buon, February 21, 2016).

Kunthea's aspirations for land security and the high personal cost involved in migration were echoed by several other Phum Buon settlers, such as Phirun (see below). Migrants who had been landless in their home villages were particularly desperate, both in their quest for land and their desire for land security once they had gained access to it.

Phirun

Phirun was a Khmer man in his forties who, like Kunthea, moved to Phum Buon as he had no land in Pohnea Kraik. Phirun had worked as a small cassava trader in the neighboring district of Memot but found it difficult to compete with other traders. In 2007, Phirun drove to Phum Buon on his motorbike to visit his aunt who had settled there. While visiting, he met an old Bunong man who asked Phirun if he would exchange his motorbike for some land. Phirun had bought the motorbike in Vietnam for around USD 350 and went ahead with what seemed like a good deal. The swap earned him a 120 m by 1,000 m block of forest that he set about clearing. At that time, he reflected, the area was heavily forested, and land was readily available to "grab." Only four families lived in Phum Buon, one of which was Bunong. He gradually cleared new blocks of land, built up his holdings and assets over time, and supplemented his farming income with trading activities, becoming relatively wealthy compared with others in this village (interview with Khmer man, Phum Buon, February 20, 2016).

Phirun and Kunthea followed quite different trajectories after arriving in Phum Buon, but both were driven by their shared desire to find land. As High (2014, 4) observed in her study of rural Laos, desires can have a personal dimension as well as being a "social force." In Phum Buon, the desire for land was often explained as a matter of material and emotional security. These personal aspirations accumulated into a social force that, through migration, expanded the market from Tbong Khmum to Mondulkiri's agricultural frontier. Migrants to Phum Buon planted cassava as a pioneer crop to clear and claim land, thus cassava played an important role in extending the market rhizome to this new location.

In this way the nexus between land and migration served to open new agricultural lands, which migrants immediately incorporated into market networks by producing commodity crops, using the knowledge and cultivars they brought from the lowlands. Phum Buon's migration stories thus illustrate the central role of land aspirations in driving the spatial spread of frontier markets from transitioning, or "postfrontiers," such as Phum Prampii, to newly opened areas, such as upland Phum Buon.

Tbong Khmum's Rhizomic Market

Evidence from Phum Prampii and Phum Prammoui in Tbong Khmum Province and Phum Buon in Mondulkiri Province shows that market formation has been an ongoing and interconnected process without a neat chronology. Fundamental to this process was the successive development of new agricultural commodity networks, which built on and coexisted with prior networks. These processes are still ongoing. As land became scarcer, these markets expanded spatially through outmigration from Tbong Khmum to new agricultural frontiers, such as Phum Buon. Tbong Khmum therefore highlights some important mechanisms that underpin and propel a rhizomic frontier market.

In Phum Prammoui and Phum Prampii, crop transitions were driven by a range of factors. Traders were influential in providing new knowledge and cultivars. One or two farmers would typically test the latest crop, drawing on advice from traders, knowledge gained through social networks in neighboring villages, and their own observations. If cultivation was successful and these early farmers achieved good returns, others would follow. This process reflected established patterns of agricultural innovation (Diederen et al. 2003). Although price shifts were an important driver of decisions to abandon certain crops or adopt new ones, the capacity of farmers to take up specific crops depended on their assets as much as their aspirations. Medium to large farmers could shift fluidly across several connected and dynamic agricultural commodity networks, while smaller farmers focused on less capital-intensive crops, such as cassava and cashew. Better-resourced farmers (such as Rachany and Montha) also helped to enroll others in the market or deepen their engagement through their assets, such as trucks and trailers, and their services and skills. Small farmers were less able to withstand low prices and poor harvests and would work for other farmers when squeezed. Landless villagers provided essential labor in these processes of market elaboration but were highly precarious in their livelihood circumstances—sometimes intergenerationally.

These patterns of market formation in Tbong Khmum have also been observed in other frontier regions in mainland Southeast Asia. Sikor and Pham (2005, 406) have found that commodity networks in the northern Vietnamese uplands were similarly intersecting and complex. Villagers there engaged in a range of commodity markets and were exposed to differentiated benefits and risks. These were not just one-off acts of market penetration that played out in predetermined ways. Instead, farmers exercised agency, but they were also constrained by political and economic institutions that mediated their access to land and financial resources, among others. Sikor and Pham (2005, 424) proposed that rather than specific commodity chains, the market was a commodity "web"—or what I call a rhizome—where "particular actors participated in multiple commodity chains at the same time, and where their actions in one chain could affect their behavior in other ones." Tbong Khmum farmers followed a similar trajectory, making active choices about which crops to adopt, which to abandon, or when to leave the village for new frontiers.

The tendency toward socially differentiated market engagements and outcomes that was visible in Tbong Khmum is also widely documented elsewhere (see Sikor 2005 for a useful summary; see also Kem 2017 on Tbong Khmum). Rigg's (2007) work on agrarian change in Laos attributed these differences to peoples' disparate knowledge and capabilities in relation to the market and the market's uneven presence. In Vietnam, Sikor and Pham (2005, 425) found that market engagements could increase social disparities over time as some actors were more able than others to accumulate and reinvest capital. The commodification of land and labor associated with new markets has been another important mechanism that reifies structural inequality (Akram-Lodhi and Kay 2009, 336; see also Li 2014). These patterns were evident in Phum Prammoui and Phum Prampii, along with emerging intergenerational inequality. The complete disruption of land tenure under the Khmer Rouge and the subsequent inequalities in postconflict land allocation in Cambodia fueled these disparities and migration in search of land (see Diepart 2015). Lack of available labor in the household was another key constraint in clearing new agricultural land. Space and data constraints meant that I could not examine such factors as gender or life-cycle stage, although this is an important area for further work (see, e.g., Beban 2014). Over time, differentiated advantages and disadvantages accumulated and were carried between generations, an enduring pattern that Rigg and his coauthors (2016) call "vulnerability," to distinguish it from more situational forms of precarity.

The material characteristics of specific cultivars further influenced cropping patterns. Cashew, for instance, could be easily planted around cultivated land and near houses, making it accessible to a wide spectrum of farmers alongside their other crops. Cassava too was quick to grow, served land clearing activities, but required dedicated areas of land. Rubber and particularly pepper required far more capital investment, usually gained through credit, to cover the labor and material costs of establishment and the protracted maturation period. In this way, crop characteristics interacted with farmers' assets and resources to influence market networks.

While Sikor and Pham (2005) have shown the importance of diverse and intersecting commodity networks in market formation, the rhizome concept draws specific attention to market fluxes over time and the spatial expansion of the market. Market crops were taken up and disseminated through social and material networks. Meanwhile, farmers' entanglements across multiple commodities arose from their pattern of growing several crops simultaneously. While crops like pepper were altogether new in this area, others, such as cashew, had been cultivated since before the Khmer Rouge era and went through a renaissance.

Although migrants were crucial agents for market expansion, their motivations differed from other market actors, such as traders. Migrants from Tbong Khmum to Mondulkiri kept returning to their personal aspiration for land security in our discussions. In Cambodia more broadly, this remains a continuing driver of migration to upland frontiers and is the reason that Cambodia bucks the "urban transition" model of migration that prevails in other parts of Southeast Asia (Diepart and Ngin 2020). The story of Kunthea clearly demonstrates that even when beset with hardships, migrants continued to pursue the ultimate prize of securing a plot of land. Their desire for land security became a mechanism for the market's geographical spread to new agricultural frontiers.

Ultimately, the case studies from Tbong Khmum illustrate the development and fluxes of a market rhizome. The return of dislocated people and the arrival of new migrants after the Khmer Rouge marked the reestablishment of market crops. Over time, the province transitioned from a frontier to an established agricultural landscape intersected by a rhizome of emerging and connected commodity networks. While specific commodities waxed and waned, the overall trajectory was one of market intensification and expansion.

MOBILIZING CASSAVA NETWORKS IN MONDULKIRI

A group of elderly Khmer villagers gathered in Phum Prambei in December 2013 to share stories of their migration to Mondulkiri. Their collective history reached back to 1997, a time when the village was still surrounded by a blanket of dense forest and Khmer settlers were a minority in this predominantly Stieng and Bunong region. They recounted negotiating with these communities to borrow land or exchange sacks of rice for land access, or if there was no clear "owner," they would simply seize and clear plots of forest. Within a year, around fifty families were living in Phum Prambei. Some settlers found the conditions too taxing and quickly left. But this elderly group counted themselves among the hardened few who survived successive bouts of malaria, food shortages, and rudimentary living conditions to make their lives in Phum Prambei. Phnom Penh was a distant place for these migrants, who relied for their daily provisions on the Vietnamese traders that visited these Cambodian border districts every few weeks. Encouraged by these traders, they started to grow cash crops, and by 2005 cassava cultivation started booming. This brought a new rush of migrants to Phum Prambei, eager to take up land and work opportunities. By 2012, however, land was increasingly scarce, and newcomers either had to buy land from established settlers—worth around USD 1,000 per hectare by that time—or sell their labor to these families. In 2013, the Cambodian government's rapid land titling policy (Order 01) generated another flurry of small-scale land grabbing and clearance of protected forest areas in order to expand and consolidate landholdings. Villagers called this the time "when the students came" (group discussion with Phum Prambei villagers, December 12, 2013; see introduction for more on Order 01).

Although these Khmer settlers recounted their interactions with Indigenous communities in neutral terms, land claiming by new migrants to upland areas of the Cambodia-Vietnam borderlands has dislocated Bunong and Stieng peoples (see chap. 4). As first referenced in Surya's story in the introduction, this chapter describes the close involvement of military and other state actors in land-claiming arrangements in Mondulkiri. Despite being ostensibly a project to strengthen land security, Order 01 represented another example of uneven state intervention in land markets that have shaped this frontier.

These accounts from early Khmer migrants to Mondulkiri Province also highlight the central role of migration in market formation, a connection that I introduced in the preceding chapters. Smallholder commodity production first started in lowland areas of Mondulkiri, such as Phum Prambei, in the early 2000s, before expanding into more remote upland areas. In the process, cash crops such as cassava have generated new forms of settlement and market-oriented agriculture, expanding the frontier market. At this time, the burgeoning of Vietnamese processing industries in adjacent border districts created high demand for Cambodian cassava. New migrants embraced it as a pioneer crop since it provided a good annual return. Chinese and Asian Development Bank (ADB) investments in road improvements during the early 2000s (Hughes and Un 2011) further enabled migration to Mondulkiri and the cross-border cassava trade.

In this context, two distinct cassava networks have emerged through subtle geographical variations in transport infrastructure, migration patterns, and the availability of uncleared land—or the sociomaterial context. The first network supplied dried cassava chips to Vietnamese and international markets for bio-ethanol and livestock production. After being cut and sun-dried, these more highly priced semidried cassava chips could be stored for several months before being transported to Vietnamese warehouses and ultimately to Chinese livestock and ethanol industries. The second network supplied fresh cassava to Vietnamese starch and food-processing factories. Fresh cassava needed immediate transport to Vietnamese factories within a day or two of harvesting, where it was rapidly processed into starch and glucose and the derivative monosodium glutamate (MSG). Vietnamese producers then shipped these products to China and other East Asian destinations for secondary processing into foods, paper, and pharmaceuticals.

The case of cassava also illustrates how new commodity networks form and evolve over time. Some years after cassava networks were mobilized in Mondulkiri, they were demobilized by environmental, economic, and social pressures, such as disease and price volatility (Callon 1986). This chapter shows the significance of network fracture and dissipation as sources of change within the frontier market. At the same time, fundamental market formation processes, based on land commodification and debt, continued throughout these specific network disruptions. As with the preceding chapters, I use the term *actant* in this chapter to describe the material (more than human) entities that sustain cassava networks (Latour 1996, 7).

It is noteworthy that fresh and dried cassava represent only part of Mondulkiri's frontier market. Chapter 2 showed the diverse range of commodity crops grown by smallholders. Beyond this, timber has been a key commodity here for many years. Since 2008, the development of large-scale *Hevea* plantations on economic land concessions (ELCs) has become a major factor in market formation, as I elaborate in chapter 4. In this chapter, however, I focus on cassava not only as one of Mondulkiri's primary smallholder crops but also for its potential to reveal the sociomaterial foundations of market formation. My discussion of fresh cassava networks centers on Phum Prambei, which is in the southern lowland region of Mondulkiri (see fig. I.1 in the introduction), where I worked in 2013 and 2016. The dried cassava data are drawn from the upland villages of Phum Muoi, Phum Pii, Phum Bei, Phum Buon, and Phum Pram, where I worked in 2016 and 2017.

Networks for Cassava Chips and Fresh Cassava

As outlined, the province's differentiated geography has shaped Mondulkiri's two cassava networks (see fig. 3.1). Upland areas of Mondulkiri, where cassava was an initial crop of choice for new lowland migrants, were best suited to dried cassava chip production. For fresh cassava, transport time was critical as it needed to reach Vietnamese processing factories within one to two days, before starch levels deteriorated. In Mondulkiri, these conditions only existed in the more established farming areas of the lowlands that were relatively close to the Cambodia-Vietnam border.

In 2005 Vietnamese traders initiated cassava cultivation in Mondulkiri at Phum Prambei. These traders advised farmers on cultivation techniques, loaned them seed stock and materials, and promised to return at the end of their first few growing seasons to buy their harvest (group discussion with Phum Prambei villagers, December 11, 2013). Farmer networks then quickly disseminated the crop, which first gained a foothold in lowland Mondulkiri and gradually spread to upland areas as migration targeted new lands for farming.

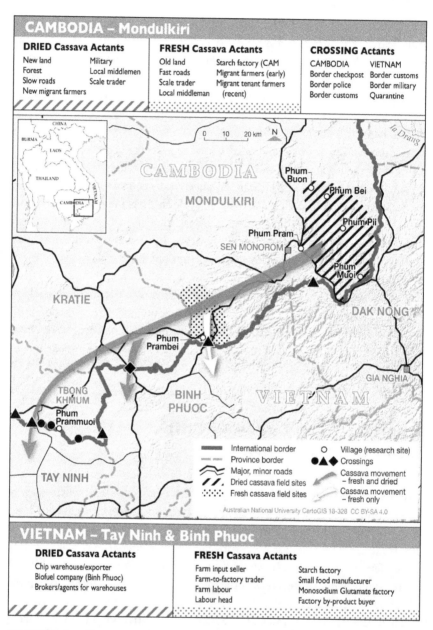

FIGURE 3.1. The geography of dried and fresh cassava in Mondulkiri

Source: Prepared by ANU CartoGIS from author's data.
Note: For legibility, only a subset of the actants discussed in chapter 3 appear in figure 3.1.

FIGURE 3.2. The precarious road to Phum Moui, which is impassable in the rainy season

Source: Photograph by author.

As mentioned, Mondulkiri's differentiated road infrastructure was an important influence in the unfolding of the two cassava networks—a pattern that has been more broadly documented in the development literature (Dalakoglou and Harvey 2012; Harvey and Knox 2012). Roads overcome the "friction of terrain" (Scott 2009) by enabling access into and out of ostensibly remote areas (Rigg 2002). In lowland Mondulkiri, Chinese and ADB finance progressively upgraded road infrastructure from the early 2000s (Chan 2017; Hughes and Un 2011). This produced a lowland road system of sealed or packed dirt roads that could support large trucks and rapid transportation of fresh cassava to Vietnamese factories over the border. In contrast, only motorbikes or the hardiest cars and trucks could service the villages in upland Mondulkiri (see fig. 3.2). The ability to transport dried cassava after weeks of storage made it suitable for these relatively inaccessible localities.

A second crucial difference between the two cassava networks was the timing of migration and land clearance in cassava production areas. Lowland Mondulkiri's ease of access made it the first part of the province to be settled during postconflict migration. As discussed at the start of the chapter, this commenced in the early 2000s and intensified—alongside cassava cultivation—from 2005 on-ward (group discussion with Phum Prambei villagers, December 11, 2013). By 2016, the population in lowland Phum Prambei was dominated by established migrant farmers whose landholdings were more than five years old. The remain-ing population consisted of a small number of Bunong and Stieng families and relatively new migrants. Accessible lowland forests had diminished by 2013, and only elites had the political connections and paid labor to clear and secure any remaining land (Mahanty and Milne 2016). Landholdings were also fixed by Or-der 01 during 2013 (see below). With little scope to claim land in lowland Mon-dulkiri, new migrants instead moved on to upland locations or took on work as day laborers for established lowland migrants. It was this settled or relatively "old" agricultural landscape, serviced by relatively good roads, that character-ized the fresh cassava network.

In contrast, the upland cassava network involved new migrants, cultivating freshly cleared or "new" lands. The development of upland chip-producing areas, such as Phum Buon and Phum Pii, was part of this later migratory surge (group discussion with Phum Buon villagers, February 10, 2016; discussion with male hamlet leader, Phum Pii, January 26, 2016). In Phum Pii, the allocation of several ELCs brought an additional influx of workers, which boosted the steady drift of lowland migrants that had already commenced around 2005 (see also chap. 4).

Cassava's ease of cultivation on newly cleared lands made this crop central to land-claiming processes and therefore to landscape change in these agricul-tural frontiers. New migrants were still continuing to clear land in remote areas of Mondulkiri during 2016 and 2017 (see figure 4.1). The nexus between upland cassava chips, land clearance, and land claiming also brought local state actors into this commodity network, particularly village and commune officials. New migrants had to seek the approval of these local officials to clear and occupy land. During Order 01, local authorities also verified and approved the land measure-ments and ownership status—demonstrated by active cultivation—that were needed for land titling. In this way, dried cassava emerged from interactions between forests, new migrants, state actors, and newly cleared lands. In both the dried and fresh cassava networks, district, commune, and village officials mediated land access networks and authorized land titles. These relationships tied cassava cultivation to land use change in these frontiers, which was histori-cal in fresh cassava areas and ongoing in dried cassava areas during my field-work period.

Embedded in these commodity networks was a complex set of relationships between settlers and Indigenous peoples, both in relation to land transactions and Indigenous engagements in cassava production, which I examine further in chapter 4. Relationships between Khmer farmers and Vietnamese traders were significant to the development of both cassava networks. As detailed below, these commercial relationships were also built on historical migration patterns that have intersected these borderlands over many decades.

Vietnamese traders were equally influential and active in both the dried and fresh cassava networks of Mondulkiri, although their arrangements for buying and transporting cassava chips differed from those for fresh cassava. Large Vietnamese warehouses in the adjacent border province of Tây Ninh were the primary destination for cassava chips, where they were held for onward distribution and export, primarily to China. Typically, Vietnamese warehouses did not directly purchase their chips from Khmer farmers but instead relied on Vietnamese traders to aggregate the chips and transport them over the border. Sometimes these traders would use Khmer middlemen (fee-for-service agents) to connect them with farmers that could supply cassava chips. In some rare cases, warehouses would facilitate this process by extending credit to their trusted Khmer traders in Cambodia.

In contrast, the primary destinations for Mondulkiri's fresh cassava tubers were Vietnamese starch factories, also clustered in adjacent border districts. By 2015, Tây Ninh was Vietnam's most important cassava-processing province and relied heavily on Cambodian fresh cassava. Starch factories ranged in size, depending on the number of production lines they contained. As I observed during field research in 2015 and 2017, the largest factories had up to four production lines and a production capacity of up to 300 tons of dried starch per day. This level of output required about 1,200 tons of fresh cassava per day, of which factories sourced up to 60 percent from Cambodia (interview with factory manager, Bình Phước, January 13, 2018). By 2018, however, all of these factories were producing well below their capacity due to cassava shortages.

These starch factories—or *lò mì* (stoves), as Vietnamese cassava traders called them—each had five to six loyal traders that they regularly dealt with. After tracking and communicating with a core group of nine traders between 2015 and 2017, it became clear that Vietnamese traders specialized in either dried chips or fresh tubers. Some tuber traders, known as "farm-to-factory" traders, used networks of paid Khmer middlemen to connect them to farmers, while others approached farmers directly. It was this type of farm-to-factory Vietnamese trader that first introduced cassava to Phum Prambei. Over time, Khmer middlemen graduated to become fully fledged cassava traders in their own right, often operating weighing and aggregation facilities. Farmers who owned or could hire a tractor would transport their cassava to these recently established Khmer traders. The Khmer traders would then either sell and transport the goods directly to Vietnamese factories—bypassing the Vietnamese traders that they collaborated with previously—or collaborate with the Vietnamese traders to arrange transport to factories. For chips, on the other hand, the main buyers were large Vietnamese warehouses. For both fresh and dry cassava, specialized Vietnamese agents at the border would take care of the border paperwork and informal fees (see below).

Khmer farmers and traders often viewed Vietnamese factories as powerful network actors, but the factory owners instead saw themselves as being at the "very end of the chain," as one Tây Ninh factory administrator described, referring to the company's relative powerlessness, since buyers in China set the price (interview with factory administrator, Tây Ninh, April 26, 2015). In 2007 the Vietnamese government attempted to develop a domestic biofuel industry, but the policy was poorly designed and implemented so did not create a secure domestic market for chips (see chap. 5). One large warehouse owner confirmed that China provided a more consistent and lucrative market for chips than the unstable Vietnamese biofuel market (interview with warehouse owner, Tây Ninh, January 7, 2018). My visits to two medium-sized and two large chip warehouses thus confirmed that China was the key cassava chip buyer for animal feed and biofuel production.

Although dried and fresh cassava circulated through different trading networks, both passed through common Cambodian and Vietnamese state actors at the border. The specific government agencies represented at a border check post depended on its location and classification (see table 3.1). State actors at small local border crossings were usually limited to border police in Cambodia and military officers in Vietnam, while the larger and more highly monitored international crossings were staffed by several agencies on both the Vietnamese and Cambodian sides. The roads traversing borders similarly ranged from unsealed and narrow tracks at local crossings, to "smooth as silk" highways at international crossings (military official, interview, Tây Ninh, April 2015).

Check post officials routinely required informal payments for fresh and dried cassava shipments, making check posts and their personnel important actants in the dried and fresh cassava networks. Interviews with traders revealed that they made strategic decisions as to which border crossing to use, based on the volume and type of commodities being transported and their connections to officials. Importantly, although more government agencies were present at international crossings, Cambodian border police and Vietnamese border military were present at all crossings. These actors played a central role in mediating cross-border commodity flows. Cassava producers, middlemen, buyers, and processors all mentioned regular interactions with these actors, while more specialized agencies, such as Cambodia's Cam-control and Vietnam's Agricultural Quarantine, only became relevant when documentation was needed to reexport goods and for large commodity shipments. Payments were usually made as a

TABLE 3.1 Border crossings and attending agencies

CROSSING TYPE[1]	CAMBODIAN ATTENDING AGENCY	VIETNAMESE ATTENDING AGENCY
Local	Border police	Military
Bilateral or "national"	Border police	Military
	Customs	Customs
	Cam-control[2]	Agricultural Quarantine
International	Border police	Military
	Customs	Customs
	Cam-control[2]	Agricultural Quarantine
	Immigration	Immigration

Source: Mahanty 2018, based on interview data and observations.

[1] "Informal" crossings are a fourth category of crossing that is completely unmonitored and was not studied in this research.

[2] Cam-control is the Cambodian agency responsible for inspecting goods for quality assurance and quarantine purposes.

lump sum to one official, to be distributed through established mechanisms and practices among the different agencies represented at particular check posts. Traders cited border payments of this kind as an integral cost of doing business that was accommodated, albeit grudgingly, as part of trading practices and sale price. At the time of my fieldwork, cassava traders reported check post fees of about USD 50 per truck on the Cambodian side of national and international check posts and less for smaller-scale crossings, with a further USD 10 on the Vietnamese side. Depending on the strength of their relationships with border officials, these payments were either made through an agent, involving additional agent fees, or directly by the trader.

Traders therefore needed both sufficient capital to cover these illicit fees and personal connections to check post officials in both Cambodia and Vietnam to facilitate their operations. Those with such capital and connections could work directly with customs and border officials, which cut costs and streamlined the border crossing process. Personal networks were helpful for small-scale traders but were essential for large-scale traders, to facilitate the necessary paperwork and payments for large shipments at international check posts (interview, Tây Ninh, May 2015). As one medium-sized trader summed up: "Without a network you cannot trade" (interview, Tây Ninh, April 2015). Those with weak networks had to resort to agents, involving additional costs.

The spatial configuration of crossings gave check post officials a larger role than simply collecting rent and waving on trucks. Some of these officials actively and informally governed the space between the two border check posts (the "inter-check-post space"). This space could extend for several hundred meters, sometimes dissected by a water feature but more often was an uninterrupted tract of farm or forest land. National crossings in my study areas had a border marker to delineate where Cambodian territory ended and Vietnamese territory began. At such crossings, the land between the border marker and the Vietnamese check post was controlled by the Vietnamese military. At one Tây Ninh crossing, the military illicitly rented out this land to traders to store their goods while they waited for customs clearance. Some of the larger Vietnamese cassava traders had built semipermanent storage sheds on such rented land as a holding space when they transferred goods from Cambodian to Vietnamese vehicles. This was necessary if the goods were being taken beyond Vietnamese border districts (known as the "border belt") as only trucks with Vietnamese registration could do this.

Among state actors, vertical networks were also important. For example, traders reported that a particular check post between Mondulkiri and Bình Phước was "reserved" for cassava being bought by a large Taiwanese-owned MSG producer. Through connections to the central government hierarchy in Vietnam and to local Cambodian authorities, the factory owner had become the sole buyer at this crossing. This enabled the Taiwanese company to set the price for several contracted Khmer traders on the Cambodian side. To circumvent this monopsony, traders sometimes traveled to check posts that were two hours' drive to the south in Tbong Khmum.

In summary, the example of dried and fresh cassava illustrates how commodity networks were interactively shaped by the social and physical conditions in Mondulkiri's lowland and upland areas, as well as the material qualities of cassava. Specialized Vietnamese traders and buyers were significant in both networks, as discussed in chapter 2. Check post officials were also critical to both networks, and, due to the specific spatial configuration of the border, opportunities for state engagement went beyond collecting rent at check posts to governing the ambiguous inter-check-post space at the border. These revenues not only enriched border officials but also flowed upward to senior officials and, in Vietnam, to provincial governments (see Mahanty 2018), highlighting the broader and systemic political-economic role of these networks. While these actors were instrumental in mobilizing cassava networks, the networks were ultimately susceptible to broader pressures and disruptions, which I discuss next.

Demobilization: Network Disruptions and Risks

As a "flex crop" with diverse applications, cassava competes in global markets with other starch crops (Borras et al. 2016). For this reason, although the initial market outlook for cassava was strong, demand for the crop and its price was closely coupled to that of its key competitors: maize and sugarcane (Smith, Newby, and Cramb 2018). When the Chinese government removed subsidies and reduced the price of maize in 2016, cassava networks experienced sudden shifts in demand and price. The price paid to farmers by Khmer and Vietnamese buyers more than halved between January 2016 and January 2017, from riel 240/kg (USD 0.06/kg) to riel 108/kg (USD 0.026/kg). Another issue, specific to the cassava chip network, was the volatile nature of the biofuel market in East and Southeast Asia, as well as policy uncertainty regarding the introduction of a 5 percent ethanol fuel in Vietnam (Smith, Newby, and Cramb 2018; interview with Vietnamese official, January 18, 2018; see also chap. 5). The effects of these price and policy shifts, while geographically remote from cassava producers and traders in Mondulkiri, created significant uncertainty and disrupted both cassava networks.

By late 2017, a distinct pattern of demobilization had emerged in frontier cassava-producing districts. In Phum Prambei, financial losses pushed some farmers into distress land sales or landlessness due to debt defaults (see chap. 4 for details). Those with sufficient assets to buffer a poor season moved to different crops, such as green bean, cashew (relatively low cost), rubber (higher cost due to the longer wait for production) or even the most capital-intensive crop of pepper, taking on major loans of up to USD 20,000 for the latter. This suggests that commodity disruptions could also drive the agricultural innovations discussed in chapter 2. In relatively remote areas such as Phum Buon, some farmers left their cassava crop in the ground, unable to afford the labor to harvest it, with the hope of harvesting the crop in the following season if the price improved. These trends created a decline in cassava production during 2017, which was acutely felt by downstream processing industries in Vietnam. In January 2018, only about 50 percent of the expected volume of cassava was being transported over the border, and Vietnamese starch factories were consequently running at a fraction of their capacity (interview with factory manager, Bình Phước, January 13, 2018). Adapting to these changing cropping patterns and the downturn in the cassava market, smaller Khmer traders started to buy and aggregate other types of commodities. Although the price of cassava rebounded in subsequent years, this only confirmed the crop's price volatility.

Although Khmer farmers tended to view traders as the ones who framed market conditions, Vietnamese traders outlined several challenges that ate away their financial margins. Price volatility affected farmers and traders alike. For instance, Duc, a large-scale Vietnamese trader based in Tây Ninh, shared the stresses he faced due to the fluctuating price of cassava: "This year is much more challenging. First, the price is down. Secondly, the market was stable last year, not up and down during the harvesting season—so it was easy to buy and sell. This year, the price is up one day then down the next day. I cannot do business [làm ăn không được]—it is hard work but leaves me with no money for Tết [Vietnamese New Year]" (interview with Vietnamese trader, Tây Ninh, January 19, 2016). By early 2018, these pressures were becoming untenable for several traders.

Aside from price volatility, traders were further squeezed by delays in factory payments. Hanh, another large-scale Vietnamese cassava trader, spoke of the effect of a factory closure where "one dead person pulled down a bunch of others [một thằng chết lôi theo một đống]" (interview with Vietnamese trader, Tây Ninh, April 19, 2015). Indeed, the metaphor of the dead trader, or corpse, was commonly used to describe traders who had hit bankruptcy. One trader described a man who was once one of the biggest traders in the district as a "corpse" (còn cái xác)—a dead trader (interview with Vietnamese trader, Tây Ninh, April 19, 2015)—implying a final and untimely end wrought by the market's unpredictable twists and turns. Another observed that traders like him would "die with their tongue out" (chết lè lưỡi) because of the fallout from market volatility (interview with Vietnamese trader, Tây Ninh, January 2018).[1] Large traders in particular struggled to shift their trading operations between commodities as their investments and networks were usually framed around one type of commodity.

Vietnamese traders cataloged several other risks associated with working in Cambodia, which could force unpredictable losses. As trucks were often overloaded, fines from traffic police were a constant threat. For lump-sum traders, another key risk was the need to commit to purchasing a crop before they were sure of its quality (interview with Vietnamese traders, Tây Ninh, April 20 and 23, 2015). Cambodia was regarded as a space where connections and caution were essential, but personnel changed unpredictably, captured in this statement by a large-scale trader: "When this Mr. is in power, he lets you work. When another Mr. is in power, he takes everything from you. It's tricky. You dare not invest" (interview with Vietnamese trader, Tây Ninh, January 19, 2016). They also faced competition from other traders, which created risks in openly sharing information with each other. These stories highlight the range of potential network disruptions for dried and fresh cassava.

In this already uncertain cassava trading climate, cassava pathogens gained a foothold in Mondulkiri during 2017. The cassava mosaic disease, a virus transmitted by the whitefly (Bemisia tabaci), entered Cambodia in 2015 (Wang et al. 2015). Mondulkiri was initially less affected than Tbong Khmum, since Tbong Khmum was the first port of call for diseased Vietnamese cassava stems coming across the border. On the Vietnamese side of the border, this disease reached a crisis point during 2017, with the Tây Ninh People's Committee declaring an epidemic on July 28, 2017 (interview with Tây Ninh official, January 25, 2018). The Cambodian government similarly released a statement in mid-2018 that advocated urgent action to stem the spread of cassava disease, which was gripping all of Cambodia's eastern border provinces, particularly Ratanakiri, Mondulkiri, Tbong Khmum, Kratie, and Kampong Thom (Chan 2018). Disease provided further impetus to farmers who were already considering other crops because of cassava's depressed price. Although the associated fall in cassava production buoyed its price during 2018 (Sokhorng 2018), this did not overcome deepening disruptions to cassava's production and trading networks.

Meanwhile, government policies to regulate environmental waste from these industries amplified the pressure on Vietnamese processing factories. The wastewater from cassava processing can be high in biological contaminants and cyanide. Citing these concerns, the provincial environmental agency in Tây Ninh closed eight factories for wastewater violations during 2015 (interview with Department of Natural Resources and Environment official, Tây Ninh, April 13, 2015). Several other processing plants were being closely monitored for environmental violations. Although their tough standards disadvantaged smaller operators the most, officials argued that it served environmental protection interests to limit production to only those factories that had the capacity to comply with waste processing regulations—which, in practice, were the larger factories. In January 2018, factory owners cited environmental compliance as a key financial stressor along with reduced cassava production.

It is noteworthy that while both cassava networks experienced disruptions, the overall trend of market intensification through commodity agriculture continued. In this sense, market formation pressed on regardless of the fortunes of one specific commodity. The commodification of land and farmers' uptake of loans to finance new crops fueled broader processes of market formation. These processes were crucial in enabling the market to continue its evolution in spite of disruptions to specific commodity networks.

Embedding the Market: Land Commodification and Credit

Although cassava networks were volatile, the land claiming that cassava facilitated had a pervasive influence on market formation across the province's agricultural frontier. Migrants composed a particularly large proportion of Phum Buon and Phum Pii households (see fig. 3.3). Prior to the arrival of migrants, Bunong people typically grew a mix of subsistence crops and traded nontimber forest products, an activity that preceded European colonization (see the introduction).

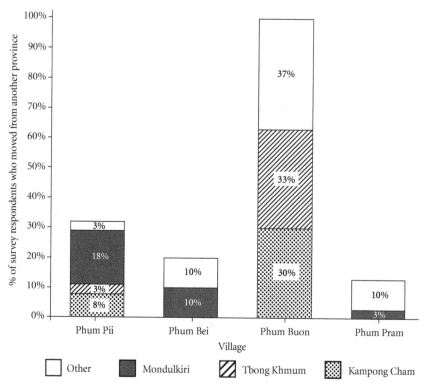

FIGURE 3.3. Proportion of migrant households in four Mondulkiri villages and their province of origin

Notes: (i) Phum Muoi and Phum Prambei were not included in the household survey and are therefore missing from this graph; (ii) figures reflect the place of origin of the survey respondent, who was the female or male household head; (iii) the category "other" includes (in order of prevalence) Prey Veng, Kratie, Kandal, and Battambang.

In contrast, new settlers would solely produce agricultural commodities from the outset, which Bunong and Stieng farmers would gradually adopt (interview with Bunong man, Phum Pii, January 26, 2016). Chapter 2 established that migrants were driven by a desire for land, which served to spatially extend the reach of the market. Here, I turn to the crucial role of land commodification in embedding frontier markets.

In Mondulkiri, the first wave of postconflict migrants would either clear and seize land without permission or negotiate access with existing Bunong and Stieng residents. An example of forcible land seizure was provided by Borey, an early Khmer settler in Phum Buon, and his Bunong wife, Rachany. Borey came to Phum Buon because his brother, who was already living there, said that land was being "distributed." In 2007, the year that Borey married Rachany, there was only one Bunong family left in the thickly forested area and a few Khmer settlers. From 2007 onward, new settlers seemed to arrive on a daily basis. Borey and Rachany recalled that they were unable to clear and take land like these new settlers because they "didn't have the money for labor, and only used axes to cut the trees, not like the Khmer, who had chainsaws and could clear two to three hectares of land in a day compared to our two to three trees." In addition, Rachany reported that the number of Bunong families living there was so small that they could not prevent Khmer migrants from taking the land or stand up to the threats made by these new settlers (interview with Bunong woman, Phum Buon, February 21, 2016).

Bartering for land was more common in settlements with a visible Bunong community. An elderly Bunong man in Phum Pram explained that when migrants started arriving in their community in 2005, they would come to the Bunong asking to buy land. He did not initially engage in land sales: "At first, I didn't sell land, but later when the Khmer came to ask me for land, I exchanged one hectare of land for a few sacks of rice" (interview with Bunong man, Phum Pram, February 17, 2016). In other cases, land barters involved valued goods, such as motorcycles (interview with Khmer man, Phum Buon, February 2016). Post-2010, however, financial transactions were the norm. By this time, settlers were not typically buying land from the Bunong but from other migrants who had moved earlier to the area. For example, a Khmer woman named Chanthavy and her family moved to Phum Buon from Memot District in 2013 when they heard there was cheap land available. By selling a half hectare of land in Memot, Chanthavy could buy two hectares in Phum Buon from a family of early migrants that had gained many hectares of land. In 2013, her land purchase cost USD 2,500 (interview with Khmer woman, Phum Buon, December 16, 2017). By 2016, the land price in Phum Buon had risen to USD 4,000–5,000 per hectare, illustrating the rapid escalation of land values from this high demand.

State officials, such as the border police and the military, also sold land to new migrants. In the postconflict period, the military gained control over forests in the border regions—repeating patterns observed in other parts of Southeast Asia (Dwyer, Ingalls, and Baird 2016; Peluso and Vandergeest 2011; see the introduction). In areas very close to the border, such as Phum Muoi and Phum Prambei, they became key land brokers. When migrants first arrived in 2013, border officials sold uncleared land to newcomers for around USD 400 per hectare. After clearing the land, a secondary land market developed among the migrants. By 2016, land values in this very remote settlement had risen to USD 1,500 per hectare (field notes, February 22, 2016). Phum Muoi illustrates the key role of government officials in early land transactions.

In addition to acquiring their own land, migrants played an important role in speculative land accumulation by elites. A migrant farmer in Phum Prambei who cultivated land for an absentee owner explained:

> Besides daily labor, farmers can produce their own crops by borrowing land. First, we clear the land and grow cassava for the landowner for three years. After the land is well cleaned [i.e., the stumps and tree roots have been removed], we give it back to the landowner, or we grow green beans, new rubber, or cashew nut trees for the landowner. When the rubber produces resin or the cashew tree provides nuts, we can either leave the land or still work for the landowner and get a share of the income, for example, one-quarter of it. This is only possible for the landowner who has no available time to monitor the farming activities themselves—mostly government officers. (interview with Khmer man, Phum Prambei, December 4, 2013)

This farmer's account shows that government actors who had acquired land would enter leasing or land-lending arrangements with migrants. Through such arrangements, migrants helped elites to consolidate their position by clearing new land and demonstrating its active use by initially growing cassava. The owners would then hold this land speculatively, lease it, or resell to new migrants.

Land accumulation and resale thus occurred under the benevolent eye of state actors, who either claimed newly cleared lands for themselves or received payments from those undertaking forest clearances. Although the clearance of land by migrants was officially forbidden under the 2001 Land Law and the 2002 Forestry Law (Article 97), I routinely witnessed this during my fieldwork. Occasionally, state agencies like the Forestry Administration acted to prevent clearance in protected forests, but migrants would typically buy their complicity or override them by appealing to more senior authorities, as seen in this account from Phum Buon: "In 2009, two houses were burned by the Forestry Administration or the district authority—I'm not sure which. Then we heard that Prime Minister Hun Sen was coming to Keo Seima, so we wrote a protest letter to him" (interview with Khmer man, Phum Buon, February 20, 2016). This informant implied that he and other Phum Buon residents could win the support of the highest authorities to secure their land claims. While villagers were typically in a less powerful position than state officials in almost all interactions, this account shows that those in high office could easily override lower-ranked agencies, such as the Forestry Administration, to facilitate or condone land grabbing when it suited their interests.

Land titling further embedded land commodification and unleashed the possibility of using land for secured loans. It was the growing pressure for land security in frontier areas that prompted the Cambodian Peoples' Party to launch Order 01 in 2012 (see introduction). In this initiative, uncleared lands and lands under conflict were supposed to be excluded, but in practice this rule was implemented according to the connections and influence of landholders (Grimsditch and Schoenberger 2015). Order 01 teams targeted four of my Mondulkiri study sites: Phum Pii, Phum Bei, Phum Buon, and Phum Prambei. The opportunity to gain titles under Order 01 produced a flurry of anticipatory land clearance and seizure in these villages. In Phum Prambei, data from a conservation NGO revealed that Order 01 led to a land rush and a six-hundred-hectare sprawl of new farms inside a designated protected area. Elite and state networks were instrumental in this land rush, and Order 01 teams subsequently titled these lands (Mahanty and Milne 2016). Because cassava could be easily planted and could therefore demonstrate the active use of newly cleared lands—a criterion of ownership—it was integral to the formalization of illicit landholdings. In this way, state tenure interventions such as Order 01 contributed to land commodification. It helped migrants to secure titles for informally claimed lands that, once titled, could gain a higher price in subsequent land sales. Titles also opened access to secured loans for farmers to transition from cassava to more capital-intensive commodity crops, such as rubber and pepper.

The use of land as collateral for secured loans was a relatively new development during my research, echoing suggestions in the wider literature that debt is integral to the "advance of capital" to frontiers (Harvey 2007, 368; Gerber 2014; Graeber 2011; see table 3.2). Among middle-income and wealthier farmers in Phum Pii in particular, debt enabled these farmers to transition to new and more lucrative crops (as per the Tbong Khmum case studies in chap. 2) or enter business, both of which contributed to the deepening of frontier markets. My other Mondulkiri field sites also found families with the high levels of debt using funds for similar purposes.

Within the debt typology developed by Gerber (2014), four forms of credit prevailed in Mondulkiri. The first, particularly among Bunong and Stieng families,

TABLE 3.2 Median debt and debt range in four Mondulkiri villages

VILLAGE	% HOUSEHOLDS WITH DEBT	MEDIAN DEBT (USD)	RANGE OF DEBT (USD)
Phum Pii	44%	2,500	500–20,000
Phum Bei	57%	1,000	70–5,000
Phum Buon	73%	1,750	125–20,000
Phum Pram	44%	1,750	250–3,000

Source: 2016 household survey.

Note: Phum Prambei was not covered in the survey.

was the use of informal loans among kin. Second was personal loans, which usually took the form of cash or in-kind support. For example, traders sometimes provided farmers with in-kind credit (e.g., seed stock, herbicide, and hormone sprays) at key points in the cassava season, such as during planting, spraying, and harvesting. Upon harvest, farmers would repay these debts, sometimes at up to 10 percent interest. Initially such loans came from Vietnamese traders, but with the opening of Cambodian chip warehouses in 2012, Khmer traders took on the lending role (group discussion with Phum Prambei residents, December 11, 2013). By building codependent relationships with farmers, traders would gain access to the cassava on concessional terms (interview with Khmer trader, Phum Prambei, December 14, 2013; see also To, Mahanty, and Dressler 2016). The third form of credit was from local savings and credit associations, which were the usual port of call when farmers needed funds for things like medical expenses, home improvements, and ceremonial events, such as weddings and funerals. These first three categories of loan were unsecured, requiring no collateral.

The fourth category of credit, which most influenced market formation, came from microcredit institutions and banks. These formal, secured loans required land as collateral. Before Order 01, the only collateral available to farmers were "soft" titles—proof of land ownership verified in a letter from commune chiefs. After Order 01 however, farmers who had secured "hard" (or formal) land titles could more easily gain secured loans. The rush for loans after villagers obtained land titles produced a concurrent boom in lending institutions in the provincial and district centers, eager to meet this demand for loans. It was no coincidence that in this environment, two former microcredit institutions—ACLEDA and Sathapana—scaled up their operations to become fully fledged commercial banks, opening many new branches in previously unserved district centers. These bigger institutions primarily offered large loans of USD 2,000–5,000 or more for activities needing more capital, such as setting up a new trading operation or planting long-term crops, such as rubber, cashew, and pepper. Smaller commercial microfinance institutions, such as Angkor Mikroheranhvatho Kampuchea (AMK), Prasac, Hatta Kaksekar, and Crédit Mutuel Kampuchea (CMK), also flocked to Phum Prambei, competing to offer smaller loans of USD 1,000–2,000 for smaller-scale farming activities, housing, and social commitments, such as weddings. This flood of capital initially supported market evolution through the adoption of high-value commodity crops, along the lines documented earlier (see chap. 2).

Monthly interest rates at these institutions ranged from 2.4 to 2.7 percent (or 28–32 percent annually). Lower risk (secured or repeated) loans attracted lower rates, while unsecured loans or loans for first-time borrowers came at higher rates (interview with ACLEDA Bank manager, Phum Prambei, December 9, 2013). Informal discussions with roving representatives from these financial institutions, who regularly visited villages to elicit new clients, revealed that their salaries were contingent on growing their client base.

Not all villagers visited by Order 01 teams could gain land titles, and such families were then also sidelined from credit access. The student teams tasked with carrying out land titling often demanded gifts of food or other bribes to prepare title documents (Grimsditch and Schoenberger 2015). Those landholders who were unable to meet these demands were made to wait and ultimately excluded. Borey and Rachany—the Bunong-Khmer family that I met in Phum Buon—had lamented that their chances of gaining a title disappeared when Rachany's elderly father "cursed" the Order 01 students upon their arrival, thinking that they had come to take their land. After this incident, the family also failed to meet the students' demands for "two chickens or ducks" before they would measure the land, and therefore it was never titled (interview with Bunong-Khmer family, Phum Buon, February 21, 2016). Several households in my study sites that were visited by Order 01 student teams were unable to secure land titles for similar reasons. Sometimes the student teams missed entire villages within their targeted districts. Phum Prammuoi in Tbong Khmum Province, being one such village, was ostensibly overlooked because the village chief and community members lacked the political connections of the leaders in neighboring villages. Although these farmers could still engage in informal land sales and gain unsecured loans, the lack of a title constrained their capacity to move into more capital-intensive cash crops.

In summary, while cassava assisted migrants to clear and claim land, their actions to secure these newly acquired landholdings served to deepen and expand market formation beyond the cassava network. Land was commodified through titling, land sales, and leasing arrangements, which supported elite land accumulation and speculation. Even where a secure title was not gained, these negotiations had a generative effect on frontier land dynamics through informal land transactions. Land formalization also catalyzed higher rates and levels of debt than ever before, particularly for the establishment of capital-intensive crops, such as rubber and pepper.

Mobilizing Networks and Embedding the Market Rhizome in Mondulkiri

Like *Hevea* in the early period of French colonization, cassava has been the global commodity crop that has further populated, expanded, and intensified this frontier market in the past two decades. In their quest for land, lowland migrants were key players in this process. As discussed in chapter 2, Cambodia's high levels of rural-rural migration from lowland areas to Mondulkiri contrasts with the steady rural-urban migration trend noted throughout mainland Southeast Asia. Migrants' stories show how individual motivations and desires, such as the quest for land, can feed into larger-scale processes of land commodification and environmental change. Frontier migration and settlement are in this sense profoundly unsettling, not least for Indigenous populations, whose perspectives I explore further in the next chapter.

In the contemporary context, global connections and shifts, such as the rise of China and the liberalization of Southeast Asian economies (Vietnam in particular), have catalyzed the current intensive and ongoing pattern of commodity booms and market formation. These developments rekindled the integration of these borderlands into global markets and provided the impetus for cassava production and processing as well as the diversification of commodity networks. Land governance changes and the emergence of political elites in the postconflict period further supported market development. This provided a set of conditions that converged in time and place—a frontier assemblage or conjuncture (Li 2014)—to embed markets.

Through the dried and fresh cassava cases, we saw that the variegated character of this frontier landscape framed these markets. In the 1990s and 2000s, the cessation of conflict and road network improvements promoted migration—first to lowland areas and then to progressively more remote upland areas with poor road infrastructure. These latter upland localities were only suited to the production of dried cassava due to the time taken to transport cassava crops to prospective buyers. Here, key material actants, such as roads and forests, were influential in framing market opportunities and formations to coproduce two distinct commodity networks. For both networks, proximity to the border enabled Khmer farmers to access novel markets via Vietnamese traders and buyers and enabled state border officials to draw illicit rents.

These cases show why we need to look beyond the mobilization of one or two specific commodity networks to understand frontier market formation. When cassava networks tipped toward demobilization, land commodification and credit continued to embed and evolve market transactions. Some farmers engaged with new commodity crops, such as rubber, cashew, or pepper. Those with fewer resources, however, were squeezed in their livelihood opportunities, as chapter 4 will further explore. My findings resonate with the work of Bair (2009) and her colleagues (2013), who recognize the influence of dispossession and "disarticulation" in commodity networks. The Mondulkiri case adds that, even where specific commodity networks are disrupted, land commodification and access to credit can deepen and expand market engagements in diverse ways. Mondulkiri's market appeared to be transitioning to a similarly diverse web of interconnected commodity networks as seen in Tbong Khmum but with novel constraints that are discussed in the next chapter.

Like the market rhizome described in Tbong Khmum, market formation in Mondulkiri emerged from historical, geographical, and social relationships. Cassava illustrated how differentiated and nuanced opportunities in resource frontiers actively contribute to the development and form of specific commodity networks. Closely related trends, such as migration, land commodification, and the mobilization of credit, served to deeply embed markets for cash crops and enabled the proliferation of new agricultural commodity networks. Mondulkiri's case therefore shows that market formation is driven by not only innovation but also dissonance and disruption within ongoing processes of commodification.

FRONTIER RUPTURE

Chea and Chanlina were a Khmer couple who moved with their son from the lowland province of Kampong Cham to Phum Pii, Mondulkiri, in 2012. Chea's friend, Leap, who was from the same village, had moved to Phum Pii two years earlier to work on a new French-owned rubber estate. Leap encouraged Chea to also make the move, telling Chea that he would easily find work in Phum Pii, because he was educated and "knew things." He helped Chea to find work as a security officer, and Chanlina was employed as a company laborer. After three years, both Chea and Chanlina resigned, as Chea explained: "I was paid twenty thousand riel a day [USD 5]. I would wake up at two A.M. to prepare food to take to work and finished work at four P.M. That much money was not even enough to buy food here—it is so expensive. The work was very hard, and we couldn't stand it, so Chanlina and I decided to quit. My friend Leap had already left a year earlier." After resigning, they lived off their small karaoke store, and Chanlina's wholesale business that supplied Khmer cakes to local vendors. They had been able to buy a small plot of land on which they built a home, but life was hard. Chea added that his situation was not unique: "Most people feel the same; they hoped that when they came here, life would be better than in Kampong Cham. Some do OK because they have money—and also because of their ideas and way of working. But others who came before me, they are still renting a house and on a daily wage." Chea bought their tiny residential plot for USD 4,500 from a Khmer family that was among the first to migrate to Phum Pii after the Khmer Rouge fell in 1979. Chea explained, "The man got this land when it was forest.

They cleared it and gave rice to the Bunong—one sack of rice for one hectare of land. That family owned a large area of land, which they subdivided and sold to newer Khmer migrants." I asked Chea what advice he would give to others considering a move to Phum Pii. He paused before saying, "If they are poor, they should not come here" (interview with Khmer man, Phum Pii, February 25, 2016).

Chea's story illustrates the interactive processes of change that continue to shape Mondulkiri's frontier market, in which new rubber plantations colonize forest spaces, Indigenous communities are dislocated, resources dwindle, and migrants face crushing livelihood stresses. For Chea and others who lacked money and agricultural land, conditions worsened over time—sometimes leading to onward migration. Examining two "postboom" villages in Mondulkiri—Phum Pii and Phum Prambei—this chapter considers the landscape and social pressures wrought by frontier markets. While rhizomes have the inherent capacity to rupture—to break and reform (Deleuze and Guattari 1987)—this chapter shows the human and material costs of such market rupture. In contrast with Tbong Khmum, where market disruptions produced change and spatial expansion, here we witness the frontier market's limits. If, as Lund (2016, 1202) describes, rupture is an "open moment . . . when opportunities and risks multiply," we need to better understand such risks and who bears them. To address this, I examine the disruptive synergies between smallholder agriculture, large-scale plantations, and other landscape transitions in Mondulkiri.

Mondulkiri's once heavily forested landscape has undergone significant transformation in the last two decades (see fig. 4.1). Two of my study sites illuminate the connections between smallholder commodity production and these changes. The first site, Phum Pii, where I did fieldwork in 2016, reveals how land and migration interact with smallholder crop booms and economic land concessions (ELCs) for rubber. Although Phum Pii is in an upland location, road connections and proximity to the provincial capital of Senmonorom made this an early hub of postconflict migration and plantation development. The second site, the lowland village of Phum Prambei, illustrates how a combination of smallholder markets, timber extraction, ELCs, land depletion, and debt have escalated livelihood pressures and environmental change (see also chap. 3). In both villages, some groups experienced greater precarity, while others exercised relative forms of agency within the depleted landscape by working within illicit economies or leaving to find seasonal and long-term work elsewhere. The experiences of Bunong communities, smallholders, and recent migrants in these two villages demonstrate the physical and social limits to market formation and the risks these pose for the most vulnerable within frontier landscapes.

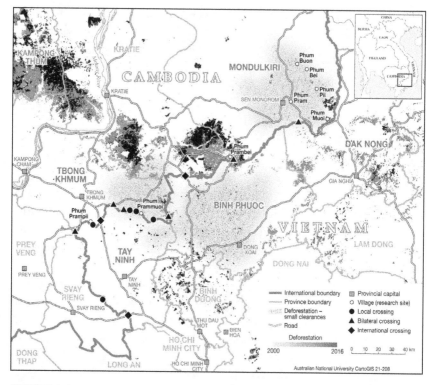

FIGURE 4.1.   Forest cover and land use change in Mondulkiri, 2000–2016

Source: Based on Hansen et al. 2013. The authors annually update data on this open-access website:
http://earthenginepartners.appspot.com/science-2013-global-forest.

The Role of Timber in Mondulkiri's Transitioning Frontier

I have discussed the long history of frontier crops in earlier chapters, particularly rubber (see chap. 1). The extraction of such raw resources as timber, however, was an important precursor to commodity crops in these borderlands. In addition to Indigenous communities' precolonial trade and tribute networks for natural resources, forested provinces like Mondulkiri fed a thriving cross-border timber trade in the 1850s (see the introduction). As timber was very loosely regulated by the Cambodian royalty, Cambodian forests could be more readily exploited than those across the border in what became French Cochinchina. Vietnamese and Chinese traders particularly targeted bamboo and high-value timber, such as rosewood (*trac*, in Vietnamese; sp. *Dalbergia cochinchinensis*). The Vietnamese operated as small-scale local brokers who would procure the timber, while the Chinese and Malays took care of transport to Vietnam and beyond. These extractive activities in the border region became so intense that they caused a market glut and a dramatic fall in the price of timber by the turn of the nineteenth century (Cooke 2004, 142).

The French attempted to govern these existing frontier networks, both to gain a share of timber revenues and to manage political risks. The colonial administration installed border stations and customs officials at major crossings, imposed taxes on timber imports from Cambodia to Cochinchina, and created forest reservations, first in Vietnam and later Cambodia, to prevent unauthorized timber cutting and stem the trade at its source.[1] In addition, the French tried to quell exploitative practices by Chinese and Khmer traders, which were viewed as a political liability. For example, when the administrator of Kratie was assassinated by Bunong people in 1915, the French blamed this incident on the "excessive need for profit" among Chinese and Khmer traders, exercised through "practices of intimidation." The incident report stated, "Naturally the Phnongs became tired of being exploited and fought back against any kind of foreign officer, without distinction. It was in this context that the militia under the direction of Mr. Truffot was attacked in retribution for the injustices carried out by their predecessors."[2] French responses to this event reveal that their control of timber networks served a mix of political, security, and economic ends, pointing again to the nexus between market formation and state formation.

Timber has remained a key commodity for state formation in Cambodia, especially in the postconflict period. As discussed in the introduction, timber exploitation on both sides of the border has funded armed conflict and enabled capital accumulation by state elites and their networks over an extended period, and Cambodian and Vietnamese military and state actors continue to control the sector (Cock 2016). These groups not only gained direct revenues from timber (Le Billon and Springer 2007) but also accumulated the partially cleared lands after timber was extracted. Timber revenues became increasingly important for the Cambodian ruling party following the 1991 peace agreement and the scaling back of postconflict donor support (Milne 2015).

In response to the rapid deforestation that ensued, donors pressured the Cambodian government to implement tighter forest regulations, and a system of logging concessions was installed in the 1990s (FAO 2000; Le Billon 2000, 798–99). Between 1994 and 2001, some 39 percent of Cambodia's land area—over half of its forests—was placed under timber concessions (Diepart and Schoenberger 2016). In Mondulkiri, the Malaysian company Samling was a key operator, holding a timber concession near Phum Prambei. Within this new regulatory regime, state and military elites remained influential beneficiaries, and unsustainable levels of timber extraction continued (Global Witness 2002). As international pressure grew again about Cambodia's rapid forest depletion, the government banned the export of logs and rough timber in December 1996 (Durst et al. 2001). It then specified more stringent management of the Permanent Forest Estate (2002 Law on Forestry), effectively terminating the existing timber concessions. Illicit extraction has continued apace, however, in such provinces as Mondulkiri (Mahanty 2018; Milne 2015).

Mondulkiri's next significant wave of forest clearance came after 2005, when an amendment to the 2001 Land Law enabled the large-scale development of economic land concessions (ELCs). Cambodian and foreign companies gained leases for up to ninety-nine years to develop thousands of hectares of land at a time (Sub-decree No. 146 on Economic Land Concessions (2005); Davis et al. 2015). Although many protected forests had been established in Cambodia under a 1993 royal decree (Paley 2015), several of these areas were handed over as ELCs, especially for rubber production. By 2012, an estimated 2,547,718 hectares (or 14 percent [FAOSTAT 2015]) of Cambodia's land area was held in agricultural concessions, much of it forested (Diepart and Schoenberger 2016). In practice, these ELCs enabled timber extraction under the guise of agro-industrial development (Milne 2015). Land conflicts between concessionaires and resident communities also started proliferating at this time (NGO Forum on Cambodia 2015). As local concerns grew, and a key national election loomed, the government placed a moratorium on the granting of new concessions in May 2012 (see table I.1 in the introduction). By this time, however, the government had already allocated substantial areas of land across Cambodia, including in Mondulkiri. Near Phum Pii, a total area of 11,964 hectares was allocated for rubber production by three French-Cambodian ventures that were later taken over and consolidated by the French investor Socfin. Near Phum Prambei, a Vietnamese rubber company acquired 11,625 hectares. Indeed, most of my study villages were located near ELCs. Figure 4.2 shows these ELC boundaries and the extensive deforestation that was already evident during my fieldwork (2016).

This history has produced an assemblage of protected forest areas, rubber concessions, small-scale farms, and shifting cultivation in Mondulkiri. According to available remote sensing data, the greatest forest depletion occurred between 2008 and 2012 in connection with the granting of ELCs, since these required complete forest clearance rather than the selective removal of trees that occurred under timber concessions (Davis et al. 2015). While colonial-era plantations were driven by and served European capital, these postconflict land-use changes additionally served the interest of predatory Cambodian elites, as well as Vietnamese and Chinese capital.

Aside from agro-industrial development within Mondulkiri, the province was also affected by ELCs in neighboring provinces. Migrants from Kratie and Tbong Khmum often commented that colonial-era and new plantations had exacerbated land pressures in their home districts. For example, my informal discussions in Phum Pii revealed that the largest migrant influx to Phum Pii came from Snuol in Kratie Province, where a Vietnamese company opened a ten-thousand-hectare rubber concession in 2011. My 2016 household survey in Phum Buon also found that migrants primarily came from districts in Kratie and Tbong Khmum that hosted or neighbored large rubber concessions. Migrants seeking agricultural land melded with those who came to work on Mondulkiri's new rubber plantations. Similar findings are emerging in other parts of Cambodia, suggesting that the labor and land demands of ELCs have broadly served to boost frontier migration (Fox et al. 2018).

Thus the formation of commodity networks for smallholder crops such as cassava in Mondulkiri sat within broader processes of land commodification, migration, and landscape change. Timber extraction and agro-industrial development were important factors in this mix. The next two sections explore specific social and environmental interactions between these frontier commodity networks for timber, land, and smallholder cash crops.

Synergistic Change in Phum Pii

Like my Mondulkiri study sites discussed in chapter 3, Phum Pii was a hub for lowland migration from the early 2000s. The development of three neighboring rubber concessions, however, significantly boosted migration and market formation. By 2016–2017, when I undertook field research in Phum Pii, the French company Socfin had consolidated three existing Khmer-held concessions into one large landholding (see ELC #3, fig. 4.2). Socfin counts among its founders two early investors in colonial Indochinese rubber, who received large land allocations in French Cochinchina: Adrien Hallet and the Rivaud Group (see chap. 1). This colonial-era company still holds substantial agro-industrial investments in Southeast Asia, Africa, and South America.

In a contemporary echo of the problems that plagued the rubber sector during French rule, conflict has shrouded Socfin's plantation near Phum Pii. After gaining control of the first of these three concessions in 2008, the company commenced forest clearance in December of that year to prepare the land for *Hevea* cultivation. The absence of free prior and informed consent from the Bunong community, who held customary rights to that land, became an unhealed wound. A 2012 NGO investigation confirmed that "Socfin KCD cleared their lands without giving them any notice" (Liu et al. 2012, 181).[3] For the Bunong, this clearance brought sudden exclusion from their ancestral lands. As noted earlier, Bunong people in Phum Pii, like those in other areas of Mondulkiri, historically

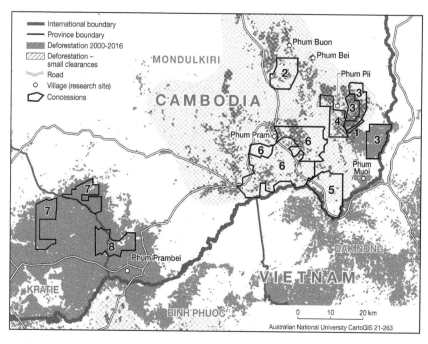

FIGURE 4.2. Economic land concessions near Mondulkiri study sites

Source: Open Development Cambodia 2016; LICADHO 2018; forest cover data from Hansen et al. 2013 (updated 2016). See table 4.1 for key to the numbered regions on this map.

relied on shifting cultivation in their surrounding forests and on nontimber forest products, such as wild vegetables, fuelwood, honey, fish, and wild meat (Nikles 2006). The loss of land and forest access through Socfin's rubber operations restricted access to these important livelihood resources, pushing Bunong people in Phum Pii to rely more heavily on market-oriented agriculture. Later, when tourism took off at a local waterfall, many Bunong families started to sell food to tourists or to work as guides. Through these processes, Socfin's exclusion of the Bunong community and subsequent large-scale forest clearance drew this community into greater market engagement.

From the perspective of Bunong informants, however, there was an equally important affective or emotional dimension to this land exclusion (Colman 2012). Many still spoke of their personal distress after significant cultural sites, such as burial forests, were razed in 2008 and in subsequent clearing. Burial forests were regarded as sacred places whose disturbance could risk the health and well-being of villagers (Bourdier 2009; van der Eynden 2011). These events sparked a wave of community protests that were initially suppressed by the government to protect company interests. Later, in 2009, the conflict was referred to a newly established tripartite (company-community-government) committee

TABLE 4.1 Key to figure 4.2

MAP REFERENCE NO.	PROVINCE	COMPANY	INVESTING COUNTRY	AREA (HECTARES)	PURPOSE	YEAR ESTABLISHED	NEARBY STUDY SITES
1	MDK	K Peace	Cambodia	500	Agro-industry (rubber, other)	2012	Phum Pii
2	MDK	DTC	Cambodia	4,000	Rubber	2009	Phum Bei and Phum Buon
3	MDK	Varanasi (Socfin)*	Cambodia/France	2,705	Rubber	2008	Phum Pii
3	MDK	Sethikula (Socfin)*	France	4,273	Rubber	2010	Phum Pii
3	MDK	Covy Phama (Socfin)*	Cambodia	5,345	Rubber	2008	Phum Pii
4	MDK	Dak Lak MDK	Vietnam	4,162	Rubber	2008	Phum Pii
5	MDK	Mega first	Malaysia/ Singapore	9,477	Agro-industry, ecotourism, special economic zone	2012	Phum Pram and Phum Muoi
6	MDK	Wuzishan	China	20,498 +10,000	Agro-industry (pine, fruit/vegetable)	2005	Phum Pram and Phum Muoi
7	MDK/ KRA	Binh Phuoc 1 & 2	Vietnam	9,968	Rubber	2011	Phum Prambei
8	MDK/KRA	Sovann Reachsey	Vietnam	6,525	Rubber	2010	Phum Prambei

MDK=Mondulkiri; KRA=Kratie

* These three allocations are collectively referred to here as the Socfin concession.

to negotiate a resolution. Socfin also appointed a community liaison team to oversee compensation payments (van der Eynden 2011). Some Bunong families accepted compensation, but others found money to be inadequate reparation for this perceived cultural violence, causing splits to emerge within the community (interview with Bunong man, Phum Pii, March 5, 2016).

The depth of feeling over this incursion was still evident during my field visit in 2016, some eight years later, when many Bunong people were still outraged about the bulldozing of their burial sites. One woman shared photographs of the human remains and artefacts that this uncovered (see fig. 4.3), and many others stated that they had not forgotten the dark origins of Socfin's operations near Phum Pii (interviews with Bunong residents of Phum Pii, February 24, 2016; March 5, 2016; December 21, 2017; and December 23, 2017). These Bunong community members viewed Socfin's incursions on their land and these waves of migrant settlement as an act of invasion that threatened their way of life and their identity. As one Bunong informant described: "They are invading. Our sacred forest and burial forest were cleared . . . one by one. There are no more sacred forest and burial sites left. They cleared the forest, and they did not ask me" (interview with Bunong man, Phum Pii, April 23, 2016). The profound sense of loss associated with these rapid, exclusionary, and imposed landscape changes went far beyond livelihood deprivations. It was more akin to "solastalgia," a term used by psychologists to capture the distress caused by sudden environmental (and social) change among a people that is closely connected to their place (Albrecht et al. 2007).

The Socfin-Bunong land dispute continued over several years as an elderly Bunong leader, Borey, explained. Borey was born in Cambodia but spent his early years in Vietnam because his family moved there to escape heavy bombing in 1970. When Borey returned to Cambodia as a young man in 1992, he could speak Khmer but was only literate in Vietnamese. Borey led the Bunong community's protests against Socfin and their efforts to gain back rights to customary lands. The opportunity to apply for communal land title under the 2009 amendments to the 2001 Land Law (see table I.1 in the introduction) came a few years too late for the Bunong community in Phum Pii. By this time, the Socfin concession was well in train, and many of the areas they could potentially claim in a communal title application were occupied by Socfin (interview with Bunong man, Phum Pii, February 24, 2016). In 2014, mirroring trends across Cambodia (Vize and Hornung 2013), a provincially based NGO supported their application for communal land title over their customary lands. This application could not progress however, because some areas conflicted with Socfin's holdings. So the group turned instead to another land governance technology, submitting a community forest application under the national Law on Forestry, again with NGO

FIGURE 4.3.   Bunong remains and artefacts uncovered during bulldozing of burial sites by Socfin

Source: Photograph by the author of an image shared by a Bunong informant.

support. This revised area covered 660 hectares of reserved forest known as Phnom Nam Lear Sanctuary. To meet community forest status requirements, they had to keep some of the land under strict protection, which was subsequently developed for tourism. The remaining community forest land was cleared for agriculture. Through these mechanisms, the Phum Pii Bunong community was able to stitch together their claim to a far more limited area than their original customary lands (interview with Bunong leader, Phum Pii, February 24, 2016).

In addition to the divisions over compensation mentioned earlier, land titling became a source of tension among the Bunong. The opportunity for individual titling under Order 01 drew some community members away from the communal land claim (see also Milne 2013). Their reasoning for this was that only individual titles could be used as loan collateral, which was particularly valued by farmers that wanted to grow capital-intensive crops, such as *Hevea* and pepper. One Bunong woman, Vanna, who had left the community land claim for a private title observed that those who had persevered with the communal land claim had missed out on market opportunities as they were "not trusted to take a loan" (interview with Bunong woman, Phum Pii, February 23, 2016). Although access to secured loans came at the high price of weakened relationships with her community, Vanna had no regrets about gaining a secure individual land title. Her case highlights that the Bunong had diverse aspirations. These differences became deeper rifts during community negotiations with Socfin and subsequent land-titling and commodification processes.

Socfin's initial forest clearance work and *Hevea* planting increased the demand for both labor and agricultural land in Phum Pii. Estimates of employment numbers during Socfin's establishment phase vary between 10,000 (Liu et al. 2012, 181) to a more realistic 187 permanent workers and 1,169 day laborers by late 2009 (FIDH 2011). By 2014, the reported workforce had fallen to 844. Bunong people gained only about one-fifth of these positions, reflecting a sizeable influx of migrants to the formerly small and predominantly Bunong settlement (Foster and Gray 2016). According to the 1998 census, the entire district population stood at just 2,425 (National Institute of Statistics 2002). A decade later it had more than doubled to 6,540, mainly through migration (Royal Government of Cambodia 2018). A Phum Pii District official explained that Socfin's flood of workers brought significant transformations to the area: "In 2007–2008 there was a big change when the company arrived. Groups of people came from Kampong Cham, Memot, and Snuol to work for the company. . . . Some of the company workers quit because of their low daily pay—only 20,000 riel/day (USD 5). So, within one or two years, the numbers went down, but some of those workers settled here and bought land from the Bunong" (interview with Phum Pii official, February 23, 2016).

These migration patterns reflected the company's changing labor needs. As with other natural resource projects, rubber plantations have a high demand for manual labor during the initial clearance and cultivation period; once established, plantation workforce numbers are reduced, and new skills are required. For example, latex tapping requires a more elaborate and specialized skill set than cultivation (Liu et al. 2012). Many of the retrenched Socfin workers that provided the labor to establish the plantation looked for land to purchase in order to settle in Phum Pii.

While Socfin's labor force increased the demand for land in Phum Pii, the plantation itself had reduced the available land for these new migrants to clear or purchase (interview with Khmer man, Phum Pii, February 24, 2016). As in Chea's case at the beginning of this chapter, these relatively recent migrants could only purchase land from older, more established migrant families, who had acquired large tracts of land in the immediate postconflict years and during the early 2000s (interview with Khmer man, Phum Pii, February 25, 2016). If they could not afford to purchase land, the only other pathway to gain agricultural land in Phum Pii was through a social land concession (SLC). Under the 2001

Land Law, the 2003 Sub-Decree on Social Land Concessions (No. 19) enabled the government to allocate small areas of less than five hectares to poor and dislocated families for residential and agricultural purposes. In Phum Pii, an SLC was allocated to several reportedly well-connected Cham migrants from Kampong Cham. Like the Socfin concession, the new SLC overlaid Bunong lands that, according to a report by the Cambodian Center for Human Rights (CCHR), included "burial sites, spirit forests, land reserved for rotational agriculture and residential land, displacing nearly 100 indigenous families" (CCHR 2013; interview with Bunong man, Phum Pii, March 5, 2016). Coming on top of Socfin's earlier incursions, Bunong concerns about land security further heightened social tensions in Phum Pii. In my 2016 household survey, for example, about 25 percent of Phum Pii respondents itemized specific land conflicts.

In Phum Pii, there was a mutually reinforcing relationship between Socfin's rubber plantation, Bunong dispossession, migration, and growing smallholder demand for farmland. All of these conditions interacted to squeeze land availability. The Phum Pii case particularly exposes how as the frontier market took hold, it escalated land conflicts and disrupted Bunong ties to land.

Postboom Phum Prambei

Landscape and social stressors were even more prominent in the older and predominantly migrant settlement of Phum Prambei. Featuring twenty-two hamlets and a total population of 4,036 in 2012, this "village" was already on the verge of becoming a small district town in the early stages of my field research (WCS 2012). Over a period of five years (2012–2017), however, the booming cassava and timber economy that had driven Phum Prambei's growth hit a visible downturn. This postboom environment saw the exhaustion of high-value timber, depleted soils, unsustainable household debt, and, increasingly, a shift toward seasonal and long-term outmigration. Cash crops, such as cassava, had transitioned from a lucrative to a risky venture, and high levels of debt left farmers unable to adopt new crops.

The initial economic boom which occurred in Phum Prambei around 2010 arose from the conjuncture of rich forests, the postconflict military presence at the border, and Vietnamese-owned plantation development. Although timber trade was not permitted under the Law on Forestry, proximity to the Vietnamese border provided a ready market for illicitly harvested timber. These conditions fueled a local economy that thrived on timber in the postconflict years. By 2013, villagers estimated that about 80 percent of their community was involved—directly or indirectly—in the timber network (group discussion in Phum Prambei,

FIGURE 4.4.   Modified vehicles of this kind were used to transport timber to Vietnam during Phum Prambei's timber boom; this vehicle had been impounded by the Forestry Administration

Source: Photograph by author.

December 11, 2013). Migrants provided a crucial labor force, whether they operated chainsaws for elite-owned operations or transported timber to Vietnamese and Khmer buyers in modified vehicles (see fig. 4.4). The Phum Prambei village head confirmed that those running the logging operations would often import labor from other provinces. At the start of the boom, some of these migrant workers were lucky enough to be paid two to three hectares of land for their clearing work, but by 2013 this window of land access was rapidly closing, and new migrants were more likely to be loaned land by provincial elites than to gain their own plot (interview with male Phum Prambei official, December 12, 2013; see also chap. 3). Latecomers were locked into manual labor or timber clearing due to the lack of arable land and livelihood alternatives. Yet by this time, even work in timber extraction was rapidly declining.

During Phum Pii's timber boom, young Bunong men also joined logging operations. Initially recruited as assistants to Khmer chainsaw operators, they gradually gained chainsaw skills in their own right. Prak, a young Bunong man from a neighboring village, explained the challenges of learning to operate a chainsaw:

It was very tough to use a chainsaw. When I first started doing it, if you didn't know how to use it properly, the wood could hit you. Using the chainsaw was painful because you have to hold it without any strap—you have to use your hands directly and just do it. I learned how to use it from a Khmer person. First he didn't want to teach me because he was worried I may stop working for him as an assistant. I told him, "No, that's OK—I'll still work as an assistant for you." . . . Both *chuncheat* and Khmer may be teachers now, but first the chainsaws came in from the Khmer.[4] The chuncheat didn't know anything [about chainsaws]. (interview with Bunong man, Phum Prambei hinterland, February 6, 2014)

Bunong and Stieng youth like Prak described their participation as a way of securing something from their rapidly disappearing forests: "If we don't do it, the forest will still be gone, and we will feel stupid—just like with land grabbing" (interview with Bunong man, Phum Prambei, December 11, 2013; see also Dara and Chen 2018). This informant's direct comparison with land grabbing reflected a broader view among Indigenous groups that they felt like bystanders in processes of land and resource colonization—this time by lowland Khmer settlers and elites.

The former deputy village head, a Khmer man called Dara, was well informed about timber operations because he ran the local mechanic shop, servicing many of the vehicles that transported timber from the forest to Vietnam. When I first met him in 2012, Dara expressed dismay at the recent downturn in the local economy now that the "forest was gone." I asked what he meant, since the village was next to a protected area that still attracted international finance to secure its forest carbon reserves. Another villager at the coffee shop clarified, "There are only small trees left now." Dara blamed well-connected elites for this situation: "If you are powerful—like the military—you can cut many hectares without consequences. At worst, the forests will last six months, and at best, twelve months." His gloomy prediction was well founded. A year later, Dara reported that there was a nightly procession of at least ten large trucks and thirty small cars loaded with timber that sped through Phum Prambei. The largest trucks, owned by a prominent Khmer businessman, went straight to the port at Sihanoukville, while the others headed for the Vietnamese border. Dara admitted, "The drivers come back in the evening for repairs—they are my customers!" By 2017, however, the timber boom was over and, with it, prospects for local businesses like his. The small roughly cut blocks of timber that were now being transported in broad daylight on the backs of motorcycles were hewed from lower value species and far smaller trees than before. Dara's wife recalled that in the heady days of Phum Prambei's timber boom, truck and car drivers came to them daily for repairs and to buy new tires. In 2017, customers came only weekly or monthly. She concluded that the loss of forests had seriously damaged local businesses (interview with former village official, Phum Prambei, December 13, 2013).

From 2016 onward, as timber became smaller and scarcer, violence over the remaining spoils was more flagrant. Timber cutters had to work deep within the protected forest, usually under the oversight of the military and border authorities. Sometimes clashes would emerge between competing elite- and government-supported groups. For example, a forest patrol group was shot in early 2018, allegedly by military and border officials. The incident resulted in the deaths of three men, who were employed by the Ministry of Environment, the Wildlife Conservation Society, and the military police (Chakrya, Dara, and Sassoon 2018). The decline in timber stocks and competition for dwindling resources that ensued thus made the lives of timber workers and regulators more precarious.

In addition to this decline in Phum Prambei's timber network, migrants had other pressures to contend with. Chapter 3 detailed the central role of migration during the early 2000s in Phum Prambei's market formation. As in Phum Pii, however, opportunities were significantly more constrained for subsequent migrants, who had to buy agricultural land rather than clear it from standing forests. In 2013, the average price of land per hectare was around USD 1,000—more or less, depending on proximity to roads and water—but by 2016, the land price had risen to between USD 3,000 and 5,000 per hectare. Titled lands near roads were the most costly. This dramatic jump in land price made it impossible for the majority of new arrivals to purchase land in Phum Prambei, making land acquisition the province of only wealthy migrants and elites.

Declining land fertility and the onset of crop disease (see chap. 3) also squeezed farmers, because they needed to invest more time and money on cultivation but gained lower returns. The fertility of newly cleared frontier lands was a major asset in the early stages of cultivation but had rapidly depleted. Hall (2011, 841) compares this initial soil fertility of frontier lands to a form of "forest rent" that can be rapidly drawn down. Informal discussions in the village revealed that five years was the average time frame before soil fertility became depleted, after which farmers observed a visible decline in cassava production. My 2016 household survey confirmed that average yields had halved, from about twenty tons of cassava per hectare to ten tons or less, in five years. Farmers would try various strategies to extract greater productivity from their tired soils, including experimenting with new cassava varieties from across the border. Those with money or access to loans would use chemical inputs, such as fertilizers and a hormone spray that was reputed to increase yield. Unlike their Vietnamese counterparts, however, most Phum Prambei farmers typically lacked the capital and knowledge to use such inputs. Consequently, in both Phum Pii and Phum Prambei, falling yields were a major concern by 2016 and 2017.

Newly arrived migrants who were unable to acquire land joined a growing pool of laborers who could be hired by earlier settlers for cassava planting and harvest and by elites overseeing the final throes of timber extraction and land clearance. New migrants like Thyda, a young Khmer woman I interviewed in Phum Prambei, reported they had to take whatever work was available and found it hard to make ends meet but stayed on as they had nowhere else to go: "It's getting harder. Mum doesn't get paid quite often because there is no work opportunity. But we don't think of returning to Kampong Cham as we have no land there. My sister has only ten meters of land there.[5] We cannot go back to depend on my sister, so we must keep on struggling here" (interview with Khmer woman, Phum Prambei, January 18, 2016). To add to their difficulties, Thyda and her mother had to compete with seasonal laborers for work, who came from Prey Veng and Kampong Cham during harvest season. Seasonal workers had the advantage that they could stay on the owner's farm, which allowed them to find work farther away from the village. In contrast, because of lack of transport options, Thyda and her mother could only work close to their small shack, limiting their employment options. Theirs was one among several cases of hardship I encountered among recent migrants.

In Phum Prambei, this lack of work meant that newly arrived migrants who had the capacity to move to new locations would often leave before they were able to put down roots. One laborer's account explained the uncertain future for migrants: "The new migrant coming here is not sure that they will be here next year. They may go to Thailand, where there are better work opportunities than here. Workers for the rubber plantation also complain that they must live day to day because of difficulties in their workplace regarding the amount of work and salary. So migration to another country seems more attractive than being in this place right now" (interview with Khmer man, Phum Prambei, January 19, 2016).

The village chief confirmed this trend of outmigration and the shift to temporary or seasonal forms of migration in Phum Prambei. By 2016, many migrants would come for one or two months or for the cassava harvest season and then return to their place of origin or move on to a new location (interview with Khmer man, former Phum Prambei official, January 18, 2016). While this trend was possibly the most striking in Phum Prambei, surveys in my other Mondulkiri study sites also revealed a fresh pattern of outmigration from the earliest sites of inmigration, such as Phum Prampii (see fig. 4.5).

In Phum Prambei, debt was the other factor constricting farmers. By 2016, after the rapid uptake of secured loans following Order 01, debt became a pressing concern for many Phum Prambei farmers as well as those at other Mondulkiri

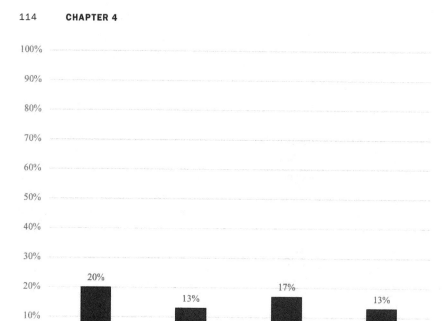

FIGURE 4.5. Percentage of households in Mondulkiri study sites where one or more people had left the village during the preceding twelve months

Source: 2016 household survey.
Note: Phum Prambei was not part of the survey.

study sites. Combined with the price volatilities, soil depletion, and declining harvests discussed earlier, many faced the risk of defaulting on their loan and losing their land. The case of Daevy, a Khmer woman from Phum Prambei, exposes the lived experience of these pressures. Daevy used three hectares of farmland and a house to secure a loan of USD 4,000 from the local branch of ACLEDA Bank. She also held a small unsecured loan of USD 250 from the microfinance company AMK. Daevy explained that her husband's family, who came to Phum Prambei in the early migration wave of 2005, worked hard to seize and clear her land. She married into the family in 2009, moving from Battambong Province. Like many others in the village, Daevy's husband gained a land title when the Order 01 teams visited their village in 2013, which helped them to get the ACLEDA loan. But when we met in 2013, repaying the ACLEDA loan was already a daily worry for Daevy, as she contemplated the difficulties of meeting the bank's end-of-year deadline. They had started to work for other farmers to keep up repayments and were ready to borrow money from other people if needed: "If we don't pay the ACLEDA loan, then the bank will put a 'for sale' sign on our land and sell it off at a discounted price [*lai long*, in Khmer]. Everyone is afraid of having no land or house and will do their best to borrow from other sources to avoid this" (interview with Khmer woman, Phum Prambei, December 7, 2013). These circumstances often caused farmers like Daevy to borrow money from relatives or take unsecured loans from secondary microfinance institutions to maintain payments—ultimately an untenable situation.

By 2016, land loss in Phum Prambei started to drive onward migration. Visiting the village that year, I found that at least twelve (or one-half) of the indebted households that I had interviewed two years earlier had left the village after defaulting on loans and losing their land. Their neighbors reported that these families had moved as far afield as Malaysia and Thailand in search of laboring work. The growth of debt-related land loss was confirmed in a 2015 Cambodia-wide study that found that most land sales in rural areas were distress sales, to reimburse loans or to deal with health emergencies (World Bank 2015, 26; see also LICADHO 2019). Some commentators have viewed this as an inevitable process of agrarian change, whereby more "efficient" agricultural producers can accumulate land and newly landless farmers transition to industrial work in cities (see Deininger and Jin 2007 on Vietnam). The Phum Prambei case, however, highlights the anxieties and social disruption associated with such a shift.

After the cassava price slump of 2016 (see chap. 3), farmers in other areas of Mondulkiri also reported that the weight of their land mortgages sat heavily on their shoulders. The household survey that I undertook that year in the Mondulkiri villages of Phum Pii, Phum Bei, and Phum Buon and Phum Pram found that half the households with an existing debt also reported a reduced level of well-being due to such factors as insufficient funds to cover health care, food, and social commitments and because they needed to work harder to make ends meet. Consequently, many of these households—particularly small to medium landowners—were left without funds to meet daily needs, such as food and health care.

In summary, Phum Prambei's postboom malaise emerged as timber dried up and agricultural commodity production became increasingly uncertain, difficult, and expensive. The village's large base of landless workers was deployed to extract the remaining timber resources and by landed farmers who were still able to grow cassava. There was little new land and work, however, causing these laborers as well as many new arrivals to remigrate on a seasonal, temporary, or permanent basis. In both Phum Prambei and Phum Pii, successive waves of migrants to the frontier had few opportunities to gain land (see also chap. 3). The most recent arrivals, who had come late in the postboom period, had the most precarious situation. Although many of these settlers arrived with the intent to stay, they lacked the funds to buy land.

From Market Rupture to Frontier Rupture

In the preceding discussion, I have explored the evolution of smallholder commodity networks within broader environmental and social transformations in this frontier. While smallholder land clearing was a gradual process, it interacted with relatively abrupt and large-scale disruptions, such as Socfin's *Hevea* plantation. The effects of these profound and synergistic processes crossed over between commodity networks: resource depletion, loss in soil fertility, crop disease, debt, reports of reduced well-being, and onward migration. As supply and demand dwindled and intensified across these commodities, elements of physical and emotional violence were also characteristics of this frontier market, echoing the colonial "contact zone" of chapter 1 (see also Li 2017). These cumulative changes pushed the frontier socionature to its brink.

Responses to these processes of social and ecological stress were highly differentiated. Life became more precarious for many, while some consolidated their power and land, shifted to different commodity networks, or left (see also Cramb and McCarthy 2016; Kelly 2011; Rigg, Salamanca, and Thompson 2016). People who found themselves in a marginal situation were not simply passive either, as seen in the expanding political space occupied by Bunong protesters and the capacity of migrants to move on when life became unworkable in Phum Prambei. In both cases, though, such agency was highly contingent—a "capacity to act" (Giddens 1984, 9) rather than to shape outcomes or exercise influence over others. Migration from an unviable setting, for instance, could equally place people in even greater precarity, as seen in recent accounts of the exploitation of Cambodian labor on Thai fishing boats (Marschke and Vandergeest 2016) and as domestic workers in Malaysia (Viajar 2018). With civil society support, the Bunong community amplified their voices through collective action, but this was less evident among new migrants, given their recent or transient history in my study sites. In both Phum Pii and Phum Prambei, household and community circumstances shaped the forms and extent of agency (collective or individual).

Rather than being continually "reinvented" (Rasmussen and Lund 2018), the frontier market started to waver between incorporating new commodity networks and hitting constraints in the form of environmental and social stress. This was most evident in Phum Prambei, where the village economy had slumped, unemployment and outmigration were increasing, and farmers did not appear to shift as readily to new commodity crops as they had in Tbong Khmum (see chap. 2). Phum Prambei therefore challenges the notion of frontier reinvention, revealing that the frontier can also rupture to a point where markets and lives start to become unviable, particularly for the most vulnerable people.

Such ruptures can also look different at various scales of analysis. At a provincial level, we saw exhausted landscapes and forest depletion. At the individual and household level, rupture manifested in financial and emotional uncertainty and stress. Migrant smallholders and the Bunong community also experienced rupture through specific dramatic incidents, such as the desecration of a burial forest or a failed crop. These experiences in turn mobilized different forms of agency. The affective dimensions of loss and change provided a strong motivator for Bunong resistance. The costs were also social, for example, as farmers lost their land and left their support networks for new and uncertain settings. In some cases, gradual pressures on household finances and falling yields seemed to be absorbed as a new norm. Either way, local actors were conscious of an overall decline in well-being due to experiences of land dispossession, debt, loss of soil fertility, crop failure, declining employment, and market uncertainty, with the emerging sense that the boom was over in Phum Pii and Phum Prambei.

The notion of an environmental crisis arising from the unbridled growth of markets is not new. Marx proposed that this was a natural outcome of capitalism, which would ultimately break down the socioecological metabolism that joins society to its natural and physical foundations—a process he called "metabolic rift" (J. Foster 1999). More than a biophysical process, Marx's metabolic rift also encompassed social alienation through the "material estrangement of human beings in capitalist society from the natural conditions of their existence" (J. Foster 1999, 383). In the agricultural sphere, Marx argued that despite technological revolutions in fertilizers, intensive agricultural production would ultimately deplete the soils in order to meet market demands and provide for industrial and urban centers. Thus, although technology—in this case, agricultural innovation—could mediate the timing and extent of the metabolic rift, it could not fully prevent it. This was certainly visible among the poorest farmers in Phum Pii and Phum Prambei, who had little capacity to engage in soil improvement technologies. Moore (2017, 2018) has since emphasized that because markets ultimately thrive on the exploitation of frontier resources and human labor, ruptured socioecological relationships may be unavoidable.

This chapter adds to my mapping of a rhizomic market, showing that the frontier market involves not only incorporation, intensification, and expansion but also rupture. Rather than an end state, the frontier ruptures documented here were ongoing, synergistic, and cumulative. At times, the effects were dramatic, as with Socfin's land grab, while at other times they were slow and processual, as with smallholder debt and land exhaustion. The risks were disproportionately felt among the most vulnerable groups. The stories in this chapter question whether ruptured rhizomes can inevitably reform and whether frontiers can be continually reinvented after resources are depleted and labor shortages set in.

5

INTERVENING IN MARKET FORMATION

In January 2018, I met Binh, a young, internationally trained Vietnamese policy adviser. Based in a state-affiliated research center in Hanoi, Binh worked on Vietnam's biofuel policy and had unique insights into its turbulent history. The policy was introduced in 2007 to initiate domestic ethanol production and to move the transport sector toward using an ethanol-petrol mix known as E5. "That was the plan," Binh said, "but it all went bad." Domestic demand for E5 failed to develop, in part because people did not trust it and worried about cheating on the part of fuel outlets. Public hesitation peaked when media reports drew a link between E5 and cases of cars and motorcycles that exploded while in use. Upon investigation, these incidents were shown to have other causes, but the damage to public trust was done. Furthermore, Vietnamese production trials struggled to compete with ethanol imports in terms of efficiency and price. By the time of our interview, only two of the six state-run factories built to produce ethanol remained in operation. When I asked Binh why Vietnam had embraced biofuels so enthusiastically, he replied, "The scientific community agreed that biofuels are better for the environment, so we took this as given." Binh added that the government also saw an opportunity to strengthen markets for agricultural products, particularly cassava, which farmers were adopting in droves. High-level corruption cases during 2017 added to the public's lack of trust in this state-run initiative. Vietnam's car and motorcycle industries further undermined the policy by continuing to assemble vehicles that were unable to use E5. Politically, the government wanted to see this initiative succeed after investing so much. "But in the end," Binh concluded, "they did not consider the market and consumer habits enough. It takes too long to get this aspect of the market working well" (interview with Vietnamese official, Hanoi, January 17, 2018).

In chapter 1, I argued that the French colonial state played a central role in catalyzing frontier rubber production. The colonial administration facilitated access to new land, created the conditions that mobilized labor for rubber estates, and provided favorable incentives for European capital. Ultimately, however, the French administration struggled to govern the Indochinese rubber market in the context of labor unrest and global price volatility. Here I return again to the uneasy role of states in market formation, this time for the contemporary commodity of cassava.

Comparing government-backed programs in both Cambodia and Vietnam, I find that state influence in relation to markets remains indirect and contingent, raising important implications for market governance. We see this through two case studies where state actors, supported by international donors, have attempted to influence market development. The first case study comprises two value-chain development interventions (hereafter, value-chain interventions) that have tried to influence Cambodia's cassava sector. One project encouraged international investment in cassava processing and contract farming, while the other concentrated on improving farm-level technologies and market linkages. The second case concerns Vietnam's biofuel market where—as Binh described earlier—the Vietnamese government attempted to establish a new green market for mixed ethanol fuel to meet environmental and energy security goals. From its inception, this strategy was premised on the availability of cassava chips as input for ethanol production from upland frontiers in Vietnam and Cambodia, as well as other agricultural inputs. In light of the ultimate failure of this policy, it provides important insights on the state's role—and limitations—in building new markets.

These examples add to the rhizomic picture of frontier agricultural networks developed in the preceding chapters. While state actors and others were able to influence aspects of the cassava and biofuel markets, these markets were ultimately unruly and beyond direct control. Like the French colonial context, contemporary market interventions still feed into projects of state formation, in this case by enhancing the revenue base from commodity exports, responding to populist demands for agricultural development or promoting new technologies to keep up with regional and international expectations. The outcomes of these particular interventions, however, remained captive to disparate social, economic, and political relationships and interests that are beyond direct state influence.

Market "Strengthening": Cambodia's Cassava Value-Chain Projects

Value-chain interventions have gained wide purchase as a pathway to strengthen agrarian livelihoods. Following the technocratic green revolution approaches of the 1960s and 1970s, value-chain interventions adopted a more prominent emphasis on market mechanisms (Moseley 2016). Although the language of value chains resembles the notion of commodity chains that grew from Marxist world systems theory, the goals of commodity-chain analysis and value-chain interventions differ significantly (Neilson, Pritchard, and Yeung 2014). While they share a focus on commodity networks, value-chain interventions embrace market formation in the belief that market incorporation and a flourishing private sector will "trickle down" and deliver better welfare for rural populations. In contrast, commodity-chain analysis exposes the unequal structures of global capitalism in relation to labor, production, and consumption (Bernstein and Campling 2006). Political ecologists have further highlighted that domestic resource-access institutions multiply the differentiated risks and benefits in commodity chains (Neimark 2010; Ribot 1998). The two approaches thus do not concur on the developmental benefits of the market.

Agricultural value-chain development is an integral part of the Cambodian government's Trade Sector-Wide Approach (Trade SWAP), an umbrella initiative led by the Ministry of Commerce (Royal Government of Cambodia 2014). With donor support, the government mapped a suite of interventions to expand and support cassava production, partly due to the emerging boom discussed in preceding chapters and due to cassava's export and processing potential. Through this approach, they aimed to achieve the win-win outcome of improved national trade revenues from cassava exports, which would also improve returns to smallholders. The first intervention discussed here, supported by the multilateral donor UNDP (United Nations Development Programme), initially tried to build a better understanding of value-chain functioning and to form new farmers' associations (UNDP 2013). Later, the focus shifted to promoting domestic cassava processing. The UNDP hoped to achieve this by expediting international investment in cassava processing factories, along with the development of new institutions—such as contract farming—to secure inputs for these fledgling factories (UNDP Cambodia 2018). The second value-chain intervention, supported by a bilateral donor, the Australian Centre for International Agricultural Research (ACIAR), targeted more efficient and cost-effective production at the farm level to benefit smallholders (ACIAR 2014). The two projects differed in their specific aims, but both worked to influence the ongoing formation of the cassava market in ways that embedded cassava as a commercial crop and strengthened domestic returns from cassava exports.

UNDP Cambodia Export Diversification and Expansion Program

The UNDP Cambodia Export Diversification and Expansion Program (CEDEP) was funded through the World Trade Organization's (WTO's) Enhanced Integration Framework (EIF).[1] When Cambodia joined the WTO in 2004, it was eligible for funding under the EIF, which supports developing countries to use trade as a vehicle for growth and poverty reduction (UNDP 2017). On its website, the EIF is described as a "co-pilot" for national governments who occupy the "driver's seat" in determining specific pathways to trade development, while the EIF is there to guide them "every step of the way" to "identify sectors with export potential and help countries become more competitive in regional and global markets" (EIF 2019). Housed within the Cambodian Ministry of Commerce, the EIF hub coordinated several donor-financed value-chain interventions. An interview with officials in the Ministry of Commerce found that they were well inducted into the EIF's trade-for-development discourse. One senior official explained that he had recently moved to the ministry because he "could pick a good leader when he saw one." He was referring to the then minister for commerce, whom his team viewed as a dynamic person with a drive to develop Cambodia's exports. The group was also well versed in the kind of approach that the EIF aimed to promote, including the practice of designating priority crops as a basis for export development (interview with Cambodian official, Phnom Penh, September 15, 2014). While senior state and government personnel were supportive of these value-chain interventions, much of the implementation work was facilitated by donors. The WTO's trade-for-development initiatives typically followed this kind of joint approach (Hoekman and Kostecki 2009).

In this context, the UNDP export program was rolled out in three phases. The first phase (CEDEP I) focused on milled rice and high-value silk. In the second phase (CEDEP II, 2014–2018), the program targeted cassava, marine fisheries, and hospitality as priority sectors. A suite of sector-specific activities was implemented to build jobs, strengthen expertise, reduce vulnerability to external shocks, and nurture collaboration with the private sector (UNDP 2017). Phase II was funded for a total of USD 6.4 million (from various sources), of which USD 1.3 million was designated for cassava development. In the early stages of this initiative, CEDEP project staff focused on capacity building among cassava actors

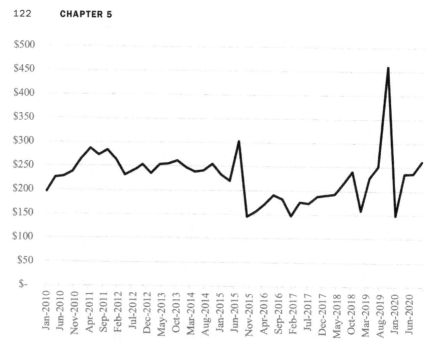

FIGURE 5.1. Vietnamese starch export price (USD/Ton), 2010–2020

Source: Government of Vietnam 2021.
Notes: Vietnam customs data showing FOB (Freight on Board) prices for starch exports. Figures are taken from the first fortnight of the month shown, except for January 2010, January 2011, and October 2015. For these months, data from the second fortnight of the month was used to address a data gap.

(interview with government official, Phnom Penh, September 20, 2014). A midterm review (UNDP 2017), which came after the 2016 cassava price slump, warned of the deterioration of the "cassava sector business environment." It noted that the market had become volatile and the profitability of cassava had slipped, leaving "farmers either locked in a downward spiral of debt and poverty or going into crop diversification" (UNDP 2017, 19). The dramatic price shifts for cassava starch exports from Vietnam (see Figure 5.1) devastated Cambodian farmers, because the lack of a domestic processing sector in Cambodia forced producers to export to established industries in Thailand and Vietnam. The midterm review called for a realignment of project activities to address this issue, criticizing the project team for their slow response to changing conditions and challenges (UNDP 2017, 7). On the face of it, several of these findings aligned with my own field observations about the challenges facing cassava producers during this period (see chaps. 2, 3, and 4). Yet the review did not fundamentally question the capacity of value-chain interventions to manage global market volatility, beyond creating a "better business environment" and helping the government to develop a dedicated cassava policy (UNDP 2017, 49).

By December 2017, the UNDP was planning for the third phase of CEDEP. In a meeting to discuss the findings from my research, the lead adviser outlined the program's future focus on bringing foreign investment to the cassava sector, pollution control for the new processing activities, and improving farmer productivity and disease management to facilitate farmers' closer integration into domestic markets (interview with UNDP official, Phnom Penh, December 13, 2017). Together with key government actors, the UNDP facilitated Chinese investment in cassava processing within the rubric of "south-south" cooperation. The minister for commerce enthusiastically advocated for such investment during his visit to China in January 2018, where he explained, "We have the raw material, but we don't have so many factories. Our doors are always open for Chinese investors who want to build factories and warehouses in Cambodia." He particularly urged Chinese investment in cassava-processing plants, highlighting Cambodia's production rates of fourteen million tons of cassava per year as well as its favorable investment climate (Chan 2018).

From their intervention armory, the UNDP selected contract farming as the best means to assist farmers. They viewed annual cropping contracts as a means to provide farmers with a steady seasonal price, while assuring fledgling processing industries of guaranteed cassava inputs (UNDP Cambodia 2018). Here, UNDP personnel were repeating the logic that has driven contract farming's growth across the developing world: that it provides a "win-win" approach by supporting farmer incomes (Eaton and Shepherd 2001) and providing certainty for start-up firms (Humphrey and Navas-Alemán 2010). In Cambodia, the UNDP partnered with the Chinese company Green Leader, which already had global operations in energy and land-based commodities (Green Leader 2017). The two parties signed a memorandum of understanding in April 2018, which the UNDP country director for Cambodia lauded as a much-needed "private catalyst to a new phase in which more value is generated for the cassava industry, redistributing value-added [sic] downwards to different actors and towards the end of the value chain" (Chin 2018). His statement reflected the trickle-down assumption that value creation at the company level would flow through to actors lower down on the value chain.

The collaboration also had an important geopolitical dimension. Chinese commentators viewed these cassava ventures as part of broader Chinese regional engagements across agriculture, tourism, and manufacturing and as a quid pro quo for Cambodia's acceptance of Chinese "Belt and Road" infrastructure investments (Mao and Nguon 2019). Another geopolitical dimension was the government's desire to cut out Vietnam as a "broker" in the cassava sector and instead deal directly with China, who was a major buyer of Vietnamese products. This point was affirmed by Green Leader's CEO, who pitched their plans to develop twenty processing factories in Cambodia over five years on the basis that it would reduce the vulnerability of farmers to the demand and price fluctuations inflicted by "adjacent countries and buyers" (Green Leader 2018). Thus, the next phase of CEDEP saw a convergence of state, donor, industry, and Chinese agendas around cassava production and domestic processing.

It was too early at the time of writing to predict the results of the UNDP's cassava experiment, but Thailand's mixed experience with three decades of contract farming is instructive (Glover 1992). While the UNDP has presented farming contracts as a secure basis for farmers' production, contract defaults by farmers and companies were commonplace in Thailand (Saenjan 1998). Some years on, Thai industry and farmers had "all kinds of arrangements in place in the name of contracting" (Singh 2005, 5579), echoing the changeable market networks that they intended to replace. Brokers retained an important role in this shifting farming landscape. At the same time, there were concerning instances where contract farming worsened labor conditions, disrupted intrahousehold relationships, and expanded the gap between those who benefited and those who lost out from farming contracts, leading some to conclude that contract farming was no silver bullet (Singh 2005, 5585). It was also clear that being tied to cassava production contracts would likely restrict the scope for Khmer farmers to adopt and abandon crops in response to shifting conditions and opportunities, such as market volatility or disease, given the flexible basis of farming livelihoods outlined in chapter 2. The UNDP project leader was quick to cast aside as "fake news" my findings about debt and the broader social and environmental disruptions in cassava-producing localities (outlined in chap. 4; interview with UNDP official, Phnom Penh, December 13, 2017). His staff subsequently shared a two-page dossier on "myths and facts" about cassava to correct my misconceptions about the risks associated with the frontier cassava market.

ACIAR Value-Chain Project

In contrast with the private sector and contract farming focus of the UNDP project, ACIAR concentrated on farmer-level interventions in its multicountry cassava value-chain project (henceforth, the ACIAR value-chain project). The Cambodian-Lao project component was part of a larger initiative that also covered cassava markets in Vietnam, Indonesia, and Myanmar.[2] ACIAR's model of research-led practice involves partnerships between Australian universities and country-based affiliates of the Consortium of International Agricultural Research Centers (CGIAR), which usually instills an agronomic and agroeconomic focus to their interventions. Accordingly, ACIAR's AUD 1.5 million (USD

1.1 million) Cambodian-Lao intervention aimed to strengthen linkages between value-chain actors at the farm level, in government and research institutions, and from industry. Farm-level interventions targeted cassava cultivation practices and disease management through extension agencies, and the project also contributed to the development of a national cassava policy in Cambodia—all in support of smallholder-based cassava markets. According to project documents, smallholder markets provided the opportunity to shift agro-industries away from large-scale land concessions, with their well-documented and serious impacts on communities and environments (ACIAR 2014). ACIAR cited cassava's growing economic and livelihood importance as the reason for the intervention's focus on this commodity (ACIAR 2014). As such, like the UNDP intervention, the ACIAR project aimed to understand and influence market conditions, but ACIAR's approach had a greater emphasis on smallholder livelihoods than was evident in the later phases of the UNDP project. In this sense, the ACIAR value-chain intervention appeared more sensitive to social conditions. Since 2016, however, the project's efforts were diverted to addressing market volatility and, especially, disease.

The cassava mosaic disease, a virus transmitted by the whitefly (*Bemisia tabaci*), entered Cambodia in 2015 (Wang et al. 2015). ACIAR research suggests that Ratanakiri Province was the first infection site in the Cambodia-Vietnam region, but the same study acknowledges that the first point of infection might have been elsewhere (Minato et al. 2019, 10). Infection occurred early in such border regions as Tbong Khmum (see chap. 3). Other diseases that have affected cassava cultivation include cassava witches broom disease and mealybug (Smith, Newby, and Cramb 2018). By 2018, stemming the spread of these diseases was viewed as an urgent priority to secure cassava production. The ACIAR project team acknowledged the challenges created by the weak "incentive structures" around disease management and the complex social networks that share and sell seed stock in Cambodia (Smith, Newby, and Cramb 2018, 16). Previous chapters have affirmed the importance of farmer-farmer and farmer-trader networks in disseminating cassava stems and seeds for other crops (see also Delaquis et al. 2018; Thavat 2010). These same networks also, perversely, spread diseased stems and made it challenging to remove these from circulation.

ACIAR supported technical efforts to develop disease-resistant crops in Vietnam (project official, pers. comm., March 23, 2019), while Cambodian activities centered on traditional extension approaches, such as crop trials for new varieties (Smith, Newby, and Cramb 2017). These strategies did not prove effective, however, as the Cambodian project officer divulged to the project's social media group in April 2019. Posting images of trucks transporting cassava stems from Vietnam into Cambodia, he observed that the spread of disease was very difficult to prevent since these trucks were transporting thousands of diseased cassava stems (project official, pers. comm., April 26, 2019). Several of his earlier posts documented farmers saving or purchasing planting materials that were already riddled with disease. Thus, collaborations between this project and agricultural agencies struggled to quell the spread of disease as, like the market itself, the rhizomic tendencies of the disease networks became evident.

Traditional political economy critiques of value-chain projects point to the role of market intensification in widening existing social and economic disparities (Neilson 2014). Ethnographic critiques add that social relations are insufficiently recognized in value-chain approaches, which concentrate on financial value and transactions (Freeman 2013; Thavat 2010). These two Cambodian projects further illustrate that value-chain interventions also struggle to work with the complex and changeable relationships that constitute these commodity networks and their place within broader market formation processes. The UNDP and ACIAR interventions both emphasized individual commodities in the face of inherent uncertainties, including volatile markets and hazards, such as disease, that any market intervention must grapple with. At the same time, by concentrating on—in effect, fetishizing—one specific commodity, the projects were less able to holistically engage with agrarian livelihoods and land dynamics, a recognized failing of value-chain interventions more broadly (Staritz 2012).

Creating Green Markets: Vietnam's Biofuel Sector

The Vietnamese government's attempts to establish a domestic biofuel market provides additional insights on the challenges of market governance. The case differs in some key ways from the Cambodian value-chain interventions just discussed. Rather than attempt to modify an existing commodity network, as the UNDP and ACIAR interventions did, here the state attempted to develop a brand-new domestic market for a 5 percent mixed ethanol fuel known as E5. The E5 fuel was ostensibly part of the government's policy of reducing transport sector carbon emissions (Nguyen et al. 2009). As is often the case with green economy programs, however, this environmental agenda coalesced with several other interests. The government expected its E5 policy to contribute to energy security and stronger markets for agricultural products (Nguyen et al. 2009). International audiences also figured in this policy, as Vietnam was the first to respond to the ASEAN commitment in its January 2007 Cebu Declaration that member countries would move toward biofuels and other renewable energy sources.[3] Less than a year later, in November 2007, the Vietnamese government had already approved its *Strategy for Biofuel Development to 2015 and Vision 2025* (Decision No. 177/2007/QD-TTg on November 20, 2007).

Vietnam has a record of rapidly adopting new policies in the environmental sector, such as payments for ecosystem services (PES) (To, Mahanty, and Dressler 2016) and community forestry (Sunderlin 2006), to capitalize on donor support and enhance its international reputation. While influenced by donor imperatives, the E5 initiative was state funded and proposed legal institutions and other measures to create a favorable environment for a new domestic biofuel industry. The aim was to replace a portion of conventional transport fuel with ethanol through the national adoption of E5 and eventually E10 (10 percent ethanol fuel). Government support would center on scientific research and technology, demonstration programs, new biofuel manufacturing plants, and international cooperation. The Ministry of Industry and Trade (MOIT) was placed at the helm of policy implementation, although several other agencies were involved—notably the Ministry of Agriculture and Rural Development (MARD)—because ethanol production relied on agricultural inputs. Early studies flagged cassava as one of several potential inputs; others included sugarcane, maize, and Jatropha. After analyzing the costs and benefits of each, the government prioritized cassava (Nguyen et al. 2009). It also committed significant funding (VND 259.2 billion or USD 11 million during 2007–2015) and planned to mobilize additional private investment to support the policy (Nguyen et al. 2009, 51).

From the earliest days of Vietnam's biofuel plan, frontier cassava became an essential input. A 2009 MARD study documented new areas for cassava cultivation across Vietnam—primarily in the uplands—to support ethanol production. It also noted that cross-border inputs were likely to play an important role in building a viable biofuel production industry because cassava expansion was reaching its limits in Vietnam (Nguyen et al. 2009). The study suggested Vietnamese cross-border investment as one potential model for securing biofuel inputs, in preference to operating through a network of intermediaries to access supply from Khmer smallholders (Nguyen et al. 2009, 47). The emphasis in these early analyses was on getting ethanol production up and running in Vietnam rather than on the overall question of how fuel substitution in vehicles would be implemented. As Binh explained at the beginning of this chapter, several factories were developed and located as close as possible to input sources. Some of these were joint ventures, but most were state financed, as was the case with the Orient Biofuels factory in Bình Phước Province, which I studied during my field research.

By 2015, cracks were appearing in the government's biofuel strategy. Initially, the plan was to mandate the use of E5 by December 1, 2015, and E10 by December 1, 2017 (Hieu 2015), but in an interview, the input manager for the Orient Biofuels factory disclosed that two key constraints had emerged. The first was the question of how to set an ethanol price that encouraged end users to switch to this unfamiliar product. The second constraint was the cost of technological change for petrol distributors:

> The money was invested, and factories were built, but we have not yet been able to produce bioethanol. Since December 2014 the government has been applying its road map to move to E5 fuel and forcing the provinces and suppliers to provide E5 so that the market can go ahead. For example, each station will have to have one pump that supplies E5. But there are many difficulties with this, like the costs to the station owner of changing their pumps. . . . Another challenge is price. The government is trying to keep the cost of bioethanol low at the pump, but there is not enough of a price difference to send a signal—a price difference of 1 percent from standard fuel is not enough of a difference for buyers. (interview with factory manager, June 6, 2015)

The manager was responsible for securing dried cassava for the Orient Biofuels factory and was therefore well informed about input sources. The factory's primary input source was Cambodian cassava chips from such provinces as Mondulkiri and beyond, because Vietnamese cassava farmers near the factory sold fresh cassava tubers to starch factories rather than preparing dried chips. To access Cambodian cassava, the factory tapped into networks of commune-level traders who would aggregate and bring dried cassava to a border warehouse. As the Orient Biofuels factory was not yet in production mode, however, they were unable to use the growing stock of chips that was piling up at their border warehouse. So they exported these chips through established private export businesses and then hired out the empty warehouses to cross-border traders for their own use. Our discussion revealed that while the government was building factories and implementation of the plan appeared to be underway, on the ground things were stalling. The E5 market, fed with ethanol produced from cassava and other inputs, needed more than state fiat to mobilize it.

The difficulties in constructing this new market were even starker three years later. In January 2018, after the government's own deadlines for national E5 implementation had lapsed, I visited the Orient Biofuels factory in Bình Phước (see fig. 5.2; interview with factory manager, January 12, 2018). Built in 2009, nine years later the factory resembled a ghost town. The boardroom displayed two framed awards from 2012. The first was awarded by PetroVietnam and the second by the Red Cross, both for successful construction of the factory. The room also housed several sporting trophies that the underutilized staff at the factory had won in the intervening years. The two staff whom I interviewed explained that the factory had only run five times in its history. These operations

FIGURE 5.2.   Orient Biofuels factory, Binh Phuoc; built in 2009, the factory was one of six purpose-built government-run facilities and had operated only five times

Source: Photograph by author.

were to check on the machinery, each time producing around ten thousand liters of ethanol. "After that," one of them added, "there were complications with the E5 policy, so the factory stopped operation." He explained some of the challenges they would face should the factory start producing ethanol as intended:

> Production techniques may not be efficient after so long under the blanket. The factory will need upgrading. . . . Usually to reach good productivity, you need to learn during operations. If we start operations now, it will take a certain amount of time before we know which parts need an upgrade and how. We can't decide it now. For that trial period, we will need a government subsidy as we will not be competitive in relation to costs. The next challenge is the market trend., . . . The [government] will is there but implementation is very hard. . . . Another challenge is that Vietnam has imposed an import tax on imported ethanol. But if the E5 policy is actually implemented, the government cannot impose this tax anymore because it violates the international free trade agreement. . . . Currently there is a misunderstanding that E5

can cause fires and explosions in vehicles. One or two years ago, there was big media coverage when a motorbike suddenly caught fire. But I think it was caused by the cheating practices of traders who sometimes mix ethanol and methanol to increase their profits. Methanol can cause those problems. (interview with factory manager, January 12, 2018)

This employee flagged additional technical challenges to those raised by the input manager three years prior. The staff were now conscious of limitations to state subsidies and tariffs, and the issue of trust in the E5 fuel by end users had risen to prominence after sensational media coverage about the exploding vehicles. This deficit in public trust for mixed fuels echoes findings in other Vietnamese research (Chaiyapa et al. 2018).

Aside from their distrust of E5 itself, the Vietnamese populace has also been losing faith in state institutions overall due to the perceived corruption of senior state officials (To and Mahanty 2019). These public suspicions were vindicated on April 25, 2017, when the government's Central Inspection Commission recommended disciplinary actions against Dinh La Thang, a high-level official who was closely involved with implementation of the E5 policy. Between 2009 and 2011, Thang was secretary of the Party Committee at the Vietnam National Oil and Gas Group (PetroVietnam) and chairman of the corporation's board, before being promoted to minister for transport (2011–2016). He was subsequently elected to Vietnam's elite nineteen-member politburo, appointed secretary of the Ho Chi Minh City Party Committee, and became a member of the National Assembly. In other words, Thang was a powerful and influential player, making the sanctions that followed unprecedented and of enormous public interest and symbolic importance. Ethanol factories that never officially started operation, including the Orient Biofuels factory in Bình Phước, were among the many projects that Thang and other PetroVietnam officials were accused of mismanaging, costing the country millions of US dollars in revenue. These projects were based on loans with a total investment value of VND 5.4 trillion (USD 237.4 million). Thang was further accused of contracting irregularities that enabled him and other board members to gain kickbacks by awarding contracts to companies and individuals of their own choosing (D. Ha 2017). In January 2018, Thang was sentenced to thirteen years in prison for "deliberate violation of state regulations on economic management that caused serious consequences" (Nguyen and Pearson 2018). His part in another high-level case of financial mismanagement saw this sentence extended by a further eighteen years (Bao 2018; Viet Nam News 2018c). Thang's corruption case intensified public skepticism about the E5 policy, leaving consumers less likely than ever to unquestioningly follow state edicts to pump this new and untrusted fuel into their vehicles.

Vietnam's biofuel market ultimately "failed to launch," affecting government investments as well as frontier farmers. In 2018, the government was pressing on with its E5 rollout, optimistic that Vietnamese drivers would adopt this new fuel. Many consumers, however, continued to question the product's quality and pricing (*Viet Nam News* 2018a, 2018b). By January 2019, after clear evidence that consumer uptake was well below expectations, the government proposed a review of its E5 policy (*Viet Nam News* 2019). This was perhaps a face-saving acknowledgment by the state of its inability to shift the behavior of millions of Vietnamese consumers, on which a viable E5 market depends. The intermittent and controversial character of the policy has not only kept major state investments like the Orient Biofuels factory in mothballs but also wreaked havoc on the cassava chip market (*Viet Nam News* 2016). Although biofuel manufacturers are not the only buyers for cassava chips—domestic and regional animal husbandry being the other major buyers—the variations in chip price across four years imposed visible hardships at the farm level in Cambodia (see chaps. 3 and 4). The Chinese government had also made commitments for a mixed ethanol fuel in the transport sector—in their case as a remedy for urban pollution—but planned on using diverse input sources, such as maize and straw waste, as well as cassava (Hao et al. 2018; *Shanghai Daily* 2017). These factors also made the Chinese market for cassava chips inconstant, since sources could be readily substituted.

With its E5 policy, the Vietnamese government was responding to several agendas—environmental, political, and economic. In part, government officials followed international trends, as Binh had explained in our interview. Once adopted as a goal, the government, with technical assistance from the ADB, ran studies to assess how best to facilitate this new policy (Chaiyapa et al. 2019) but paid little attention to how these fuels would be received in the marketplace. The ultimate lack of E5 uptake, together with the widespread loss of faith in such state institutions as PetroVietnam, served to undermine these market formation efforts.

Governing Rhizomic Markets

The case studies covered in this chapter represent two contemporary modes of market intervention in frontier cassava networks in Cambodia and Vietnam. The two Cambodian value-chain interventions aimed to consolidate cassava production and processing as a basis to secure trade revenues and returns to producers. The UNDP's CEDEP model of intervention echoes the French colonial state's efforts to expand commodity production and trade for specific commodities via private investment, while ACIAR's smalholder focus was a departure from the era of French Indochinese rubber. In the second example of Vietnam's biofuel policy, state efforts centered on developing an entirely new market ostensibly driven by an environmental agenda but in which political, economic, and social considerations were ultimately more influential. All three cases reveal important insights on state engagements in market formation.

Two decades of donor support for value-chain interventions have produced a significant literature on experiences and challenges with this approach. Evaluations from within the value-chain paradigm show that historical transitions and earlier interventions can significantly shape the effectiveness of these programs. Furthermore, they flag that broader development goals—beyond specific commodities and sectors—need to be considered. Finally, the strong reliance on lead firms as a basis for value-chain development has been questioned (Neilson 2014, 48). The UNDP approach appeared blind to such lessons, with its premise that the development of a domestic processing industry together with contract farming would secure both trade and rural development outcomes. In other words, it emphasized a lead-firm approach to value-chain development, without recognizing the scope for conflicts of interest along the value chain (Staritz 2012).

The UNDP's push toward contract farming was particularly concerning. In Thailand, where contract farming has been underway for three decades, many of the problems that cropping contracts were intended to solve have been left unresolved. Farmers and companies often reneged on agreed production targets and prices (Singh 2005). Over time, many farmers abandoned farming contracts to regain flexibility and independence, including the opportunity to negotiate better prices. At the same time, some farmers stayed with farming contracts, because they thought these provided better access to markets, updated knowledge, and farming inputs (Schipman and Quaim 2011; Sriboonchitta and Wiboonpoongse 2008). Concerningly, given the land pressures discussed in previous chapters, the mixed outcomes of contract farming were causing some firms in Thailand to venture into direct production in periurban areas in order to guarantee supply (Schipman and Quaim 2011). If Khmer farmers were to renege on their contracts, processing companies might similarly acquire land for cassava production as a logical next step. One such cassava concession already existed in Tbong Khmum. These potential risks made contract farming a crucial space to watch in the wake of the UNDP intervention.

Both value-chain interventions discussed here worked with a theory of change that viewed smalholder market incorporation as a pathway to development. UNDP's pathway was through private-sector investment and industry development, while ACIAR's centered on technical development and support to producers. Market incorporation was not brought about by these interventions, however. In my study sites, commodification of land and labor were well in train, as was the growth of social inequality (see also Akhram-Lodhi 2005; Harvey 2007; and Kem 2017 on Cambodia). Yet both interventions, with their single-commodity emphasis, had the effect of entrenching and fetishizing one crop—cassava—with its associated risks of market volatility and disease. By promoting such strategies as contract farming that could expose farmers with fewer assets and safety nets to greater precarity and debt, value-chain interventions also intensified potential risks.

The UNDP and ACIAR interventions' narrow commodity focus may have added to existing risks while leaving little scope to address such risks. The tendency for value-chain interventions to have a limited sectoral approach has been observed elsewhere (Gereffi, Humphrey, and Sturgeon 2005; Neilson and Pritchard 2009). Here, this depoliticized approach overlooked highly influential political and economic factors that were an inherent and important facet of commodity networks, such as inequities in land and financial access or the unfair operations of credit agencies, as discussed in the preceding chapters. The neglect of these indirect but significant influences not only made the interventions less likely to achieve their espoused goals but also added to the core challenges already faced by smallholders.

Turning to Vietnam's biofuel experiment, biofuels have a growing record of relying on inputs that replace food crops or expand cultivation in agricultural frontiers (Hought et al. 2012; Overmars et al. 2011). In China's Yunnan Province, failed Jatropha projects for the biodiesel industry inflicted environmental and social costs on ethnic minority farmers while corporate and state actors benefited from state subsidies (Rousseau 2018). In other instances, such projects have extended territorial control by international companies (Harnesk 2019). Vietnam's biofuel case followed similar patterns. Cassava chips became a major input for ethanol production, drawn from frontier cassava networks in Vietnam and Cambodia. Yet the capacity of green markets to mask the inner workings of these "green" commodities, including resource exclusions, environmental change, and labor exploitation, call for caution with such interventions (Kosoy and Corbera 2010; Milne and Mahanty 2019; Neimark et al. 2020). These impacts could make any net environmental benefits of so-called green economy interventions marginal or even negative. Furthermore, the political and economic constraints faced by the Vietnamese biofuel policy underscored clear viability questions. The government's limited grasp of market formation processes ultimately rendered the biofuel intervention unviable. These failures in turn magnified the risks for frontier cassava chip producers in both Cambodia and Vietnam. Like other green economy initiatives, such as REDD+, the Vietnamese government promoted the E5 policy as a win-win outcome for the transport sector and farmers, but in practice it drew on unsustainable modes of input production in frontier regions of Cambodia and Vietnam.[4]

E5 differed from rubber in French Indochina, whose establishment was a matter of "planting" a market rhizome. This green economy experiment required the state to govern inputs, set up processing industries, and promote consumption of a new commodity. Effectively, the state needed to govern the entire commodity network. Yet the nuanced and interconnected set of relationships and change processes embedded in such networks were beyond the state's grasp and made more complex by such issues as public distrust and the emerging decline in state legitimacy (To and Mahanty 2019). The government's established approach of directing state investment and engaging appropriate (but rapidly outmoded) technologies proved ineffective. The case therefore affirms the view that the stakes are shifting for former developmental states (Yeung 2014). State agents can be particularly challenged by new approaches to economic development, such as the green economy, that differ from their usual work of regulating citizens and from their past infrastructure, labor, and industrial investments. Regardless of the causes of the E5 policy failure, its implications have nonetheless been profoundly felt in the frontier locations where cassava chips are produced.

Like colonial rubber, this chapter has also shown that efforts to direct or encourage market formation are inherently contingent, whether the goal is new market development or using markets to achieve positive environmental outcomes. The nuanced and rhizomic character of market networks lends an element of "ungovernability" to the market that states and donors are yet to grasp and acknowledge. Political scientists coined the concept of ungovernability in the 1970s and 1980s to highlight the paralyzing effect of competing pressures on states and fragmented forms of authority (Yates 1977). The ungovernability of markets observed here is different from such paralysis. Instead, markets continue to unfurl and evolve but do so in unpredictable and therefore unmanageable ways. They are more akin to Heron's (2011) notion that subjects are ultimately ungovernable because they are changeable and unruly in their motivations and actions. Applying this notion to markets, ungovernability arises from the organic, interconnecting, and volatile networks that bind complex actors, materials, and locations.

These findings raise important questions for interventions that seek to shape markets for specific developmental and political-economic ends, including green markets. Rather than controlling markets, states and donors were caught out by unseen and unanticipated influences. I do not, however, make an argument here for full market liberalization and the abandonment of state responsibility vis-à-vis markets. Instead, I suggest that we acknowledge the limited capacity of state and donor interventions to control the market and its effects. By challenging the hubris often tied to these interventions, we will be better placed to attend to their risks.

CONCLUSION

Reexamining Frontier Markets

What do these case studies from the Cambodia-Vietnam borderlands bring to our understanding of frontiers and market formation? The cases explored market formation in a specific kind of frontier: a borderland. In mainland Southeast Asia and beyond, borderlands are important spaces of market growth (Taylor 2016) since they are often rich in resources (Hall 2011). After French territorial interventions produced the Cambodia-Vietnam borderlands, this space was continually reinvented as new commodities were transplanted and exploited. Migration was central to this process. Ultimately, however, the cases have raised the question of whether this reworking of frontiers can continue in perpetuity or will ultimately falter through material and social limits.

By viewing actor networks and commodity chains as parts of a broader market rhizome, the case studies illuminate the mechanisms that produce change in frontier markets. This lens also made visible the tendency for specific commodity networks to rupture, which could produce innovation but also inflict pressures on local producers. Further, it reveals the formative role of individual and collective desires and practices within frontier landscapes and markets. A recurring theme in these network dynamics was the market's unruly and ungovernable character. Within the context of a borderland frontier, state authority and markets were coproduced. Yet even as states used market development to gain control of territories and subjects or for other forms of state building, they seemed unable to effectively govern the slippery market trajectories that followed.

Overall, these cases complicate the view of frontier landscapes as passive resource assemblages awaiting extraction and frontier populations as compliant handmaids for global capitalism. Instead, frontier peoples, landscapes, and their relationships coproduced a continually expanding market, with deep, tangled, and consequential roots.

Historical and Structural Influences on the Market Rhizome

Through the case of French rubber, we saw how historical events and institutional structures framed this frontier market, which both entrenched power differentials and provoked local expressions of agency and resistance. It is only by attending to both the structural and the relational influences in the market that we can grasp its continuous state of formation, through intersecting institutions, networks, and practices.

Although the colonial-era rubber market was expansive and fluid, it was not unstructured. The French embedded a capitalist mode of production in this frontier to feed the European and North American industries (Wolf 1982, 45). This colonial influence did not end with independence from the French, because colonization is a process, not a discrete event (Wolfe 2006). When Cambodia and Vietnam gained independence, many of the institutional structures created during the colonial era persisted. Sometimes they took on new forms, but these underlying structures nevertheless sustained market formation and resource extraction. Despite the dramatic intervention of revolutionary regimes, which completely overthrew existing property institutions in both countries, contemporary state formation reinvigorated colonial ideals, and institutional ghosts resurfaced through new waves of market formation. Cambodia's postconflict land reforms (see the introduction) were an exemplary case of this. In this postconflict period, market beneficiaries shifted from European capitalists to actors closer to home: domestic military and state elites who accumulated land and resource-based wealth (Le Billon 1999). More recently, Vietnamese and Chinese capitalists have also become beneficiaries.

These structural inequities also filtered down to the local level. In chapter 2, the Tbong Khmum case studies, which ranged from intergenerational landless laborers to wealthy entrepreneurial farmers, revealed the critical importance of land access. Those who missed out on early post-conflict land distribution, usually because they lacked political connections, continued to lack opportunities for market engagement. Providing labor for wealthier farmers or migration became the only option for landless villagers. Those with more marginal landholdings or livelihood options were also vulnerable to market fluctuations. Land tenure in turn influenced access to credit, further marginalizing those without land. At the same time, those who held land were entering unsustainable levels of debt that also made them vulnerable. These patterns resonate in broader critical agrarian studies research (see, for instance, Akram-Lodhi 2005 on Vietnam; Green 2019 and Green and Estes 2019 on Cambodia). The political and economic institutions that were integral to market formation perpetuated these inequalities and risks.

Importantly though, while prevailing political-economic institutions framed the market rhizome, my research showed that their effects were not deterministic. Even during French colonization, policies and laws to support market development faced various "frictions," such as frictions of appropriation, with local resistance to state land and resource accumulation, and frictions of distance and terrain in remote frontier areas (Scott 2009). These frictions were generative. At times they slowed market formation or shaped its specific form within localities (chap. 1; see also Tsing 2005). In other words, nuanced interactions with people and landscapes moderated these political and economic influences. This was seen in the interactions that constituted two distinct cassava networks in chapters 3 and 4 and in Bunong resistance to *Hevea* plantations in colonial Indochina (chap. 1) and contemporary Phum Prampii (chap. 4). These cases highlight the role of localized physical and social frictions in shaping the frontier market.

Relating these observations back to the market rhizome, these moderated, shifting structural impacts echo Deleuze and Guattari's (1987) principle of decalcomania. This was the idea that, rather than being simple reproductions of existing patterns, rhizomes took form through the interactions between such patterns and the environment that they encountered. The role of localized social contexts in shaping institutions is also integral to Giddens's (1984) structuration theory (see the introduction) and anthropological research on the social embeddedness of markets (see, for instance, Appadurai 1988; R. Foster 2002; Gibson-Graham 2006; and Gregory 1982). My cases from this borderland frontier additionally highlight the role of material actants in these formative processes, and confirms the highly contingent ways in which political and economic institutions are translated to local contexts.

Agency in Commodity Networks

In the introduction I explained the importance of considering individual and group agency within networks. Like other forms of network analysis, Deleuze and Guattari's rhizome does not adequately consider this influential aspect of commodity networks. My case studies show that personal and group actions were influential in several aspects of market formation (see also Hudson 2016). Two key examples I discussed in some detail were migration and farmers' adoption of new crops.

Chapters 2 to 4 demonstrated that farmers' migration in search of land was a primary mechanism for smallholder market expansion. Migration was more than an individual choice; it was a multidimensional decision that reflected individual, family, and village interests and desires. The stories of Kunthea and Phirun in chapter 2 showed that individuals faced considerable hardship when they chose to move to areas of new migration, but their strong desire for land security often guided their decision. These same cases, and subsequent examples, such as Chea and Chanlina's story in chapter 4, added that social networks were essential for information about land opportunities and support when migrants arrived in their new districts. These examples revealed that migration was simultaneously an individual and collective action, propelled by desires for land. In addition to taking commodity crops into new areas, migration extended the frontier market through land commodification, as migrants created the demand for newly cleared land. Individual and shared aspirations for land were so strong that frontier migrants often withstood significant difficulties in order to stay on their land rather than leave to seek work elsewhere. These responses echo High's (2014) view that personal and collective desire is a related and powerful source of action, often with a strong emotional quality (Skoggard and Waterson 2015).

Personal agency was also central in the formation of new commodity networks. Specific traders catalyzed the uptake of new crops, such as cassava (chaps. 2 and 3), while individual farmers would often test and disseminate these new cultivars. Assets and opportunities, such as access to land, labor, and capital, could support or constrain agency. Farmers with more land and access to credit were able to experiment with new commodities and livelihood opportunities, such as Samnang's cashew-picking contracts in Ratanakiri or Rachany's cross-border leases to Vietnamese farmers, discussed in chapter 2. Similarly, Bunong villagers, such as Vanna (chap. 4), who already had some individual assets, were more inclined to access credit to engage in markets. These examples affirmed that personal and collective agency were integral to market formation and were strongly mediated by peoples' differentiated opportunities.

Rupturing the Market

As Deleuze and Guattari (1987) foreshadowed in their discussion of the rhizome, commodity networks across my study sites were highly prone to instability and rupture. Such ruptures played a generative role, whether by driving new market trajectories or by destroying places and livelihoods. Both networked and critical analytics acknowledge such disruptive influences. I discussed the actor-network theory concept of "dissonance" in the introduction, as a force that can destabilize and transform networks (Callon 2010, 167). Critical perspectives also view rupture as an inherent facet of capitalism. Marx wrote of capitalism's inherent tendency toward "metabolic rift" between society and nature (J. Foster 1999). Marx and later Schumpeter also discussed the concept of "creative destruction." For Schumpeter (1994 [1942]), this implied that periods of crisis could drive innovation by pushing firms to adopt new modes of production. Marx used this same term to describe capitalism's universalizing tendency, whereby prior economic relations were destroyed. He also saw this as a source of change, where the dysfunctions of capitalism would ultimately drive revolution (Elliot 1980). In contrast, Deleuze and Guattari's concept of rupture is a more open framing, akin to Lund's (2016) "open moment." The concept of rupture thus speaks to the inherent instability within specific commodity networks that can produce new trajectories but also accumulate across several networks to deepen inequality and environmental transformation.

The Mondulkiri case studies in chapters 3 and 4 documented several types of disruption, whether in the form of productive pressures on farmers and landscapes or enticements to innovate. One example was the price volatility for cassava and rubber that arose from global cycles of production and overproduction. Another example was the emergence of cassava pathogens in these borderlands, a network disruption that nudged many farmers toward adopting different crops. New cultivars and techniques introduced by traders to Tbong Khmum and Mondulkiri also disrupted the market by seeding new commodities and practices. Responses to such developments were equally diverse. The middle-income and wealthier households were more able to abandon certain crops and adopt new ones, while the poorest families found it difficult to plant new capital-intensive crops and often faced escalating livelihood stresses. In both contexts, disruptions were generative, because they prompted changes to local practices and networks that affected market dynamics.

Land shortages and livelihood stress were evidence of deepening rupture, which people often coped with through migration. In Cambodia, migration has long been an important release valve for localized land shortages (Diepart and Ngin 2020). This is also the case in Vietnam, where state-sponsored schemes have supported migration from land-poor lowland regions to upland border regions as part of projects of state formation and market development (de Koninck 2000; Hardy 2000). As shown in both Tbong Khmum and Mondulkiri, however, over time land became scarcer in these destination districts. As this occurred, the opportunities for newcomers contracted, especially for those with few assets. Chapter 4 confirmed that as these later migrants faced significant livelihood stress in their new destinations, they would leave for new locations to find land or work. Migration to new frontiers thus marked spaces of agrarian stress and could temporarily ease land pressures in source locations. Yet over time, as ruptures accumulated in receiving locations, people started to leave for places beyond the frontier, especially international and urban destinations.

The Mondulkiri case studies in chapter 4 added that synergistic interactions could intensify frontier rupture. For example, the combination of depleted timber reserves and volatile rubber and cassava prices significantly squeezed local livelihoods and resources in Phum Prambei. Some villagers also found ways to survive on the "edges" of rupture (Tsing 2015), often through mobility. For example, seasonal workers circulated through different provinces and districts to follow available work. These pressures also intensified the precarity of the poorest families, adding to their existing disadvantages in terms of access to land, household composition, and credit arrangements (Rigg, Salamanca, and Thompson 2016). As disruptions accumulated over space and time to produce a more insidious level of social and landscape rupture, it was difficult to see how market formation and "frontier reinvention" could ultimately continue (Rasmussen and Lund 2018).

The case studies demonstrate that socioenvironmental stressors are integral to market formation. But these pressures can accumulate and synergize across market networks, expanding from commodity-level disruptions to frontier rupture. Here, crushing debt, social alienation among Indigenous groups and precarious laborers, and ongoing forest loss and soil degradation characterized rupture.

Ungovernable Markets

This book has explored the relationship between market formation and state formation, and the implications for market governance. In chapter 1, Indochinese rubber served the French colonial state's interest in expanding its revenue base, enhancing territorial control at the margins, and subjugating frontier communities. Yet the French administration struggled to govern the rubber industry, especially as large European investors became involved. The mutual dependencies of states and markets were also the focus of chapter 5, where value-chain interventions and new biofuel enterprises were similarly important to state agendas but proved challenging to govern.

In both the historical and contemporary context, states actively promoted market formation through a wide and dynamic repertoire of instruments. At times, these served to initiate new forms of commodity production, such as rubber, or to enlist private investors. At other times, such as in postconflict Cambodia, state actors visibly sought to accumulate private benefits. In all cases, market formation was about enhancing or entrenching state authority over its territory and peoples. State administrations were therefore supportive of the market but disinterested in mitigating community risks as they could see no direct benefit in such safeguarding work, except where they challenged state authority or market control.

As the French colonial administration discovered, states could not completely ignore these market risks and inequities. The market's inherent tendency to "misfire" and rupture can easily turn it into a testing ground for state legitimacy (To and Mahanty 2019). Two clear examples of this were labor unrest on French Indochinese plantations, which contributed to the colonial administration's downfall (chap. 1), and the failure of Vietnam's biofuel industry (chap. 5). In the example of French Indochina, the state belatedly attempted to address the escalating social problems of labor unrest on plantations—a rearguard action that was in many respects more concerned with risks to French rule than plantation workers. Likewise, in Cochinchina and the Cambodian protectorate, forest reserves were created to serve territorial control and to prevent Chinese and Vietnamese interests from exploiting forest resources. Similarly, the Vietnamese government's environmental agenda ostensibly drove the E5 policy, but donor relations and state-making economic imperatives were also influential. Ultimately, the rhizomic market evaded state attempts at regulating and addressing social and environmental risks, and the rent-seeking behavior of state actors further undermined state authority.

These elements of ungovernability challenge the view of markets as a neutral and effective mechanism to meet rural development and environmental objectives, especially in frontier settings. The environmental and social risks of cassava production for biofuel production, for instance, far outweighed any environmental benefits of mixed E5 fuel. This challenge is now recognized in other studies of environmentally focused market initiatives in mainland Southeast Asian frontiers, where advocates have typically failed to address the socially and materially embedded character of these markets (see, for instance, Giessen et al. 2016 on agricultural certification; Rousseau 2018 on biodiesel; and Milne et al. 2019 on forest carbon markets). Value-chain interventions that target individual commodities, of the kind discussed in chapter 5, face similar constraints.

Since colonization, state actors have embraced and promoted markets to meet their political, economic, and developmental goals. Yet the historical record shows that states are more adept at initiating market formation than managing the market's unruly and uncertain outcomes. This is both a matter of state *ca-*

pacity and *will.* Interventions in agrarian markets still reflect simplified and linear models of how markets work, as contemporary value-chain interventions illustrate. Furthermore, state actors frequently gain significant benefits from market formation so are often uninclined to address the market's social and environmental risks. This perfect storm of catalytic power, vested interests, and incapacity to govern accentuates the risks that frontier markets pose for vulnerable and minority populations and frontier landscapes.

In the Cambodia-Vietnam borderlands, the frontier market did not simply transplant a capitalist mode of production but emerged from diverse place-based negotiations and conditions to produce a locally contextualized form of "actually existing capitalism." The frontier market here remains unsettled—in a continual state of formation—but also approaches a critical point of rupture. By seeing the market from the edge, broader questions emerge about how states and other actors should engage with markets going forward. Market advocates today are keen to embrace market-based approaches to solve many social and environmental challenges. The findings presented in this book show, however, that once instigated, markets become challenging to govern, while potentially producing perverse and socially detrimental outcomes. Particular care is indicated in adopting linear and single-commodity market interventions. Recent work on forest carbon schemes is confirming this point (Milne and Mahanty 2019).

Now that the market rhizome has worked its way into the remotest landscapes and communities, however, it is not easily uprooted. In these settings, we may instead need to recognize and work with local and collective forms of agency that can directly speak to the desires and needs that motivate people, such as land security and the possibility of hybrid livelihoods. We also need to recognize the role of historical and structural influences that continue to shape the lived experiences of frontier communities and constrain their opportunities. In the Cambodia-Vietnam frontier these influences stem from colonization, a history of conflict, growing mobility, inequality, and uneven access to any benefits that frontier markets may provide. Ultimately, we can only address these challenges with a more holistic and nuanced understanding of markets than we currently have by grasping the networked and structural elements that animate them.

Notes

INTRODUCTION

1. This term refers to ethnically Khmer people with a history in the lower Mekong region that predates French colonization. Taylor (2014, 2) writes that in Cambodian nationalist mythology, this region (known as Kampuchea Krom) is viewed as an integral part of the Khmer kingdom that was colonized and wrongfully ceded to Vietnam by France. In contrast, the Vietnamese state counts its Khmer population as one of the nation's many ethnic minorities (3).

2. In this book, a commodity refers to "an external object, a thing which through its qualities satisfies human needs of whatever kind" (Marx [1894] 1992, 125).

3. The concept of Indigenous people (*chun cheat daeum*) is relatively recent in Cambodia and has been tied to international social movements, donor safeguards, and domestic land discourses (Baird 2011; Padwe 2013). In Vietnam, the official term for ethnically and linguistically distinct upland communities is *ethnic minorities*. The colonial French term for upland peoples was *montagnards*, which I also sometimes also use while discussing Indigenous-colonial relations. In discussing specific Indigenous communities, I recognize that colonial and postcolonial states have played a central role in defining ethnic boundaries and territories within an otherwise fluid context (Gunn 2014, 154; Taylor 2012).

4. In the Vietnamese context, the ethnohistorian Gerard Hickey (1982, 16) further divides this group into central, southern, and eastern populations, each with distinctive subgroups (see also Condominas [1977], whose work centered on a group he called the Mnong Gar). At the time of my research, however, Bunong communities in Mondulkiri simply referred to themselves as Bunong or Phnong rather than identifying with a particular subgroup.

5. Resin was tapped from the species *Dipterocarpus alatus* and used to waterproof boats, as well as in paint and varnish manufacture (Evans et al. 2003).

6. In this book, the term *Khmer* refers to the dominant Khmer-speaking population of Cambodia.

7. *1937: Commission d'enquête dans les territoires d'Outre-mer. Rapport de M. d'-Hugues adr ajt des S.C. sur les minorités ethniques Moïs*, file no. 53647, ANOM, Aix-en-Provence, France.

8. *1914: Rapport sur la situation politique du Cambodge*, file no. 2008, ANOM, Aix-en-Provence, France; *1912: Esclava dans les region Mois*, file no. 19343, ANOM, Aix-en-Provence, France.

9. *1881–1883: Soumission de la peuple des Mois à la France: établissement sur leur territoire*, file no. A50(6), ANOM, Aix-en-Provence, France.

10. The northern communist-run Democratic Republic of Vietnam was established earlier and recognized by the French in 1946 (Owen 2005).

11. Đường Hồ Chí Minh in Vietnamese.

12. The Southeast Asian scholar George Coedès (1975, 15) coined the term "Indianization" to describe the founding of Buddhist and Hindu kingdoms, which "practiced the arts, customs, and religions of India." This occurred along historical trade routes throughout Southeast Asia from the second to the fourteenth century. Coedès suggested that

although local elites adopted Indian cultural practices, the rest of the populace was often largely unchanged in their local customs (25).

13. In the context of their rhizome analytic, Deleuze and Guattari (1987, 12) define *cartography* as "a map, not a tracing," indicating that the rhizome is a representation and not a copy of an existing form; while *decalcomania* refers literally to an artistic technique where images are transferred from specialized paper to other surfaces, such as glass and porcelain. In both cases, rhizomes are not a simple reproduction but exist as representations and are ultimately shaped by interactions with their terrain.

1. RUBBER IN FRENCH INDOCHINA

1. In this chapter, I use *Hevea brasiliensis* or its shortened form (*Hevea*) to refer to the cultivar and trees, while *rubber* refers to the raw and processed latex and gum sourced from *Hevea*. In subsequent chapters, I revert to using the term *rubber* when discussing interviews and case studies since contemporary farmers use the one term *rubber* for all of these (*caousu*, in Khmer; *cao su*, in Vietnamese).

2. The colonial term "coolie" is used in this manuscript for continuity with the historical texts cited. The preferred contemporary term is indentured laborer.

3. Arrêté 7534, dated January 12, 1925: "Promoting small holder plantation by sparing," file no. M 71-1425, ANOM, Aix-en-Provence, France.

4. "Notice from the director of agricultural and commercial services on the subject of a public auction of 1350ha40 near Honquan requested by Mr Hallet," October 12, 1918, file no. 43441, National Archives No. 2, Ho Chi Minh City.

5. "Dossier No.6864 relatif à lq concession par marché de gré à gré au profit de M:M: MAHE & CREMAZY, anciens combattants, de 2 terrains domaniaux," November 8, 1927, file no. M71-1437, National Archives No. 2, Ho Chi Minh City.

6. Service du Cadastre, "Plan d'un immeuble, Domanial," August 8, 1919, in Goucoch, file no. 43441, National Archives No. 2, Ho Chi Minh City.

7. Letter from Société des Plantations des Terres Rouges to the Governor, December 3, 1928, in Goucoch, file no. 43441, National Archives No. 2, Ho Chi Minh City.

8. "DEMANDE DE MISE EN VENTE aux enchères publiques d'un Terrain Dominial," September 30, 1919, file no. M71/7990-8003, ANOM, Aix-en-Provence, France.

9. Similar patterns of frontier development and state formation have been observed more recently in the context of lowland to upland migration (de Koninck 2000; Sowerwine 2011) and forestry development (McElwee 2016) in mainland Southeast Asia.

2. MARKET FORMATION IN TBONG KHMUM PROVINCE

1. "Cuplump" (also called "cup lump") refers to latex that is allowed to coagulate in collection cups on the tree rather than being collected in its liquid form. In my study sites, sulfuric acid was placed in the cups to promote coagulation.

2. In May 2012, the Cambodian government issued a policy in response to rising levels of land conflict, economic land concessions (ELCs), and tenure insecurity due to weaknesses in the 2001 Land Law. The policy was called *Order 01 on Measures for Strengthening and Increasing the Effectiveness of Economic Land Concessions (ELC) Management* (known as Order 01). Order 01 placed a moratorium on the issuing of new ELCs and launched a national campaign to fast-track the granting of land titles to households, particularly in areas where there were overlapping claims in or near ELCs, forest concessions, forest land, and other state land. Teams of students were deployed to undertake the land registration and titling process, which was abandoned after the 2013 election, excluding many communities from receiving legal title.

3. MOBILIZING CASSAVA NETWORKS IN MONDULKIRI

1. The trader meant to imply a painful figurative death, comparable to strangulation.

4. FRONTIER RUPTURE

1. "1881–1883: Rapports au Gouverneur sur la situation politique du Cambodge," January 23, 1882, file no. 10169; "1871–1884: Réglementation de la coupe des bois au Cambodge délits forestiers," July 28, 1880, file no. 10281; "1910: Affiche sur la réglementation forestières apposé dans les salas de Kompong Chhnang," August 2, 1910, file no. 16139, ANOM, Aix-en-Provence, France.

2. "1915–1917: Assassinat de M.Truffot Administratuer Délégué de Kratie Situation politique de la region," January 24, 1915, file no. 19196, ANOM, Aix-en-Provence, France.

3. "Socfin KCD" refers to the initial joint venture between Socfin and the Khmer company Khaou Chuly Development.

4. Phum Pii residents used the term *chuncheat* to refer to ethnic minorities or Indigenous people. The term translates literally as "nationality" or "ethnicity." Bunong villagers often used the term *Khmer* to refer to lowland migrants.

5. Referring to meters of road frontage, which is a common way of measuring land in Cambodia.

5. INTERVENING IN MARKET FORMATION

1. For further information on the cassava component of the UNDP CEDEP program, see UNDP (website), "Cambodia Export Diversification and Expansion Programme (CEDEP) II—Cassava Component," undated, accessed April 5, 2021, http://www.kh.undp.org/content/cambodia/en/home/operations/projects/upgrade-value-chains/project_sample.html.

2. For further information on the ACIAR Cassava Value Chain and Livelihood Program, see ACIAR (website), "Cassava Value Chains and Livelihoods in South-East Asia," August 13, 2020, accessed May 4, 2021, https://aciar.gov.au/publication/cassava-value-chains.

3. See ASEAN (website), "Cebu Declaration on East Asian Energy Security Cebu," January 15, 2007, https://asean.org/?static_post=cebu-declaration-on-east-asian-energy-security-cebu-philippines-15-january-2007-2.

4. REDD+ (Reducing Emissions from Deforestation and Forest Degradation in Developing Countries) is a mechanism developed by Parties to the United Nations Framework Convention on Climate Change (UNFCCC). See UNFCCC REDD+ Web Platform, homepage, undated, accessed April 5, 2021, https://redd.unfccc.int/.

References

ACIAR (Australian Centre for International Agricultural Research). 2014. *Project Proposal: Developing Cassava Production and Marketing Systems to Enhance Smallholder Livelihoods in Cambodia and Laos*. Bruce, Australia: ACIAR.

Akram-Lodhi, A. Haroon. 2005. "Vietnam's Agriculture: Processes of Rich Peasant Accumulation and Mechanisms of Social Differentiation." *Journal of Agrarian Change* 5 (1): 73–116. https://doi.org/10.1111/j.1471-0366.2004.00095.x.

Akram-Lodhi, A. Haroon, and Cristóbal Kay, eds. 2009. *Peasants and Globalization: Political Economy, Rural Transformation and the Agrarian Question*. London: Routledge.

Albrecht, Glenn, Gina-Maree Sartore, Linda Connor, Nick Higginbotham, Sonia Freeman, Brian Kelly, Helen Stain, Anne Tonna, and Georgia Pollard. 2007. "Solastalgia: The Distress Caused by Environmental Change." *Australasian Psychiatry* 15 (1): S95–S98. https://doi.org/10.1080/10398560701701288.

Allen, John. 2011. "Powerful Assemblages?" *Area* 43 (2): 154–57. https://doi.org/10.1111/j.1475-4762.2011.01005.x.

Appadurai, Arjun, ed. 1988. *The Social Life of Things: Commodities in Cultural Perspective*. Cambridge: Cambridge University Press.

——. 1996. *Modernity at Large: Cultural Dimensions of Globalization*. Minneapolis: University of Minnesota Press.

Applbaum, K. 2012. "Markets: Places, Principles and Integrations." In *A Handbook of Economic Anthropology*, 2nd ed., edited by James G. Carrier, 257–74. Cheltenham, UK: Edward Elgar.

ASEAN (Association of Southeast Asian Nations). 2007. *Cebu Declaration on East Asian Energy Security Cebu*. Philippines, January 15, 2007. https://asean.org/?static_post=cebu-declaration-on-east-asian-energy-security-cebu-philippines-15-january-2007-2.

Association des Planteurs de Caoutchouc de L'Indochine. 1911. *Les Annales des Planteurs de Caoutchouc de L'Indochine*. Saigon: Association des Planteurs de Caoutchouc de L'Indochine. https://gallica.bnf.fr/ark:/12148/bpt6k97435075/f3.image.

——. 1912. *Les Annales des Planteurs de Caoutchouc de L'Indochine*. Saigon: Association des Planteurs de Caoutchouc de L'Indochine. https://gallica.bnf.fr/ark:/12148/bpt6k97450465?rk=21459;2.

——. 1914. *Les Annales des Planteurs de Caoutchouc de L'Indochine*. Saigon: Association des Planteurs de Caoutchouc de L'Indochine. https://gallica.bnf.fr/ark:/12148/bpt6k9745268f/f1.image.

Association des Planteurs de Caoutchouc en Cochinchine. 1913. *Les Annales des Planteurs de Caoutchouc de l'Indochine*. Saigon: Association des Planteurs de Caoutchouc en Cochinchine. https://gallica.bnf.fr/ark:/12148/bpt6k9744296f/f7.image.

Aso, Michitake. 2009. "The Scientist, the Governor, and the Planter: The Political Economy of Agricultural Knowledge in Indochina during the Creation of a 'Science of Rubber,' 1900–1940." *East Asian Science, Technology and Society* 3 (2–3): 231–56. https://doi.org/10.1215/s12280-009-9092-7.

——. 2011. "Forests without Birds: Science, Environment, and Health in French Colonial Vietnam." PhD diss., University of Wisconsin–Madison.

——. 2012. "Profits or People? Rubber Plantations and Everyday Technology in Rural Indochina." *Modern Asian Studies* 46 (1): 19–45.

——. 2018. *Rubber and the Making of Vietnam: An Ecological History, 1897–1975.* Chapel Hill: University of North Carolina Press.

Bair, Jennifer. 2009. "Global Commodity Chains: Genealogy and Review." In *Frontiers of Commodity Chain Research*, edited by Jennifer Bair, 1–34. Stanford, CA: Stanford University Press.

Bair, Jennifer, Christian Berndt, Marc Boeckler, and Marion Werner. 2013. "Dis/articulating Producers, Markets, and Regions: New Directions in Critical Studies of Commodity Chains." *Environment and Planning A* 45 (11): 2544–552. https://doi.org/10.1068/a46297.

Bao, Ha. 2018. "Fallen Vietnamese Oil Exec Given 18-Year Sentence in $35 Million Graft Case." *VN Express International*, March 29, 2018. https://e.vnexpress.net/news/news/fallen-vietnamese-oil-exec-given-18-year-sentence-in-35-million-graft-case-3729693.html.

Beban, Alice. 2014. "How the Leopard Got Its Spots: Gender Dimensions of Land Reform in Cambodia." Sylff Association (website), October 10, 2014. https://www.sylff.org/news_voices/14378/.

Beeson, Mark, and Hung Hung Pham. 2012. "Developmentalism with Vietnamese Characteristics: The Persistence of State-Led Development in East Asia." *Journal of Contemporary Asia* 42 (4): 539–59. https://doi.org/10.1080/00472336.2012.706481.

Berndt, Christine, and Marc Boeckler. 2009. "Geographies of Circulation and Exchange: Constructions of Markets." *Progress in Human Geography* 33 (4): 535–51. https://doi.org/10.1177/0309132509104805.

Bernstein, Henry. 2010. *Class Dynamics of Agrarian Change.* Halifax, Canada: Fernwood.

Bernstein, Henry, and Liam Campling. 2006. "Commodity Studies and Commodity Fetishism I: Trading Down." *Journal of Agrarian Change* 6 (2): 239–64. https://doi.org/10.1111/j.1471-0366.2006.00121.x.

Biddulph, Robin. 2010. "Geographies of Evasion: The Development Industry and Property Rights Interventions in Early 21st Century Cambodia." PhD diss., University of Gothenburg.

——. 2014. *Cambodia's Land Management and Administration Project.* WIDER Working Paper no. 2014/086. Helsinki: WIDER.

Bignall, Simone. 2008. "Deleuze and Foucault on Desire and Power." *Angelaki* 13 (1): 127–47. https://doi.org/10.1080/09697250802156125.

Black, John, Nigar Hashimzade, and Gareth Myles. 2017. *A Dictionary of Economics*, 5th ed. Oxford: Oxford University Press.

Blanchard, Michel. 1999. *Vietnam-Cambodge, Une Frontiere contestée.* Paris: L'Harmattan.

Borras, Saturnino. 2009. "Agrarian Change and Peasant Studies: Changes, Continuities and Challenges—an Introduction." *Journal of Peasant Studies* 36 (1): 5–31. https://doi.org/10.1080/03066150902820297.

Borras, Saturnino M., Jennifer C. Franco, S. Ryan Isakson, Les Levidow, and Pietje Vervest. 2016. "The Rise of Flex Crops and Commodities: Implications for Research." *Journal of Peasant Studies* 43 (1): 93–115. https://doi.org/10.1080/03066150.2015.1036417.

Boucheret, Marianne. 2008. "Les Plantations D'Hevers en Indochine (1897–1954)." PhD diss., Pantheon-Sorbonne University.

——. 2014. "Les Grandes Plantations Hévéicoles au Temps de la Colonisation, Entre Dynamiques Régionales et Mondiales." In *L'Or Blanc: Petits et Grands Planteurs à L'épreuve du "Boom" de L'hévéaculture*, edited by Frederic Fortunel and

Cristophe Gironde, 25–40. Bangkok: Institut de Recherche sur l'Asie du Sud-Est Contemporaine.

Bourdier, Frédéric, ed. 2009. *Development and Dominion: Indigenous Peoples of Cambodia, Vietnam and Laos*. Bangkok: White Lotus.

Bourdieu, Pierre. 1977. *Outline of a Theory of Practice*. London: Cambridge University Press.

Brakman, Steven, Peter Frankopan, Harry Garretsen, and Charles Van Marrewijk. 2019. "The New Silk Roads: An Introduction to China's Belt and Road Initiative." *Cambridge Journal of Regions, Economy and Society* 12 (1): 3–16. https://doi.org /10.1093/cjres/rsy037.

Brenier, Henri. 1914. *D'Atlas Statistique de L'Indochine Française*. Gouvernement General De L'Indochine, file no. E468/u161.02, ANOM, Aix-en-Provence, France.

Brenner, Neil. 1999. "Beyond State-centrism? Space, Territoriality, and Geographical Scale in Globalization Studies." *Theory and Society* 28 (1): 39–78. https://doi.org /10.1023/A:1006996806674.

Brenner, Neil, and Nik Theodore. 2002. "Cities and the Geographies of 'Actually Existing Neoliberalism.'" *Antipode* 34 (3): 349–79. https://doi.org/10.1111/1467-8330 .00246.

Brocheux, Pierre, and Daniel Hémery. 2009. *Indochina: An Ambiguous Colonization, 1858–1954*. Berkeley: University of California Press.

Bryceson, Deborah Fahy. 1996. "Deagrarianization and Rural Employment in Sub-Saharan Africa: A Sectoral Perspective." *World Development* 24 (1): 97–111. https:// doi.org/10.1016/0305-750X(95)00119-W.

Bui, Thi Hue. 2012. *Tỉnh Bình Phước thời Pháp thuộc*. Hanoi: Tu Dien Bach Khoa.

Çalışkan, Koray, and Michel Callon. 2009. "Economization, Part 1: Shifting Attention from the Economy towards Processes of Economization." *Economy and Society* 38 (3): 369–98. https://doi.org/10.1080/03085140903020580.

Callon, Michel. 1986. "Some Elements of a Sociology of Translation: Domestication of the Scallops and the Fishermen of St. Brieuc Bay." In *Power, Action and Belief: A New Sociology of Knowledge?*, edited by J. Law, 196–233. London: Routledge.

——. 1998. "Introduction: The Embeddedness of Economic Markets in Economics." *Sociological Review* 46 (1): 1–57. https://doi.org/10.1111/j.1467-954X.1998.tb03468.x.

——. 2010. "Performativity, Misfires and Politics." *Journal of Cultural Economy* 3 (2): 163–69. https://doi.org/10.1080/17530350.2010.494119.

Carrier, James G. 2017. "Moral Economy: What's in a Name?" *Anthropological Theory* 18 (1): 18–35. https://doi.org/10.1177/1463499617735259.

Caouette, Dominique, and Sarah Turner, eds. 2009. *Agrarian Angst and Rural Resistance in Contemporary Southeast Asia*. London: Routledge.

Castree, Noel. 2002. "False Antitheses? Marxism, Nature and Actor-Networks." *Antipode* 34 (1): 111–46. https://doi.org/10.1111/1467-8330.00228.

CCHR (Cambodian Center for Human Rights). 2013. *Cambodia: Land in Conflict—an Overview of the Land Situation*. Phnom Penh: Cambodian Center for Human Rights.

CDRI (Cambodia Development Resource Institute). 2009. *Agricultural Trade in the Greater Mekong Sub-Region: Synthesis of the Case Studies on Cassava and Rubber Production and Trade in GMS Countries*. CDRI Working Paper Series no. 46. Phnom Penh: Cambodia Development Resource Institute.

Chaiyapa, Warathida, Khuong Nhat Nguyen, Abubakari Ahmed, Quan Thi, Marlet Bueno Hong Vu, Zhe Wang, Khang Tuan Nguyen, Ngoc Thi Nguyen, Uyen Thi To Dinh Thuy Thu Duong, Alexander Sjögren, Phung Thi Kim Le, Hang Thi An

Nguyen Thao Danh Nguyen, Izumi Ikeda, and Miguel Esteban. 2018. "Public Perception of Biofuel Usage in Vietnam." *Biofuels* 12 (1): 21–33. https://doi.org/10.1080/17597269.2018.1442667.

Chakrya, Khouth Sophak, Mech Dara, and Alessandro Marazzi Sassoon. 2018. "Three Killed in Jungle when Patrol Comes Under Fire; Fellow Authorities Suspected." *Phnom Penh Post*, January 31, 2018. https://www.phnompenhpost.com/national/three-killed-jungle-when-patrol-comes-under-fire-fellow-authorities-suspected.

Chan, Sok. 2017. "Cambodia a Key Country in Belt and Road Initiative." *Khmer Times*, October 31, 2017. https://www.khmertimeskh.com/5088419/cambodia-key-country-belt-road-initiative/.

——. 2018. "Chinese Delegation Explores Local Market." *Khmer Times*, January 5, 2018. https://www.khmertimeskh.com/100169/chinese-delegation-explores-local-market/.

Chandler, David P. 2008. *A History of Cambodia*. 4th ed. Boulder, CO: Westview.

Chevalier, Auguste. 1949. *L'Agriculture Coloniale: Origines et Évolution, Que Sais-Je?* Paris: Presses Universitaires de France.

Chevalier, Auguste, and Jean Le Bras. 1955. *Le Caoutchouc, Que Sais-Je?* Paris: Presses Universitaires de France.

Chhak, Sarin. 1966. *Les frontiers du Cambodge*. Paris: Dalloz.

Chin, Stephen. 2018. "Cambodian Cassava Catches Mosaic Virus." *ASEAN Post*, August 20, 2018. https://theaseanpost.com/article/cambodian-cassava-catches-mosaic-virus.

Chomitz, Kenneth M. 2007. *At Loggerheads: Agricultural Expansion, Poverty Reduction, and Environment in the Tropical Forests*. Washington, DC: World Bank.

Clarence-Smith, William. 1997. "The Rivaud-Hallet Plantation Group in the Economic Crises of the Inter-War Years." In *Private Enterprises during Economic Crises: Tactics and Strategies*, edited by P. Lanthier and H. Watelet, 117–32. Ottawa: Legas.

——. 2010. "'La SOCFIN (Groupe Rivaud) entre l'Axe et les Alliés.'" In *Les Enterprises et L'outre-mer Français Pendant la Seconde Guerre Mondiale*, edited by Hubert Bonin, Christophe Bouneau, and Hervé Joly, 99–113. Pessac, France: Maison des Sciences de l'Homme d'Aquitaine.

Cock, Andrew. 2016. *Governing Cambodia's Forests: The International Politics of Policy Reform*. Copenhagen: NIAS Press.

Coedès, George. 1975. *The Indianized States of Southeast Asia*. Canberra: Australian National University Press.

Cohn, Avery S., Peter Newton, Juliana D.B. Gil, Laura Kuhl, Leah Samberg, Vincent Ricciardi, Jessica R. Manly, and Sarah Northrop. 2017. "Smallholder Agriculture and Climate Change." *Annual Review of Environment and Resources* 42 (1): 347–75. https://doi.org/10.1146/annurev-environ-102016-060946.

Colman, A. M. 2012. *A Dictionary of Psychology*. Oxford: Oxford University Press.

Cons, Jason, and Michael Eilenberg, eds. 2018. *Frontier Assemblages: The Emergent Politics of Resource Frontiers in Asia*. Hoboken, NJ: John Wiley and Sons.

Cooke, Nola. 2004. "Water World: Chinese and Vietnamese on the Riverine Water Frontier, from Ca Mau to Tonle Sap (c. 1850–1884)." In *Water Frontier: Commerce and the Chinese in the Lower Mekong Region, 1750–1880*, edited by Nola Cooke and Tana Li, 139–58. Singapore: Rowman and Littlefield.

Cramb, Rob, and John F. McCarthy. 2016. *The Oil Palm Complex: Smallholders, Agribusiness and the State in Indonesia and Malaysia*. Singapore: National University of Singapore Press.

CRUMP (Cambodian Rural Urban Migration Project). 2012. *Report of the Cambodian Rural Urban Migration Project*. Phnom Penh: Ministry of Planning, Royal Government of Cambodia.

Curzon, Lord G. 1907. *Frontiers: The Romanes Lecture.* Oxford: Clarendon.

Dalakoglou, Dimitris, and Penny Harvey. 2012. "Roads and Anthropology: Ethnographic Perspectives on Space, Time and (Im)Mobility." *Mobilities* 7 (4): 459–65. https://doi .org/10.1080/17450101.2012.718426.

Dara, Mech, and Daphne Chen. 2018. "As Logging Changes Mondulkiri, Ethnic Phnong Are Reaping Only Meagre Gains from Major Loss." *Phnom Penh Post,* March 23, 2018. https://phnompenhpost.com/national-post-depth/logging-changes-mondulki ri-ethnic-phnong-are-reaping-only-meagre-gains-major.

Das, Veena, and Deborah Poole, eds. 2004. *Anthropology in the Margins: Comparative Ethnographies.* Santa Fe: SAR Press.

Daughton, J. P. 2006. *An Empire Divided: Religion, Republicanism, and the Making of French Colonialism, 1880–1914.* Oxford: Oxford University Press.

Davis, Kyle, Kailiang Yu, Maria Cristina Rulli, Lonn Pichdara, and Paolo D'Odorico. 2015. "Accelerated Deforestation Driven by Large-Scale Land Acquisitions in Cambodia." *Nature Geoscience* 8 (10): 772–75. https://doi.org/10.1038/ngeo2540.

De Koninck, Rodolphe. 2000. "The Theory and Practice of Frontier Development: Vietnam's Contribution." *Asia Pacific Viewpoint* 41 (1): 7–21. https://doi.org/10.1111 /1467-8373.00103.

De Soto, Hernando. 2000. *The Mystery of Capital: Why Capitalism Triumphs in the West and Fails Everywhere Else.* London: Bantam.

Deininger, Klaus, and Songqing Jin. 2007. "Land Sales and Rental Markets in Transition: Evidence from Rural Vietnam." *Oxford Bulletin of Economics and Statistics* 70 (1): 67–101. https://doi.org/10.1111/j.1468-0084.2007.00484.x.

DeLanda, Manuel. 2006. *A New Philosophy of Society: Assemblage Theory and Social Complexity.* London: Bloomsbury.

Delaquis, Erik, Kelsey F. Andersen, Nami Minato, Thuy Thi Le Cu, Maria Eleanor Karssenberg, Sophearith Sok, Kris A. G. Wyckhuys, Jonathan C. Newby, Dharani Dhar Burra, Pao Srean, Iv Phirun, Niem Duc Le, Nhan Thi Pham, Karen A. Garrett, Conny J. M. Almekinders, Paul C. Struik, and Stef de Haan. 2018. "Raising the Stakes: Cassava Seed Networks at Multiple Scales in Cambodia and Vietnam." *Frontiers in Sustainable Food Systems* 2 (73). https://doi.org/10.3389/fsufs.2018.00073.

Delarue, Jocelyn, and Naomi Noël. 2008. *Developing Smallholder Rubber Production: Lessons from AFD's Experience: Cambodia Report.* Paris: Agence Française de Développement. https://www.afd.fr/fr/media/download/11431.

Deleuze, Gilles, and Felix Guattari. 1983. *Anti-Oedipus: Capitalism and Schizophrenia.* Minneapolis: University of Minnesota Press.

——. 1987. *A Thousand Plateaus: Capitalism and Schizophrenia.* Minneapolis: University of Minnesota Press.

Desbarats, Jacqueline. 1995. *Prolific Survivors: Population Change in Cambodia, 1975–1993.* Tempe: Arizona State University.

Diederen, Paul, Hans Van Meijl, Arjan Wolters, and Katarzyna Bijak. 2003. *Innovation Adoption in Agriculture: Innovators, Early Adopters and Laggards.* Cahiers d'Economie et de Sociologie Rurales, Institut National de la Recherche Agronomique no. 67.

Diepart, Jean-Christophe. 2015. *The Fragmentation of Land Tenure Systems in Cambodia: Peasants and the Formalization of Land Rights.* Paris: French Cooperation Technical Committee on Land Tenure and Development.

Diepart, Jean-Christophe, and David Dupuis. 2014. "The Peasants in Turmoil: Khmer Rouge, State Formation and the Control of Land in Northwest Cambodia." *Journal of Peasant Studies* 41 (4): 445–68. https://doi.org/10.1080/03066150.2014.919265.

Diepart, Jean-Christophe, and Chanrith Ngin. 2020. "Internal Migration in Cambodia." In *Internal Migration in the Countries of Asia: A Cross-National Comparison,* edited by Martin Bell, Aude Bernard, Elin Charles-Edwards, and Yu Zhu, 137–62. Cham, Switzerland: Springer International. https://doi.org/10.1007/978-3-030-44010-7.

Diepart, Jean-Christophe, and Laura Schoenberger. 2016. "Concessions in Cambodia: Governing Profits, Extending State Power and Enclosing Resources from the Colonial Era to the Present." In *Handbook of Contemporary Cambodia*, edited by Katherine Brickell and Simon Springer, 157–68. Abingdon, UK: Routledge.

Do, Duc Dinh. 2016. *Manufacturing and Industry in Vietnam: Three Decades of Reform*. Discussion Paper 6/2016. Johannesburg: Brenthurst Foundation.

Donnan, Hastings, and Thomas M. Wilson, eds. 1994. *Border Approaches: Anthropological Perspectives on Frontiers*. Lanham, MD: University Press of America.

Dove, Michael. R. 2011. *The Banana Tree at the Gate: A History of Marginal Peoples and Global Markets in Borneo*. New Haven, CT: Yale University Press.

Dressler, Wolfram, Wilson, David, Clendenning, Jessica, Cramb, Rob, Keenan, Rodney, Mahanty, Sango, Bruun, Thilde Bech, Ole Mertz, and Rodel D. Lasco. 2017. "The Impact of Swidden Decline on Livelihoods and Ecosystem Services in Southeast Asia: A Review of the Evidence from 1990 to 2015." *Ambio* 6:291. https://doi.org/10.1007/s13280-016-0836-z.

Durst, Patrick B., Thomas R. Waggener, Thomas Enters, and Tan Lay Cheng, eds. 2001. *Forests Out of Bounds: Impacts and Effectiveness of Logging Bans in Natural Forests*. Bangkok: Food and Agricultural Organization of the United Nations, Regional Office for Asia and the Pacific.

Dwyer, Michael, Micah Ingalls, and Ian Baird. 2016. "The Security Exception: Development and Militarization in Laos's Protected Areas." *Geoforum* 69:207–17. https://doi.org/10.1016/j.geoforum.2015.11.002.

Eaton, Charles, and Andrew W. Shepherd. 2001. *Contract Farming: Partnerships for Growth*. FAO Agricultural Services Bulletin 145. Rome: FAO.

EIF. 2019. "Who We Are." Accessed May 10, 2019. https://www.enhancedif.org/en/who-we-are.

Elliot, John. E. 1980. "Marx and Schumpeter on Capitalism's Creative Destruction: A Comparative Restatement." *Quarterly Journal of Economics* 95 (1): 45–68. https://doi.org/10.2307/1885348.

Evans, T. D., P. Hout, P. Phet, and M. Hang. 2003. *A Study of Resin-Tapping and Livelihoods in Southern Mondulkiri, Cambodia with Implications for Conservation and Forest Management*. Phnom Penh: Wildlife Conservation Society.

FAO. 2000. *Asia and the Pacific National Forestry Programmes: Update 34*. Bangkok: FAO Regional Office for Asia and the Pacific. http://www.fao.org/3/x6900e/x6900e00.htm#Contents.

——. 2015. "FAOSTAT: Cambodia." Food and Agriculture Organization of the United Nations (website). Accessed April 6, 2021. http://www.fao.org/faostat/en/#country/115.

——. 2017. "FAOSTAT: Cambodia." Food and Agriculture Organization of the United Nations (website). Accessed April 6, 2021. http://www.fao.org/faostat/en/#country/115.

FIDH (International Federation for Human Rights). 2011. *Land Cleared for Rubber, Rights Bulldozed: The Impact of Rubber Plantations by Socfin-KCD on Indigenous Communities in Bousra, Mondulkiri*. Paris: FIDH.

Fine, Ben. 2005. "From Actor-Network Theory to Political Economy." *Capitalism Nature Socialism* 16 (4): 91–108. https://doi.org/10.1080/10455750500376057.

Fortunel, Frédéric. 2013. "Cross-Border Rubber Production in Mainland Southeast Asia: Creating a Spatial Division between Cambodia, Laos and Vietnam." *L'Espace géographique* 42 (2): 165–78. https://doi.org/10.3917/eg.422.0165.

Fortunel, Frederic, and Christophe Gironde, eds. 2014. *L'Or Blanc: Petits et Grands Planteurs Face au "Boom" de l'hévéaculture (Viêt Nam-Cambodge)*. Bangkok: Institut de Recherche sur l'Asie du Sud-Est Contemporaine.

Foster, John Bellamy. 1999. "Marx's Theory of Metabolic Rift: Classical Foundations for Environmental Sociology." *American Journal of Sociology* 105 (2): 366–405. https://doi.org/10.1086/210315.

Foster, Robert J. 2002. *Materializing the Nation: Commodities, Consumption, and Media in Papua New Guinea*. Bloomington: Indiana University Press.

——. 2005. "Commodity Futures: Labour, Love and Value." *Anthropology Today* 21 (4): 8–12.

Foster, Malcolm J., and Denis D. Gray. 2016. "Cambodia's Zeal for Rubber Drives Ethnic Group from Land." *San Diego Union-Tribune*, March 25, 2016. http://www.sandiegouniontribune.com/sdut-cambodias-zeal-for-rubber-drives-ethnic-group-2016mar25-story.html.

Fox, Jefferson, Dennis McMahon, Mark Poffenberger, and John Vogler. 2008. *Land for My Grandchildren: Land Use and Tenure Change in Ratanakiri, 1989–2007*. Phnom Penh: Community Forestry International and the East West Center.

Fox, Jefferson, Tuyen Nghiem, Ham Kimkong, Kaspar Hurni, and Ian G Baird. 2018. "Large-Scale Land Concessions, Migration, and Land Use: The Paradox of Industrial Estates in the Red River Delta of Vietnam and Rubber Plantations of Northeast Cambodia." *Land* 7 (2): 1–17. https://doi.org/10.3390/land7020077.

Freeman, Dena. 2013. "Value Chains for Development: An Ethnography of Pro-Poor Market Interventions in Ethiopia." *Anthropology of This Century* 6 (January). http://aotcpress.com/articles/chains-development-ethnography-propoor-market-interventions-ethiopia/.

Gallant, Thomas W. 1999. "Brigandage, Piracy, Capitalism, and State-Formation: Transnational Crime from a Historical World-Systems Perspective." *States and Illegal Practices* 3 (1): 25–61.

Gardère, Jean-Daniel. 2010. *Money and Sovereignty: An Exploration of the Economic, Political and Monetary History of Cambodia*. Phnom Penh: National Bank of Cambodia.

Gerber, Julien-François. 2014. "The Role of Rural Indebtedness in the Evolution of Capitalism." *Journal of Peasant Studies* 41 (5): 729–47. https://doi.org/10.1080/03066150.2014.921618.

Gereffi, Gary, John Humphrey, and Timothy Sturgeon. 2005. "The Governance of Global Value Chains." *Review of International Political Economy* 12 (1): 78–104. https://doi.org/10.1080/09692290500049805.

Gereffi, G., M. E. Korzeniewicz, and R. P. Korzeniewicz. 1994. "Introduction: Global Commodity Chains." In *Commodity Chains and Global Capitalism*, edited by Gary Gereffi and Miguel Korzeniewicz, 1–14. Westport, CT: Praeger.

Gibson-Graham, J. K. 2006. *The End of Capitalism (as We Knew It): A Feminist Critique of Political Economy*. Minneapolis: University of Minnesota Press.

Giddens, Anthony. 1984. *The Constitution of Society: Outline of the Theory of Structuration*. Berkeley: University of California Press.

Giessen, Lukas, Sarah Burns, Muhammad Alif K. Sahide, and Agung Wibowo. 2016. "From Governance to Government: The Strengthened Role of State Bureaucracies in Forest and Agricultural Certification." *Policy and Society* 35 (1): 71–89. https://doi.org/10.1016/j.polsoc.2016.02.001.

Global Witness. 2002. *Deforestation without Limits: How the Cambodian Government Failed to Tackle the Untouchables*. London: Global Witness. https://cdn.globalwitness.org/archive/files/library/deforestation_without_limit.pdf.

Glover, David. 1992. "Introduction." In *Contract Farming in South-East Asia: Three Country Studies*, edited by David Glover and Lim Teck Ghee, 1–9. Kuala Lumpur: University of Malaya.

Goodchild, Philip. 2012. *Deleuze and Guattari: An Introduction to the Politics of Desire.* London: Sage.

Goscha, Christopher E. 2012. *Going Indochinese: Contesting Concepts of Space and Place in French Indochina.* Copenhagen: NIAS Press.

Government of Vietnam. 2021. Vietnam Customs Export Data. https://www.customs.gov.vn/Lists/ThongKeHaiQuan/SoLieuDinhKy.aspx?Group=S%u1ed1+li%u1ec7u+th%u1ed1ng+k%u00ea, accessed 2 July 2021.

Graeber, David. 2011. *Debt: The First 5000 Years.* Brooklyn, New York: Melville House.

Green, W. Nathan. 2019. "From Rice Fields to Financial Assets: Valuing Land for Microfinance in Cambodia." *Transactions of the Institute of British Geographers* 44:749–62. https://doi.org/10.1111/tran.12310.

Green, W. Nathan, and Jennifer Estes. 2019. "Precarious Debt: Microfinance Subjects and Intergenerational Dependency in Cambodia." *Antipode* 51 (1): 129–47. https://doi.org/10.1111/anti.12413.

Green Leader. 2017. "Corporate Overview." Accessed May 10, 2019. https://www.greenleader.hk/EN/about1_1.

——. 2018. "Business Investment Introduction." Accessed May 10, 2019. https://www.unescap.org/sites/default/files/Green%20Business%20TF-GL_Business%20Intro%20EN%20%28no%20fin%29.pdf.

Gregory, C. A. 1982. *Gifts and Commodities.* London: Academic Press.

Greve, H. S. 1993. *Land Tenure and Property Rights in Cambodia.* Phnom Penh: United Nations Transitional Authority in Cambodia

Grimsditch, Mark, and Laura Schoenberger. 2015. *New Actions and Existing Policies: The Implementation and Impacts of Order 01.* Phnom Penh: NGO Forum on Cambodia, Land and Livelihoods Program.

Gudeman, Stephen. 2001. *The Anthropology of Economy.* Malden, MA: Blackwell.

Guérin, Mathieu. 2003. "Des Casques Blancs Sur Le Plateau des Herbes. La Pacification des Aborigènes des Hautes Terres du Sud-Indochinois, 1859–1940." PhD diss., Paris Diderot University.

——. 2009. "State Policy toward the Highlanders of Ratanakiri during the French Protectorate." In *Development and Dominion: Indigenous Peoples of Cambodia, Vietnam and Laos*, edited by Frédéric Bourdier, 115–40. Bangkok: White Lotus.

Guillou, Anne. 2006. "The Question of Land in Cambodia: Perceptions, Access, and Use since De-collectivization." *Moussons* 9–10:299–324. https://doi.org/10.4000/moussons.2060.

Gunn, Geoffrey C. 2014. *Rice Wars in Colonial Vietnam: The Great Famine and the Viet Minh Road to Power.* Lanham, MD: Rowman and Littlefield.

Ha, Duy. 2017 "Major Communist Party Official Charged with SOE Mismanagement." *Vietnam Investment Review,* April 28, 2017. https://www.vir.com.vn/major-communist-party-official-charged-with-soe-mismanagement-48915.html.

Ha, Marie-Paule. 2014. *French Women and the Empire: The Case of Indochina.* Oxford: Oxford University Press.

Hall, Derek. 2011. "Land Grabs, Land Control, and Southeast Asian Crop Booms." *Journal of Peasant Studies* 38 (4): 837–57. https://doi.org/10.1080/03066150.2011.607706.

Hall, Derek, Philip Hirsch, and Tania Murray Li. 2011. *Powers of Exclusion: Land Dilemmas in Southeast Asia.* Singapore: National University of Singapore Press; Honolulu: University of Hawai'i Press.

Hansen, M. C., P. V. Potapov, R. Moore, M. Hancher, S. A. Turubanova, A. Tyukavina, D. Thau, S. V. Stehman, S. J. Goetz, T. R. Loveland, A. Kommareddy, A. Egorov, L. Chini, C. O. Justice, and J. R. G. Townshend. 2013. "High-Resolution Global Maps of 21st-Century Forest Cover Change." *Science* 342 (6160): 850.

Hao, Han, Zongwei Liu, Fuquan Zhao, Jingzheng Ren, Shiyan Chang, Ke Rong, and Ji-uyu Du. 2018. "Biofuel for Vehicle Use in China: Current Status, Future Potential and Policy Implications." *Renewable and Sustainable Energy Reviews* 82:645–53. https://doi.org/10.1016/j.rser.2017.09.045.

Hardy, Andrew. 2000. "Strategies of Migration to Upland Areas in Contemporary Vietnam." *Asia Pacific Viewpoint* 41 (1): 23–34. https://doi.org/10.1111/1467-8373.00104.

——. 2003. "State Visions, Migrant Decisions: Population Movements since the End of the Vietnam War." In *Postwar Vietnam: Dynamics of a Transforming Society*, edited by Hy Van Luong, 107–37. Lanham, MD: Rowman and Littlefield.

Harnesk, David. 2019. "Biomass-Based Energy on the Move—the Geographical Expansion of the European Union's Liquid Biofuel Regulation." *Geoforum* 98:25–35. https://doi.org/10.1016/j.geoforum.2018.09.019.

Harvey, David. 2003. *The New Imperialism.* Oxford: Oxford University Press.

——. 2007. *The Limits to Capital.* New ed. London: Verso Books.

Harvey, Penny, and Hannah Knox. 2012. "The Enchantments of Infrastructure." *Mobilities* 7 (4): 521–36. https://doi.org/10.1080/17450101.2012.718935.

Hecht, Susanna, Anastasia Yang, Bimbika Sijapati Basnett, Christine Padoch, and Nancy Peluso. 2015. *People in Motion, Forests in Transition: Trends in Migration, Urbanization, and Remittances and Their Effects on Tropical Forests.* CIFOR Occasional Paper no. 142. Bogor, Indonesia: Center for International Forestry Research.

Heron, Nicholas. 2011. "The Ungovernable." *Angelaki* 16 (2): 159–74. https://doi.org/10.1080/0969725X.2011.591594.

Hickey, Gerard Cannon. 1982. *Sons of the Mountains: Ethnohistory of the Vietnamese Central Highlands to 1954.* New Haven, CT: Yale.

Hieu, Do Trong. 2015. "Biofuel Development in Vietnam." Paper presented at GBEP Bioenergy Week, Medan City, Indonesia, May 25–29, 2015.

High, Holly. 2014. *Fields of Desire: Poverty and Policy in Laos.* Singapore: National University of Singapore Press.

Hirsch, Philip. 2016. "The Shifting Regional Geopolitics of Mekong Dams." *Political Geography* 51:63–74. https://doi.org/10.1016/j.polgeo.2015.12.004.

Hoekman, Bernard, and Michel Kostecki. 2009. *The Political Economy of the World Trading System.* 3rd ed. Oxford: Oxford University Press.

Hopkins, Terence K., and Immanuel Wallerstein. 1986. "Commodity Chains in the World-Economy Prior to 1800." *Review (Fernand Braudel Center)* 10 (1): 157–70.

Hornborg, Alf. 2017. "Artifacts Have Consequences, Not Agency: Toward a Critical Theory of Global Environmental History." *European Journal of Social Theory* 20 (1): 95–110. https://doi.org/10.1177/1368431016640536.

Hought, J., T. Birch-Thomsen, J. Petersen, A. de Neergaard, and M. Oelofse. 2012. "Biofuels, Land Use Change and Smallholder Livelihoods: A Case Study from Banteay Chhmar, Cambodia." *Applied Geography* 34:525–32. https://doi.org/10.1016/j.apgeog.2012.02.007.

Hounshell, David. 1984. *From the American System to Mass Production, 1800–1932: The Development of Manufacturing Technology in the United States.* Baltimore: Johns Hopkins University Press.

Hudson, Ray. 2016. *Approaches to Economic Geography: Towards a Geographical Political Economy.* Oxon, UK: Routledge.

Hughes, Caroline, and Kheang Un, eds. 2011. *Cambodia's Economic Transformation*. Copenhagen: NIAS Press.

Humphrey, John, and Lizbeth Navas-Alemán. 2010. *Value Chains, Donor Interventions and Poverty Reduction: A Review of Donor Practice*. IDS Research Report 63. Brighton, UK: Institute of Development Studies, University of Sussex.

Ishikawa, Noboru. 2010. *Between Frontiers: Nation and Identity in a Southeast Asian Borderland*. Singapore: National University of Singapore Press.

Jackson, Larry R. 1969. "The Vietnamese Revolution and the Montagnards." *Asian Survey* 9 (5): 313–30.

Jasanoff, Sheila. 2004. "The Idiom of Co-production." In *States of Knowledge: The Co-Production of Science and Social Order*, edited by Sheila Jasanoff, 1–13. London: Routledge.

Johnson, Chalmers. 1982. *MITI and the Japanese Miracle: The Growth of Industrial Policy, 1925–1975*. Stanford, CA: Stanford University Press.

Jordens, Jay. 1996. "Persecution of Cambodia's Ethnic Vietnamese Communities during and since the UNTAC Period." In *Propaganda, Politics and Violence in Cambodia: Democratic Transition under United Nations Peace-Keeping: Democratic Transition Under United Nations Peace-Keeping*, edited by Steve Heder and Judy Ledgerwood, 134–59. Armonk, NY: East Gate Books.

Kaplinsky, Raphael, Anne Terheggen, and Julia Tijaja. 2011. "China as a Final Market: The Gabon Timber and Thai Cassava Value Chains." *World Development* 39 (7): 1177–90. https://doi.org/10.1016/j.worlddev.2010.12.007.

Keating, Neal B. 2016. "Kites in the Highlands: Articulating Bunong Indigeneity in Cambodia, Vietnam, and Abroad." *Asian Ethnicity* 17 (4): 566–79. https://doi.org/10.1080/14631369.2016.1145538.

Kelly, Philip F. 2011. "Migration, Agrarian Transition, and Rural Change in Southeast Asia." *Critical Asian Studies* 43 (4): 479–506. https://doi.org/10.1080/14672715.2011.623516.

Kelly, Philip F., Kris Olds, and Henry Wai-chung Yeung. 2001. "Geographical Perspectives on the Asian Economic Crisis." *Geoforum* 32 (1): vii–xiii.

Kem, Sothorn. 2017. "Commercialisation of Smallholder Agriculture in Cambodia: Impact of the Cassava Boom on Rural Livelihoods and Agrarian Change." PhD diss., University of Queensland, Brisbane.

Kiernan, Ben. 1985. *How Pol Pot Came to Power: Colonialism, Nationalism, and Communism in Cambodia, 1930–1975*. 1st ed. London: Verso.

——. 1996. *The Pol Pot Regime: Race, Power, and Genocide in Cambodia under the Khmer Rouge, 1975–79*. New Haven, CT: Yale University Press.

Kimsay, Hor. 2016. "More Cambodians Struggling to Repay MFI Loans." *Phnom Penh Post*, July 12, 2016. https://www.phnompenhpost.com/business/more-cambodians-struggling-repay-mfi-loans.

Kosoy, Nicolás, and Esteve Corbera. 2010. "Payments for Ecosystem Services as Commodity Fetishism." *Ecological Economics* 69 (6): 1228–36. https://doi.org/10.1016/j.ecolecon.2009.11.002.

Larsen, Peter Bille. 2015. *Post-Frontier Resource Governance: Indigenous Rights, Extraction and Conservation in the Peruvian Amazon*. London: Palgrave Macmillan.

Latour, Bruno. 1987. *Science in Action: How to Follow Scientists and Engineers through Society*. Cambridge, MA: Harvard University Press.

——. 1993. *We Have Never Been Modern*. Cambridge, MA: Harvard University Press.

——. 1996. "On Actor-Network Theory: A Few Clarifications." *Soziale Welt* 47 (4): 369–81.

——. 2005. *Reassembling the Social: An Introduction to Actor-Network Theory*. Oxford: Oxford University Press.

Lave, Rebecca. 2015. "Reassembling the Structural: Political Ecology and Actor-Network Theory." In *The Routledge Handbook of Political Ecology*, edited by Tom Perreault, Gavin Bridge, and James McCarthy, 213–23. London: Routledge.

Law, John. 2002. "Economics as Interference." In *Cultural Economy: Cultural Analysis and Commercial Life*, edited by P. Du Gay and M. Pryke, 23–40. London: Sage.

Le Billon, Philippe. 1999. "Power Is Consuming the Forest: The Political Ecology of Conflict and Reconstruction in Cambodia " PhD diss., University of Oxford.

——. 2000. "The Political Ecology of Transition in Cambodia 1989–1999: War, Peace and Forest Exploitation." *Development and Change* 31 (2000): 785–805. https://doi.org/10.1111/1467-7660.00177.

——. 2002. "Logging in Muddy Waters: The Politics of Forest Exploitation in Cambodia." *Critical Asian Studies* 34 (4): 563–86. https://doi.org/10.1080/1467271022000035938.

Le Billon, Philippe, and Simon Springer. 2007. "Between War and Peace: Violence and Accommodation in the Cambodian Logging Sector." In *Extreme Conflict and Tropical Forests*, edited by Wil De Jong, Deanna Donova, and Ken-ichi Abe, 17–36. Dordrecht, Netherlands: Springer.

Lee, Roger. 2006. "The Ordinary Economy: Tangled up in Values and Geography." *Transactions of the Institute of British Geographers* 31 (4): 413–32.

Lefebvre, Henri. 1974. *The Production of Space*. New York: Horizon Press.

Li, Tania Murray. 2011. "Centering Labor in the Land Grab Debate." *The Journal of Peasant Studies* 38 (2): 281–298. https://doi.org/10.1080/03066150.2011.559009.

——. 2014. *Land's End: Capitalist Relations on an Indigenous Frontier*. Durham, NC: Duke University Press.

——. 2017. "Intergenerational Displacement in Indonesia's Oil Palm Plantation Zone." *Journal of Peasant Studies* 44 (6): 1158–76. https://doi.org/10.1080/03066150.2017.1308353.

LICADHO (Cambodian League for the Promotion and Defense of Human Rights). 2018. "Land Concessions." Accessed June 30, 2018. http://www.licadho-cambodia.org/land_concessions/.

——. 2019. *Collateral Damage: Land Loss and Abuses in Cambodia's Microfinance Sector*. Phnom Penh: LICADHO. http://www.licadho-cambodia.org/reports/files/228Report_Collateral_Damage_LICADHO_STT_Eng_07082019.pdf.

Liu, Pascal, Suffyan Koroma, Pedro Arias, and David Hallam. 2012. *Trends and Impacts of Foreign Investment in Developing Country Agriculture: Evidence from Case Studies*. Rome: Food and Agriculture Organization.

Lockie, Stewart. 2006. "Networks of Agri-Environmental Action: Temporality, Spatiality and Identity in Agricultural Environments." *Sociologia Ruralis* 46 (1): 22–39. https://doi.org/10.1111/j.1467-9523.2006.00400.x.

Lund, Christian. 2016. "Rule and Rupture: State Formation through the Production of Property and Citizenship." *Development and Change* 47 (6): 1199–228. https://doi.org/10.1111/dech.12274.

Mahanty, Sango. 2018. "Contingent Sovereignty: Cross-Border Rentals in the Cambodia-Vietnam Borderland." *Annals of the American Association of Geographers* 108 (3): 829–44. https://doi.org/10.1080/24694452.2017.1374162.

——. 2019. "A Tale of Two Networks: Market Formation on the Cambodia–Vietnam Frontier." *Transactions of the Institute of British Geographers* 44: 315–30. https://doi.org/10.1111/tran.12286

Mahanty, Sango, and Sarah Milne. 2016. "Anatomy of a Boom: Cassava as a 'Gateway' Crop in Cambodia's North-Eastern Borderland." *Asia Pacific Viewpoint* 57 (2): 180–93. https://doi.org/10.1111/apv.12122.

Mahanty, Sango, Sarah Milne, Phuc X. To, Keith Barney, Wolfram Dressler, and Philip Hirsch. Forthcoming. *Rupture: Understanding Nature-Society Transformation through Hydropower Development in the Mekong Region.* Canberra: Crawford School of Public Policy, ANU College of Asia and the Pacific.

Maltoni, Bruno. 2007. "Migration in Cambodia: Internal vs. External Flows." Paper presented at the Eighth ARPMN Conference on Migration, Development and Poverty Reduction, Fuzhou, China, May 25–29, 2007.

Mao, Pengfei, and Suvon Nguon. 2019. "Spotlight: Economic Cooperation with China under BRI Helps Cambodia Diversify Economy, Strengthen Resilience." Xinhua News Agency, April 21, 2019. http://www.xinhuanet.com/english/2019-04/21/c_137995768.htm?fbclid=IwAR0NmuJabUECnyWfJye4AbyQ2CaGdVzDbOnini BNYu-vmvTNrGa9iem1G7s.

Marschke, Melissa, and Peter Vandergeest. 2016. "Slavery Scandals: Unpacking Labour Challenges and Policy Responses within the Off-Shore Fisheries Sector." *Marine Policy* 68:39–46. https://doi.org/10.1016/j.marpol.2016.02.009.

Marx, Karl. (1867) 1990. *Capital: Volume 1.* Translated by Ben Fowkes. Harmondsworth, UK: Penguin.

Mayhew, S. 2015. *A Dictionary of Geography.* 5th ed. Oxford: Oxford University Press.

McElwee, Pamela. 2016. *Forests Are Gold: Trees, People, and Environmental Rule in Vietnam.* Seattle: University of Washington Press.

McHale, Shawn. 2013. "Ethnicity, Violence, and Khmer-Vietnamese Relations: The Significance of the Lower Mekong Delta, 1757–1954." *Journal of Asian Studies* 72 (2): 367–90.

McLaughlin, Paul, and Thomas Dietz. 2008. "Structure, Agency and Environment: Toward an Integrated Perspective on Vulnerability." *Global Environmental Change* 39: 99–111. https://doi.org/10.1016/j.gloenvcha.2007.05.003.

Michaud, Jean. 2004. "French Missionary Expansion in Colonial Upper Tonkin." *Journal of Southeast Asian Studies* 35 (2): 287–310. https://doi.org/10.1010/S00224634040 00153.

Michaud, Jean, Meenaxi Barkataki-Ruscheweyh, and Margaret Byrne Swain. 2016. *Historical Dictionary of the Peoples of the Southeast Asian Massif.* Lanham, MD: Rowman and Littlefield.

Miller, Daniel. 2002. "Turning Callon the Right Way Up." *Economy and Society* 31 (2): 218–33. https://doi.org/10.1080/03085140220123135.

Milne, Sarah. 2013. "Under the Leopard's Skin: Land Commodification and the Dilemmas of Indigenous Communal Title in Upland Cambodia." *Asia Pacific Viewpoint* 54 (3): 323–39. https://doi.org/10.1111/apv.12027.

——. 2015. "Cambodia's Unofficial Regime of Extraction: Illicit Logging in the Shadow of Transnational Governance and Investment." *Critical Asian Studies* 47 (2): 200–228.

Milne, Sarah, and Sango Mahanty. 2019. "Value and Bureaucratic Violence in the Green Economy." *Geoforum* 98:133–43. https://doi.org/10.1016/j.geoforum.2018.11.003.

Milne, Sarah, Sango Mahanty, Phuc To, Wolfram Dressler, Peter Kanowski, and Maylee Thavat. 2019. "Learning from 'Actually Existing' REDD+: A Synthesis of Ethnographic Findings." *Conservation and Society* 17 (1): 84–95. https://doi.org/10.4103/cs.cs_18_13.

Minato, Nami, Sophearith Sok, Songbi Chen, Erik Delaquis, Iv Phirun, Vi Xuan Le, Dharani D. Burra, Jonathan C. Newby, Kris A. G. Wyckhuys, and Stef de Haa. 2019. "Surveillance for Sri Lankan Cassava Mosaic Virus (SLCMV) in Cambodia and Vietnam One Year after Its Initial Detection in a Single Plantation in 2015." *Plos One* 14 (2): 1–16. https://doi.org/10.1371/journal.pone.0212780.

Mitchell, B. R. 2007. *International Historical Statistics: Africa, Asia and Oceania 1750–2005*. 5th ed. London: Palgrave Macmillan.

Mitchell, Timothy. 2008. "Rethinking Economy." *Geoforum* 39 (3): 1116–1121. https://doi.org/10.1016/j.geoforum.2006.11.022.

Moore, Jason W. 2017. "The Capitalocene, Part I: On the Nature and Origins of our Ecological Crisis." *Journal of Peasant Studies* 44 (3): 594–630. https://doi.org/10.1080/03066150.2016.1235036.

——. 2018. "The Capitalocene Part II: Accumulation by Appropriation and the Centrality of Unpaid Work/Energy." *Journal of Peasant Studies* 45 (2): 237–79. https://doi.org/10.1080/03066150.2016.1272587.

Moseley, William G. 2016. "The New Green Revolution for Africa: A Political Ecology Critique." *Brown Journal of World Affairs* 23 (2): 177–90.

Müller, Nils. 2011. "Social Frontiers: Modernizing an Old Paradigm for Modern Border Research." In *Proceedings of the 2010 European Conference of the Association for Borderlands Studies: The Multifaceted Economic and Political Geographies of Internal and External Borders*, edited by Athanasios Kalogeresis, 341–52. Thessaloniki, Greece: Department of Spatial Planning and Development, Aristotle University of Thessaloniki.

Murray, Martin J. 1980. *The Development of Capitalism in Colonial Indochina (1870–1940)*. Berkeley: University of California Press.

——. 1992. "'White Gold' Or 'White Blood'?: The Rubber Plantations of Colonial Indochina, 1910–40." *Journal of Peasant Studies* 19 (3–4): 41–67. https://doi.org/10.1080/03066159208438487.

Naafs, Suzanne, and Tracey Skelton. 2018. "'Youthful Futures? Aspirations, Education and Employment in Asia." *Children's Geographies* 16 (1): 1–14. https://doi.org/10.1080/14733285.2018.1402164.

Nakamura, Goro. 2007. "Defoliation during the Vietnam War." In *Extreme Conflict and Tropical Forests*, edited by Wil de Jong, Deanna Donovan, and Ken-ichi Abe, 149–58. Dordrecht, Netherlands: Springer.

National Institute of Statistics. 2002. *General Population Census of Cambodia*. Phnom Penh: National Institute of Statistics. Accessed August 5, 2018. https://redatam.org/redkhm/census/khm1998/.

Neef, Andreas, Siphat Touch, and Jamaree Chiengthong. 2013. "The Politics and Ethics of Land Concessions in Rural Cambodia." *Journal of Agricultural and Environmental Ethics* 26 (6): 1085–103. https://doi.org/10.1007/s10806-013-9446-y.

Neilson, Jeffrey. 2014. "Value Chains, Neoliberalism and Development Practice: The Indonesian Experience." *Review of International Political Economy* 21 (1): 38–69. https://doi.org/10.1080/09692290.2013.809782.

Neilson, Jeffrey, and Bill Pritchard. 2009. *Value Chain Struggles: Institutions and Governance in the Plantation Districts of South India*. Chichester, UK: Wiley-Blackwell. https://doi.org/10.1002/9781444308723.

Neilson, Jeffrey, Bill Pritchard, and Henry Wai-chung Yeung. 2014. "Global Value Chains and Global Production Networks in the Changing International Political Economy: An Introduction." *Review of International Political Economy* 21 (1): 1–8. https://doi.org/10.1080/09692290.2013.873369.

Neimark, Benjamin. 2010. "Subverting Regulatory Protection of 'Natural Commodities': The *Prunus africana* in Madagascar." *Development and Change* 41:929–54.

Neimark, Benjamin, Sango Mahanty, and Wolfram Dressler. 2016. "Mapping Value in a 'Green' Commodity Frontier: Revisiting Commodity Chain Analysis." *Development and Change* 47 (2): 240–65.

Neimark, Benjamin, Sango Mahanty, Wolfram Dressler, and Christina Hicks. 2020. "Not *Just* Participation: The Rise of the Eco-Precariat in the Green Economy." *Antipode* 52 (2): 496–521. https://doi.org/10.1111/anti.12593.

Nevins, Joseph, and Nancy Lee Peluso. 2008. "Introduction: Commoditization in Southeast Asia." In *Taking Southeast Asia to Market: Commodities, Nature, and People in the Neoliberal Age*, edited by Joseph Nevins and Nancy Lee Peluso, 1–26. Ithaca, NY: Cornell University Press.

NGO Forum on Cambodia. 2015. *Statistical Analysis of Land Disputes in Cambodia, 2014.* Phnom Penh: NGO Forum. Accessed June 5, 2019. http://ngoforum.org .kh/files/e1f20a9889d8ae9144413f14d7b2053e-Layout-Land-dispute-report-2015 -Eng.pdf

Nguyen, Do Anh Tuan, Nguyen Anh Phong, Nguyen Nghia Lan, Ta Thi Khanh Van, Tran The Tuong, Phan Dang Hung, Vi Viet Hoang, and Ha Van Chuc. 2009. *Status and Potential for the Development of Biofuels and Rural Renewable Energy: Vietnam.* Manila, Philippines: Asian Development Bank.

Nguyen, Mai, and James Pearson. 2018. "Vietnam Jails Former Politburo Official for 13 Years in Graft Crackdown." Reuters, January 22, 2018. https://www.reuters.com /article/us-vietnam-security/vietnam-jails-former-politburo-official-for-13-years -in-graft-crackdown-idUSKBN1FB0C5.

Nikles, Brigitte. 2006. "Livelihood Strategies, Forest Resources and Conservation: Two Punong Communes in Mondulkiri, Cambodia." MA thesis, University of Zurich.

Onwueme, I. C. 2002. "Cassava in Asia and the Pacific." In *Cassava: Biology, Production and Utilization*, edited by R. J. Hillocks, J. M. Thresh, and A. Bellotti, 55–66. New York: CABI Publishing.

Open Development Cambodia. 2016. "Forest Cover Reporting." Phnom Penh: Open Development Cambodia. Last modified October 28, 2017. https://opendevelopment cambodia.net/topics/forest-cover/.

Osborne, Milton E. 1969. *The French Presence in Cochinchina and Cambodia: Rule and Response (1859–1905).* Ithaca, NY: Cornell University Press.

——. 2016. *Southeast Asia: An Introductory History.* 12th ed. Crows Nest, Australia: Allen and Unwin.

Overmars, Koen P., Elke Stehfest, Jan P. M. Ros, and Anne Gerdien Prins. 2011. "Indirect Land Use Change Emissions Related to EU Biofuel Consumption: An Analysis Based on Historical Data." *Environmental Science and Policy* 14 (3): 248–57. https://doi.org/10.1016/j.envsci.2010.12.012.

Owen, Taylor, and Ben Kiernan. 2006. "Bombs over Cambodia." *The Walrus*, October 2006, 62–69.

Padwe, Jonathon. 2009. "Customary Law, Traditional Authority, and the Ethnicization of Rights in Highland Cambodia: A Historical Contextualization." In *Development and Dominion: Indigenous Peoples of Cambodia, Vietnam and Laos*, edited by Frédéric Bourdier, 325–62. Bangkok: While Lotus.

——. 2013. "Highlands of History: Indigenous Identity and its Antecedents in Cambodia." *Asia Pacific Viewpoint* 54 (3): 282–95. https://doi.org/10.1111/apv.12028.

——. 2020. *Disturbed Forests, Fragmented Memories: Jarai and Other Lives in the Cambodian Highlands.* Seattle: University of Washington Press.

Paley, Richard. 2015. "Managing Protected Areas in Cambodia: The Challenge for Conservation Bureaucracies in a Hostile Governance Environment." In *Conservation and Development in Cambodia: Exploring Frontiers of Change in Nature, State and Society*, edited by Sarah Milne and Sango Mahanty, 141–59. New York: Routledge.

Pavie, Auguste. (1906) 1999. *Pavie Mission Exploration Work: Laos, Cambodia, Siam, Yunnan, and Vietnam*. Translated by Walter E. J. Tips. Vol. 1, *The Pavie Mission Indochina Papers, 1879–1895*. Bangkok: White Lotus.

Peluso, Nancy Lee, and Peter Vandergeest. 2011. "Political Ecologies of War and Forests: Counterinsurgencies and the Making of National Natures." *Annals of the Association of American Geographers* 101 (3): 587–608. https://doi.org/10.1080/00045 608.2011.560064.

Pham, Van Thuy. 2019. *Beyond Political Skin: Colonial to National Economies in Indonesia and Vietnam (1910s–1960s)*. Singapore: Springer. https://doi.org/10.1007/978 -981-13-3711-6.

Piper, Philip J., Hirofumi Matsumura, and David Bulbeck, eds. 2017. *New Perspectives in Southeast Asian and Pacific Prehistory*. Canberra: ANU Press.

Polanyi, Karl. (1944) 1957. "The Economy as an Instituted Process." In *Trade and Market in Early Empires*, edited by Karl Polanyi, C. M. Arensberg, and H.W. Person, 243–69. Glencoe, IL: Free Press.

——. 2001. *The Great Transformation: The Political and Economic Origins of Our Time*. Boston: Beacon.

Political Map of French Indochina. 1889. File no. ANOM (FRANOM_2PL_786ANOM), Aix-en-Provence, France.

Pratt, Mary Louise. 1991. "Arts of the Contact Zone." *Profession*, 33–40.

Rasmussen, Mattias Borg, and Christian Lund. 2018. "Reconfiguring Frontier Spaces: The Territorialization of Resource Control." *World Development* 101 (January): 388–99. https://doi.org/10.1016/j.worlddev.2017.01.018.

Ribot, Jesse C. 1998. "Theorizing Access: Forest Profits along Senegal's Charcoal Commodity Chain." *Development and Change* 29:307–41.

Ribot, Jesse C., and Nancy Lee Peluso. 2003. "A Theory of Access." *Rural Sociology* 68 (2): 153–81. https://doi.org/10.1111/j.1549-0831.2003.tb00133.x.

Rigg, Jonathan. 2002. "Roads, Marketization and Social Exclusion in Southeast Asia: What Do Roads Do to People?" *Bijdragen tot de taal-, land- en volkenkunde / Journal of the Humanities and Social Sciences of Southeast Asia* 158 (4): 619–36. https:// doi.org/10.1163/22134379-90003758.

——. 2006. "Land, Farming, Livelihoods, and Poverty: Rethinking the Links in the Rural South." *World Development* 34 (1): 180–202. https://doi.org/10.1016/j.worlddev .2005.07.015.

——. 2007. "Moving Lives: Migration and Livelihoods in the Lao PDR." *Population, Space and Place* 13 (3): 163–78. https://doi.org/10.1002/psp.438.

Rigg, Jonathan, Katie J. Oven, Gopi Krishna Basyal, and Richa Lamichhane. 2016. "Between a Rock and a Hard Place: Vulnerability and Precarity in Rural Nepal." *Geoforum* 76:63–74. https://doi.org/10.1016/j.geoforum.2016.08.014.

Rigg, Jonathan, Albert Salamanca, and Eric C. Thompson. 2016. "The Puzzle of East and Southeast Asia's Persistent Smallholder." *Journal of Rural Studies* 43:118–33. https://doi.org/10.1016/j.jrurstud.2015.11.003.

Rippa, Alessandro. 2019. "Cross-Border Trade and 'the Market' between Xinjiang (China) and Pakistan." *Journal of Contemporary Asia* 49 (2): 254–71. https://doi.org/10 .1080/00472336.2018.1540721.

Robequain, Charles. 1944. *The Economic Development of French Indo-China*. Translated by Isabel A.Ward. Oxford: Oxford University Press.

Robert, Amélie. 2016. "At the Heart of the Vietnam War: Herbicides, Napalm and Bulldozers against the A Lưới Mountains." *Journal of Alpine Research*, 104 (1): 2–15. https://doi.org/10.4000/rga.3266.

Rocheleau, Dianne E. 2015. "Networked, Rooted and Territorial: Green Grabbing and Resistance in Chiapas." *Journal of Peasant Studies* 42 (3–4): 695–723. https://doi .org/10.1080/03066150.2014.993622.

Rousseau, Jean-François. 2018. "A Failed Market Experiment and Ignored Livelihoods: Jatropha Expansion in the Sino-Vietnamese Borderlands." In *Routledge Handbook of Asian Borderlands*, edited by Alexander Horstmann, Martin Saxer, and Alessandro Rippa, 202–11. London: Routledge.

Royal Government of Cambodia. 2004. *Rectangular Strategy for Growth, Employment, Equity and Efficiency in Cambodia*. Phnom Penh: Royal Government of Cambodia.

——. 2013. *Rectangular Strategy for Growth, Employment, Equity and Efficiency Phase III*. Phnom Penh: Royal Government of Cambodia.

——. 2014. *Cambodia's Diagnostic Trade Integration Strategy 2014–2018, Phnom Penh*. Accessed June 12, 2019. http://www.kh.undp.org/content/cambodia/en/home /library/poverty/cambodia-trade-integration-strategy-2014-2018/.

——. 2018. *Commune Database*. Phnom Penh: Ministry of Planning.

Ryle, Gilbert. 1949. *The Concept of Mind*. Chicago: University of Chicago Press.

Saenjan, Veerapong. 1998. "Future Prospect of Small and Medium Size Agribusiness in Thailand." Proceedings of the Second International Seminar on Development of Agribusiness and Its Impact on Agricultural Production in South-East Asia (Dabia II), October 15–20, 1997, Khon Kaen University, Thailand.

Salemink, Oscar. 2003. *The Ethnography of Vietnam's Central Highlanders: A Historical Contextualisation, 1850–1900*. London: Routledge Curzon.

Sassen, Saskia. 2014. *Expulsions: Brutality and Complexity in the Global Economy*. Cambridge, MA: Harvard University Press.

Schipmann, Christin, and Matin Qaim. 2011. "Supply Chain Differentiation, Contract Agriculture, and Farmers' Marketing Preferences: The Case of Sweet Pepper in Thailand." *Food Policy* 36 (5): 667–77. https://doi.org/10.1016/j.foodpol.2011.07.004.

Schoenberger, Laura, Derek Hall, and Peter Vandergeest. 2017. "What Happened When the Land Grab Came to Southeast Asia?" *Journal of Peasant Studies* 44 (4): 697–725. https://doi.org/10.1080/03066150.2017.1331433.

Schoenberger, Laura, and Sarah Turner. 2008. "Negotiating Remote Borderland Access: Small-Scale Trade on the Vietnam-China Border." *Development and Change* 39 (4): 667–96. https://doi.org/10.1111/j.1467-7660.2008.00500.x.

Schumpeter, Joseph A. 1994 [1942]. *Capitalism, Socialism and Democracy*. London, UK: Routledge.

Scott, James C. 2009. *The Art of Not Being Governed: An Anarchist History of Upland Southeast Asia*. New Haven, CT: Yale University Press.

Shanghai Daily. 2017. "China to Extend Use of Ethanol Fuel." September 14, 2017. https:// archive.shine.cn/business/energy/China-to-extend-use-of-ethanol-fuel/shdaily .shtml.

Sikor, Thomas. 2005. "Rural Property and Agri-Environmental Legislation in Central and Eastern Europe." *Sociologia Ruralis* 45 (3): 187–201. https://doi.org/10.1111/j .1467-9523.2005.00300.x.

Sikor, Thomas, and Pham Thi Tuong Vi. 2005. "The Dynamics of Commoditization in a Vietnamese Uplands Village, 1980–2000." *Journal of Agrarian Change* 5 (3): 405–28. https://doi.org/10.1111/j.1471-0366.2005.00106.x.

Singh, Sukhpal. 2005. "Contract Farming System in Thailand." *Economic and Political Weekly* 40 (53): 5578–86.

Skoggard, Ian, and Alisse Waterston. 2015. "Introduction: Toward an Anthropology of Affect and Evocative Ethnography." *Anthropology of Consciousness* 26 (2): 109–20. https://doi.org/10.1111/anoc.12041.

Slocomb, Margaret. 2007. *Colons and Coolies: The Development of Cambodia's Rubber Plantation*. Bangkok: White Lotus.

——. 2010. *An Economic History of Cambodia in the Twentieth Century*. Singapore: National University of Singapore Press.

——. 2018. "Tonkinese Migrant Labour in Cambodia: A Coolie History." In *Engaging Asia: Essays on Laos and beyond in Honour of Martin Stuart-Fox*, edited by Desley Goldston, 355–74. Copenhagen: NIAS Press.

Smith, Adam. (1776) 1976. *An Inquiry into the Nature and Causes of the Wealth of Nations*. Oxford: Oxford University Press.

Smith, Dominic, Jonathan Newby, and Rob Cramb. 2017. *Annual Report: Developing Cassava Production and Marketing Systems to Enhance Smallholder Livelihoods in Cambodia and Laos*. Bruce, Australia: ACIAR.

——. 2018. *Developing Value-Chain Linkages to Improve Smallholder Cassava Production in Southeast Asia*. Cassava Program Discussion Papers. Brisbane, Australia: University of Queensland School of Agriculture and Food Sciences.

So, S. 2009. "Political Economy of Land Registration in Cambodia." PhD diss., Northern Illinois University.

Sokhorng, Cheng 2018. "Cassava Prices Up as Supply Drops, Reversing Old Trend." *Phnom Penh Post*, February 21, 2018. https://www.phnompenhpost.com/business/cassava-prices-supply-drops-reversing-old-trend.

Sopheap, U., A. Patanothai, and T. M. Aye. 2012. "Unveiling Constraints to Cassava Production in Cambodia: An Analysis from Farmers' Yield Variations." *International Journal of Plant Production* 6 (4): 409–28. https://doi.org/10.22069/ijpp.2012.757.

Soto, Hernando de. 2000. *The Mystery of Capital: Why Capitalism Triumphs in the West and Fails Everywhere Else*. London: Bantam.

Sowerwine, Jennifer. 2011. "The Politics of Highland Landscapes in Vietnamese Statecraft: (Re)framing the Dominant Environmental Imaginary." In *Upland Transformations in Vietnam*, edited by Thomas Sikor, Nghiem Phuong Tuyen, Jennifer Sowerwine, and Jeff Romm, 51–74. Singapore: National University of Singapore Press.

——. 2013. "Socialist Rules and Post-War Politics: Reflections on Nationality and Fieldwork among the Yao in Northern Vietnam." In *Red Stamps and Gold Stars: Fieldwork Dilemmas in Upland Socialist Asia*, edited by Sarah Turner, 100–120. Vancouver: UBC Press.

Sriboonchitta, Songsak, and Aree Wiboonpoongse. 2008. *Overview of Contract Farming in Thailand: Lessons Learned*. ADBI Discussion Paper 112. Tokyo: Asian Development Bank Institute.

Staritz, Cornelia. 2012. *Value Chains for Development? Potentials and Limitations of Global Value Chain Approaches in Donor Interventions*. Working Paper no. 31. Vienna: Austrian Foundation for Development Research.

Stiglitz, Joseph. 2002. *Globalization and Its Discontents*. New York: W. W. Norton.

Stuart-Fox, Martin. 2003. *A Short History of China and Southeast Asia: Tribute, Trade and Influence*. Crows Nest, Australia: Allen and Unwin.

Sunderlin, William D. 2006. "Poverty Alleviation through Community Forestry in Cambodia, Laos, and Vietnam: An Assessment of the Potential." *Forest Policy and Economics* 8:386–96. https://doi.org/10.1016/j.forpol.2005.08.008.

Swanson, H. A., A. Tsing, N. O. Bubandt, and E. Gan. 2017. "Introduction: Bodies Tumbled into Bodies." In *Arts of Living on a Damaged Planet*, edited by Anna Tsing, Heather Swanson, Elaine Gan, and Nils Bubandt, M1–M12. Minneapolis: University of Minnesota Press.

Syndicat des Planteurs de Caoutchouc de l'Indochine. 1931. *Annuaire du Syndicat des Planteurs de Caoutchouc de l'Indochine.* Saigon: Syndicat des Planteurs de Caoutchouc de l'Indochine. https://gallica.bnf.fr/ark:/12148/bpt6k899641w/f5.image

Taylor, K. W. 2013. *A History of the Vietnamese.* Cambridge: Cambridge University Press.

Thavat, Maylee. 2010. "Aiding Trade: Case Studies in Agricultural Value Chain Development in Cambodia." PhD diss., Australian National University, Canberra.

Thomas, Martin. 2012. *Violence and Colonial Order: Police, Workers and Protest in the European Colonial Empires, 1918–1940.* Critical Perspectives on Empire. Cambridge: Cambridge University Press.

Thomson, Stanley R. 1945. "The Establishment of the French Protectorate over Cambodia." *Far Eastern Quarterly* 4 (4): 313–40.

To, Phuc, Wolfram Dressler, Sango Mahanty, Pham Thuy, and Claudia Zingerli. 2012. "The Prospects for Payment for Ecosystem Services (PES) in Vietnam: A Look at Three Payment Schemes." *Human Ecology* 40 (2): 237–49. https://doi.org/10.1007/s10745-012-9480-9.

To, Phuc, and Sango Mahanty. 2019. "Vietnam's Cross-Border Timber Crackdown and the Quest for State Legitimacy." *Political Geography,* no. 75. https://doi.org/10.1016/j.polgeo.2019.102066.

To, Phuc, Sango Mahanty, and Wolfram Dressler. 2014. "Social Networks of Corruption in the Vietnamese and Lao Cross-Border Timber Trade." *Anthropological Forum* 24 (2): 154–74. https://doi.org/10.1080/00664677.2014.893505.

——. 2016. "Moral Economies and Markets: 'Insider' Cassava Trading in Kon Tum, Vietnam." *Asia Pacific Viewpoint* 57 (2): 168–79. https://doi.org/10.1111/apv.12119.

To, Phuc, Sango Mahanty, and Andrew Wells-Dang. 2019. "From 'Land to the Tiller' to the 'New Landlords'? The Debate over Vietnam's Latest Land Reforms." *Land* 8 (120): 1–19. https://doi.org/10.3390/land8080120.

Tsing, Anna Lowenhaupt. 2003. "Natural Resources and Capitalist Frontiers." *Economic and Political Weekly* 38 (48): 5100–5106.

——. 2005. *Friction: An Ethnography of Global Connection.* Princeton, NJ: Princeton University Press.

——. 2015. *The Mushroom at the End of the World: On the Possibility of Life in Capitalist Ruins.* Princeton, NJ: Princeton University Press.

Turner, F. J. 1920. *The Frontier in American History.* New York: Henry Holt.

Turner, Sarah, ed. 2013. *Red Stamps and Gold Stars: Fieldwork Dilemmas in upland Socialist Asia.* Vancouver: UBC Press.

Turner, Sarah, Christine Bonnin, and Jean Michaud. 2015. *Frontier Livelihoods: Hmong in the Sino-Vietnamese Borderlands.* Seattle: University of Washington Press.

Un, Kheang, and Sokbunthoeun So. 2011. "Land Rights in Cambodia: How Neopatrimonial Politics Restricts Land Policy Reform." *Pacific Affairs* 84 (2): 289–308. https://doi.org/10.5509/2011842289.

UNDP (United Nations Development Programme). 2013. *Cambodia Export Diversification and Expansion Program (CEDEP) II: Cassava, Marine Fisheries Products, the Royal Academy of Culinary Arts, and Program Evaluation Function.* New York: UNDP.

——. 2017. *Mid-Term Review of the Cambodian Export Diversification and Expansion Programme (CEDEP II Cassava Component).* New York: UNDP.

UNDP Cambodia. 2018. *Cassava in Cambodia: Sustainable Industrial Development.* Phnom Penh: UNDP Cambodia. https://undpcambodia.exposure.co/cassava-in-cambodia.

van der Eynden, Andreas 2011. "Rubber and Soul: Moral Economy, Development and Resistance in the Bousraa Villages, Mondulkiri, Cambodia." MA thesis, Norwegian University of Science and Technology.

van Schendel, Willem. 2002. "Geographies of Knowing, Geographies of Ignorance: Jumping Scale in Southeast Asia." *Environment and Planning D: Society and Space* 20 (6): 647–68. https://doi.org/10.1068/d16s.

———. 2005. "Spaces of Engagement: How Borderlands, Illegal Flows, and Territorial States Interlock." In *Illicit Flows and Criminal Things: States, Borders, and the Other Side of Globalization*, edited by Willem van Schendel and Itty Abraham, 38–68. Bloomington: Indiana University Press.

Vandergeest, Peter. 1988. "Commercialization and Commoditization: A Dialogue between Perspectives." *Sociologia Ruralis* 28 (1): 7–29.

———. 2008. "New Concepts, New Natures? Revisiting Commodity Production in Southern Thailand." In *Taking Southeast Asia to Market: Commodities, Nature, and People in the Neoliberal Age*, edited by Joseph Nevins and Nancy Lee Peluso, 206–24. Ithaca, NY: Cornell University Press.

Vandergeest, Peter, and Nancy Lee Peluso. 1995. "Territorialization and State Power in Thailand." *Theory and Society* 24 (3): 385–426.

Viajar, Verna Dinah Q. 2018. *Organizing Migrant Domestic Workers in Malaysia: Ways Out of Precarity*. Berlin: Friedrich-Ebert-Stiftung.

Viet Nam News. 2016. "Low Cassava Prices Plunge Farmers into Despair." November 7, 2016. http://vietnamnews.vn/economy/345695/low-cassava-prices-plunge-farmers-into-despair.html#FJ20XAR0LavFto60.99.

———. 2018a. "E5 Bio-Fuel Quality Comes under Scrutiny from Drivers." January 20, 2018. http://vietnamnews.vn/society/421536/e5-bio-fuel-quality-comes-under-scrutiny-from-drivers.html#QzwBlrKLM7ecttZ6.99.

———. 2018b. "E5 Fuel makes up 65% of Petrol Sales," February 5, 2018. http://vietnamnews.vn/economy/422434/e5-fuel-makes-up-65-of-petrol-sales.html#OpJKrGl1i2IR AvRM.99.

———. 2018c. "Đinh La Thăng Gets 18 Year, Asked to Compensate in 34.8 US$million Loss Case." March 30, 2018. http://vietnamnews.vn/politics-laws/425419/dinh-la-thang-gets-18-year-asked-to-compensate-in-348-usmillion-loss-case.html#ZVQv7Hi9vVZFX52E.99.

———. 2019. "Review of Policies for Biofuel E5 RON 92 Proposed over Disappointing Sales." May 3, 2019. http://vietnamnews.vn/economy/519389/review-of-policies-for-biofuel-e5-ron-92-proposed-over-disappointing-sales.html#15weCgr4s8l6FW61.99.

Vietnam Pictorial. 2019. "New Progress in Land Border Demarcation between Vietnam, Cambodia." October 13, 2019. https://vietnam.vnanet.vn/english/new-progress-in-land-border-demarcation-between-vietnam-cambodia/427886.html.

Vize, Jeff, and Manfred Hornung. 2013. "Indigenous Peoples and Land Titling in Cambodia: A Study of Six Villages." Paper prepared for presentation at the annual World Bank Conference on Land and Poverty, Washington DC, April 8–11, 2013.

Vuong, Quan-Hoang. 2014. "Vietnam's Political Economy in Transition (1986–2016)." *Stratfor: The Hub; International Perspectives*, May 27, 2014. https://ssrn.com/abstract=2795174.

Vuong, Quan-Hoang, Van Nhue Dam, Daniel van Houtte, and Tri Tran. 2011. "The Entrepreneurial Facets as Precursor to Vietnam's Economic Renovation in 1986." *IUP Journal of Entrepreneurship Development* 8 (4): 6–47.

Wade, Robert. 2003. *Governing the Market: Economic Theory and the Role of Government in East Asian Industrialization*. Princeton, NJ: Princeton University Press.

Wallerstein, Immanuel 1974. "The Rise and Future Demise of the World Capitalist System: Concepts for Comparative Analysis." *Comparative Studies in Society and History* 16 (4): 387–415.

Wang, H. L., X. Y. Cui, X. W. Wang, S. S. Liu, Z. H. Zhang, and X. P. Zhou. 2015. "First Report of Sri Lankan Cassava Mosaic Virus Infecting Cassava in Cambodia." *Plant Disease* 100 (5): 1029. https://doi.org/10.1094/PDIS-10-15-1228-PDN.

Watts, Michael. 2012. "A Tale of Two Gulfs: Life, Death, and Dispossession along Two Oil Frontiers." *American Quarterly* 64 (3): 437–67. https://doi.org/10.1353/aq.2012.0039.

——. 2018. "Frontiers: Authority, Precarity, and Insurgency at the Edge of the State." *World Development* 101:477–88. https://doi.org/10.1016/j.worlddev.2017.03.024.

WCS (Wildlife Conservation Society). 2012. *Census of Seima Protected Forest 2012.* New York: Wildlife Conservation Society.

Wells, Andrew. 2007. "Imperial Hegemony and Colonial Labor." *Rethinking Marxism* 19 (2): 180–94. https://doi.org/10.1080/08935690701219017.

White, J. 2009. "The Indigenous Highlanders of the Northeast: An Uncertain Future." In *Interdisciplinary Research on Ethnic Groups in Cambodia*, edited by Hean Sokhom, 333–74. Phnom Penh: Center for Advanced Study.

Wolf, Eric R. 1982. *Europe and the People without History.* Berkeley: University of California Press.

Wolf, Howard, and Ralph Wolf. 1936. *Rubber: A Story of Glory and Greed.* New York: Covici Friede.

Wolfe, Patrick. 2006. "Settler Colonialism and the Elimination of the Native." *Journal of Genocide Research* 8 (4): 387–409. https://doi.org/10.1080/14623520601056240.

World Bank. 2015. *Cambodian Agriculture in Transition: Opportunities and Risks.* Economic and Sector Work, report no. 96308-KH. Washington, DC: World Bank.

——. 2018. *Cambodia Economic Update: Recent Economic Development and Outlook; Phnom Penh, Cambodia.* http://documents.worldbank.org/curated/en/740941525786311189/pdf/126030-WP-PUBLIC-may-10-9-am-cambodia-time-Cambodia-Economic-Update-V04.pdf.

Yates, Douglas. 1977. *The Ungovernable City.* Cambridge, MA: MIT Press.

Yeung, Henry Wai-chung. 2014. "Governing the Market in a Globalizing Era: Developmental States, Global Production Networks and Inter-Firm Dynamics in East Asia." *Review of International Political Economy* 21 (1): 70–101. https://doi.org/10.1080/09692290.2012.756415.

Index

Page numbers in italic indicate figures or tables.